Color and Line in Dress

Color and Line in Dress

by

LAURENE HEMPSTEAD

SKETCHES BY SARA WHITNEY OLDS

❧ THIRD EDITION ❧

NEW YORK

PRENTICE-HALL, INC.

1947

Preface

SINCE THE FIRST EDITION of this book appeared there have been many changes of fashion, all of which have served to confirm in the author, and in other students of fashion, the belief that whatever the fashion of the moment, the basic principles of color and line and their effect upon the face and figure of the wearer remain the same. Those designs that violated the principles of design and costume selection are the ones that appear ludicrous when we look at the fashions of yesteryear. Those designs really suited to the wearer, enhancing the beauty of her face and figure, retain dignity and charm, seeming quaint, not ridiculous, to eyes accustomed to present-day fashions.

The principles of color and design in dress discussed in this book can be used as a guide for the selection of becoming costumes and as an aid in predicting styles that will be commercially successful. The garment that enhances the good points of the wearer and minimizes her defects must necessarily embody the principles of good design and selection. The dress that is worn and reworn with confidence and pleasure is the one possessing color and lines that make the wearer appear at her best. The dress that is purchased by the majority of women who try it on is the one designed to make the most of the average figure in the sizes in which it is made. Garments that remain to be marked down, those that become "mistakes," pushed back in the closet and seldom worn, may be interesting in design but difficult to wear; perhaps they are becoming only to the perfect figure or to one type of beauty alone.

In writing this book, the author's aim has been to keep basic principles of first importance, using fashion as a common language to help her explain and illustrate those principles in terms familiar to the reader. She has attempted to select for sketching styles that in some modification can be found in a number of models rather than specific designs relating to only one garment. Since we are in a period of unrest likely to be accompanied by sudden and extreme fashion changes, some of these sketches may become outmoded, but the basic principles of costume selection, of becomingness, of choosing lines that enhance the appearance of the wearer, will remain constant. However much fashion may change, lines similar to those illustrated in these sketches can be found in some of the fashions of the day, for there will always be women with figure defects, and the best designers will always produce models to flatter them.

There will be trends in color, fashions in color for mass production; yet the different color, the unusual color that is truly becoming, will always give its wearer distinction. Many a "best-dressed" woman owes her reputation largely to her faithfulness to colors that she knows to be flattering. The author does not fear that fashion changes will affect the usefulness of the chapters on color. She expects, however, that modern textile developments will give us an ever-increasing range of colors and selection of textures.

The author wishes to express her appreciation to Fairchild Publications, in whose magazines some of this material originally appeared, and who generously gave her the opportunity for disinterested research.

L. H.

Contents

PART I—FACES

CHAPTER   PAGE

I. THE HAIRDRESS SHAPES THE FACE 5

    Devices that make face seem wider 7
    Devices that add to apparent length of face . . 10
    Devices that affect apparent size of features . . 12
    Irregular features 15

II. BROOCHES, CLIPS, NECKLACES, EARRINGS CHANGE
APPARENT CONTOURS OF FACE 16

    Brooches and clips change facial picture . . . 16
    Necklaces that broaden 18
    Necklaces that slenderize 19
    Earrings almost always add width 21

III. NECKLINES FRAME THE FACE 25

    Necklines that seem to widen the face 25
    Necklines that add apparent length 27
    Irregular features 29
    Coat collars 30

IV. THE HAT IS THE BACKGROUND FOR THE FACE . 37

    The outlines of the face 38
    Veils: increase or destroy becomingness . . . 45
    Defects may be corrected 46

V. RELATING THE COLORS WORN TO THE PIGMENTA-
TION OF THE SKIN 56

    Make-up 57

❦ CONTENTS ❦

CHAPTER   PAGE

V. RELATING THE COLORS WORN TO THE PIGMENTATION OF THE SKIN (*Cont.*)

Devices that affect the color of the face 61

Devices that change becomingness of colors . . 63

Flattering colors best in case of doubt 66

VI. RELATING THE COLORS WORN TO THE PIGMENTATION OF THE HAIR AND EYES 69

The hair 69

The eyes 72

VII. CRITICAL ANALYSIS OF INDIVIDUAL COLORING . . 75

Rating scale for color reading 78

A few becoming hues preferable to many dubious colors 81

VIII. COLORS BECOMING TO INDIVIDUALS OF COOL COLORING 82

Drab or neutral blonde needs color accent . . 82

Colorful blonde permitted more colors 86

Cool, dark type wears more forceful colors . . 87

IX. COLORS BECOMING TO INDIVIDUALS OF WARM COLORING 88

Colors for the red-haired types 89

Color selections for the vivid brunette 93

The Latin type 94

X. INTERMEDIATE TYPE SELECTS COLORS TO EMPHASIZE BEST FEATURES 96

Yellow hair, cool skin, and brown eyes 97

Brown hair, brown eyes, medium or fair skin . 98

Brown hair; gray, green, or blue eyes; fair skin 99

viii

CHAPTER   PAGE

XI. COLORS VITALIZE WOMEN WITH GRAY OR WHITE HAIR 104

    Mixed dark and gray hair difficult problem . . 105
    Wider color range for definitely gray hair . . 105
    White hair permits more vivid colors 107

XII. HARMONIOUS COMBINATIONS OF COLOR 111

    Color interest 111
    Matching hues 113
    Related or analogous colors 114
    Decided contrast of hue 115
    Using color as a basis for wardrobe selection . . 117

PART II—SILHOUETTES AND SIZES

XIII. OPTICAL ILLUSIONS AFFECTING THE FIGURE . . 127

    Critical analysis of the figure 127
    Perpendicular lines 131
    Diagonals 135
    Horizontals 137
    Details 138

XIV. TEXTURE AND COLOR AFFECT SILHOUETTE AND SIZE 144

    Shiny textures increase size and reveal silhouette 144
    Dull textures decrease size and conceal silhouette 144
    Stiff fabrics increase size but conceal silhouette 146
    Heavy fabrics also increase size and conceal silhouette 147
    Transparent fabrics reveal silhouette 148
    Prints should be scaled to size of wearer . . . 150
    Light colors increase size and conceal silhouette 152

CHAPTER   PAGE

XIV. TEXTURE AND COLOR AFFECT SILHOUETTE AND
     SIZE (*Cont.*)
          Dark colors decrease size and reveal silhouette   152
          Bright colors increase size and reveal silhouette   153
          Dull colors decrease size and conceal silhouette   153
          Warm colors are difficult to wear   154
          Cool colors flatter all figures   154

XV. DEVICES THAT MAKE LARGE HIPS LESS EVIDENT   155

XVI. LINES MINIMIZING ENLARGED DIAPHRAGM AND
     ABDOMEN   163
          Maternity wear   171

XVII. LINES MODIFYING THE LARGE BUST   176
          Light-colored blouse makes upper figure heavy 182

XVIII. COSTUME LINES THAT IMPROVE ROUND SHOUL-
       DERS   183

XIX. METHODS OF HIDING LARGE UPPER ARM . . .   191

XX. FOOTWEAR, FOUNDATION FOR THE FIGURE . . .   197
          Contrasts to be avoided   197
          Long, slender shoe gives length to foot and figure 199
          Other considerations   205

XXI. THE TALL, SLENDER WOMAN   206
          Tall and slim and proud of it   206
          Too tall and thin   209

XXII. THE TALL, HEAVY WOMAN   214
          Choice of fabrics   214
          The large woman's hat   220
          Footwear   221

❦ CONTENTS ❦

CHAPTER   PAGE

XXIII. THE SHORT, SLENDER WOMAN 223

    Emphasizing petite charm 223
    Space divisions 226
    Keeping in scale 229

XXIV. THE SHORT, HEAVY WOMAN 233

    To keep figure inconspicuous 234
    To improve the figure 236
    Hats 240
    Footwear 241

XXV. LINE IN RELATION TO MOOD AND CHARACTER . 244

    Curved lines lend youth and roundness . . . 245
    Straight lines give dignity, simplicity, and maturity 245
    Diagonal, pointed lines are subtle, sophisticated 246

PART III—AGES OF WOMEN

XXVI. CHILDREN'S CLOTHES 251

    Individualized infants' clothing 251
    Little girl wants clothes like mother's 252
    Hygienic requirements of growing girl . . . 255
    Color diminishes awkwardness 259

XXVII. THE MISS IN HER TEENS 261

    Apt and inapt age emphasis 264
    Junior types 268
    Campus costumes 272

XXVIII. THE YOUNG WOMAN 275

    Accenting individuality 275
    The very feminine woman 278
    The forceful, energetic woman 280

❦ CONTENTS ❦

CHAPTER   PAGE

XXIX.   THE MIDDLE YEARS 282

        Simplicity gives distinction 283
        The hairdress 285
        The hat 289

XXX.   THE ELDERLY WOMAN 293

        Hairdress and make-up 293
        Hats 296
        Necklines 299
        Fabric and color 303
        The lines of the mode 304
        Shoes 306

XXXI.   "SHE WEARS HER CLOTHES WELL" 308

        INDEX 317

xii

Color and Line
in Dress

PART I

Faces

Faces

ANY WOMAN can approach beauty through manipulation of line and color to her advantage.

A correct and becoming costume is not only pleasing in itself, but enhances the attractiveness of the wearer. It should serve as a background for her personality. It should not be more forceful, more striking, than the woman who is wearing it. Some women have a manner so forceful, coloring and features so definite, that there is little danger of submerging their personalities with costumes of strong color or striking design. Others are so unassertive, so nondescript in coloring and physical features, that apparel of emphatic character dominates them and reduces them to further insignificance.

The face, as the key to the personality of the individual, should be the center of interest in the picture created by the costume and the wearer. The costume should be planned to accent the face. A costume that has striking footwear as its most conspicuous detail, its center of interest, detracts from the personality of the wearer because the observer doesn't notice her face. Hats, necklines, collars, scarfs, necklaces, shoulder flowers aid in making the face the focal point, concentrating interest near the face. Color accents are especially effective, particularly if they repeat the coloring of the individual.

The most pleasing faces have an oval outline. It should be the aim of every woman not naturally blessed with a face of oval proportions to frame her face in outlines that make it simu-

3

late oval contours. The following chapters tell how this may be accomplished.

It is obvious that such information is useless to a woman who has not definitely determined in what respects her own face varies from the ideal oval. Taking stock of one's liabilities as well as one's assets is the first step toward becoming as attractive as one wishes to be. Introduce yourself to yourself, to your best self, to that self that you wish to hide from the critical world.

A face that is too broad and square or too short and round requires its proportions to appear definitely narrowed and lengthened. It may be feasible to do both; or, if one has an unfortunate effect on some feature, the other alone may suffice.

Treatments of line and color, which emphasize each feature, are also studied in these chapters. An inventory of features will always result in a list of some that are pleasing and some that are out of proportion. In planning her costumes, each individual will do well to adhere to two strict rules: First, she must emphasize her pleasing features; and, second, she must center interest away from her unattractive features.

CHAPTER I

The Hairdress Shapes the Face

To THE WOMAN whose face has the perfect contours of the ideal oval, the arrangement of her hair is a pleasure, not a major problem. She may dress it to suit her mood or her gown, serene in the knowledge that her coiffure will never detract from her facial charm. But to her whose imperfect facial proportions can approach beauty only through clever grooming, the one most effective hairdress may well be the first quest and the crowning triumph; for the method of dressing the hair does materially affect the contours of the face.

The outlines of the hair may make the face seem less broad and square, less short and round, less long and thin, more nearly the ideal oval. They may even determine which features are to be prominent and which are to remain safely in the background.

Patience in combing, coaxing, training it to assume its most pleasing lines need be its chief cost, for brushing is more necessary than frequent visits to the hairdresser. Careful cutting and a good permanent, if one is necessary, should enable every woman to find and maintain a becoming style of hairdress.

It is much better to have a simple hairdress which can be kept at its best by simple daily care than an elaborate one which looks well only for a short time after periodical visits to the hairdresser. If time and income permit regular visits to the hairdresser, flattering and interesting hairdresses—impossible

5

to maintain at home—may be a charming way of emphasizing individuality. Coiffures too obviously the beauty parlor's art rather than part of the natural appearance should be avoided. Neat, well-groomed, yet soft, natural-looking hair should be the ideal.

Many of the best hairdressers gladly coöperate with women who make a sincere and intelligent effort to learn the best modern methods of daily hair care. They will show their customers how to roll the hair into pin curls nightly so that the planned, becoming lines of the hairdress can be maintained, or how to brush and comb the stylized hairdress into its smartest lines, how to pin it securely in place, how to protect it at night so that the hair may stay trained in the desired lines.

Shiny, lustrous, well cared for hair, itself a thing of beauty as well as a flattering frame for the face, is almost universal among modern young women, a feature of the "glamour gal." The too curly, too elaborate, or the too set, too rigid hairdo betrays the mind clinging to the hair style of a past decade.

Some women make the mistake of wearing the same hairdress year after year without critically appraising its becomingness with regard to features that have changed with the years. Even comparatively young women may look much older than their actual years because they wear a hairdress that was becoming to them in their school days or early womanhood. The long bob, in itself a beautiful style, showing beautiful hair to good advantage, is seldom becoming except to the young face. Its long, downward-moving lines emphasize even slightly drooping lines of the older face. This tendency, together with the observer's expectation of seeing a young, girlish face under the long bob, may seem to add several years of apparent age to the actual age of the almost-young woman.

The middle-aged woman may "date" herself by wearing a style that was youthful and modern when she was young, but that is not now worn except by a few women her own age who have continued to wear it for twenty years or more. The shingled head is an example of the hairdress that marks a woman as "set in her ways," refusing to change with the passing years. It is almost always unbecoming to the woman no longer young, as it centers attention on the back of the neck, the ears, and the jowl line, where the detrimental effects of the added years are most apparent. If a hairdress is truly becoming, it need not be ruled out because it is a period fashion, or because its wearer has clung to it for years. If it is still becoming to the face and figure of the wearer, it may be more pleasing, more youthful than a smart but trying hair style of this month's fashion. Perhaps in this category belong the pompadour, top-knot styles of the turn of the century, recently revived with modifications, but which in their original form are still worn by many older women, and which are not unbecoming, especially if the hair is softly curled or waved, although for many years this hairdress "dated" them in the same way that the shingled haircut marks the middle-aged woman who wears it today.

Devices That Make the Face Seem Wider

Center part. If the hair is parted at the middle, dividing the face at the center line, the apparent width of the face is increased. This style, therefore, is recommended to the person with long, slender face, as it will make her face seem wider. It should be avoided by the woman whose face is too broad. Persons with irregular features likewise find it trying, as it tends to reveal contours.

A center part makes the face seem wider, emphasizes irregular features. A side part with hair different at sides decreases width and minimizes irregularity of features.

The center parting emphasizes the nose and should usually be worn only by the woman whose nose is one of her best features.

Hair low on forehead. When bangs are worn covering the forehead, or the hair is combed low, giving a similar effect, the apparent length of the face is greatly decreased, with a resultant increase in the apparent width. This style, therefore, is unbecoming to the broad face, but becoming to the long, narrow face. If the forehead is unusually high or protruding, it may be

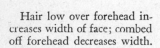

Hair low over forehead increases width of face; combed off forehead decreases width.

wise to cover it, at least partially, even though an emphasis on width is not desired. When hair is worn low over the forehead, it tends to increase the size and brilliance of the eyes and, therefore, is sometimes becoming even to the fairly broad face.

Ears exposed. When the hair is cut or combed so that the ears are exposed, the apparent width of the face is materially increased; the eye travels the full distance from ear to ear. This broadening effect is particularly apparent when a center parting is also used. Although effective in increasing width and decreasing length, this type of hairdressing cannot be recommended to all persons with narrow faces, as it reveals contours. Regular features are required for this severe arrangement.

Hair covering neck. When the hair is so arranged that it completely hides the ears and partially covers the neck, the neck is shortened and the face seems shorter and wider. The eye tends to travel beyond the face from the hair at one side to that at the other, creating additional width. This style, therefore, is usually becoming to the person with a long, thin face, especially

The pageboy bob with the hair rolled under at the bottom is simple and youthful looking, but it makes the head appear larger, the figure shorter, than does shorter hair with the ends softly waved outward.

if the neck is long and thin. The woman with too broad a face should be certain that her hair is not allowed to grow or to become disarranged so that it partially conceals her neck.

When the hair is brushed back to reveal all or part of the ears and is long behind the ears, it may give a becoming background to the face. The effect is much more slenderizing than long hair which covers the ears and the sides of the face and neck.

Close hairdress. If the hair is worn close to the head, giving no frame or background for the features, the face itself is emphasized. This frequently makes the face seem broader, fuller. A fairly close hairdress, therefore, is becoming to the woman

9

with too thin a face, but, like the too-small hat, it makes the large features of the broad face seem wider and unduly large.

When the ends of the hair are curled outward, the contour of the curls contrasting with the shape of the head, the head size seems smaller than it does when the ends are curled under, the roundness of the curls adding to the apparent size of the head. While the large head is youthful, most women finds the apparently smaller head improves their entire appearance.

Devices That Add to Apparent Length of Face

High side part. Hair parted on one side tends to decrease the apparent width of the face, making it seem longer. Hair parted definitely to one side, but high, gives the greatest appearance of length to the face, as the very low part emphasizes width at the top of the head. A parting directly in line with the beginning of the eyebrow, slightly farther to the side if the eyebrows are too close together, gives a slenderizing line for the broad face. The woman with thin face but irregular features, who cannot wear the center parting, frequently finds that the very low side parting is becoming.

Combed off forehead. Hair combed back, exposing the forehead, reveals a greater length of face, making it seem longer and narrower. This is particularly true when the hair is combed in a pompadour so that it gives added height above the head. This style, always very trying for the long face that cannot afford the added length and appearance of decreased width, may also be difficult for the person with a short, broad face, as it reveals irregularities in contour and emphasizes defects in the skin. The upswept hairdress has an upward movement that seems to lift the lines of the face. Unless its lines are stiff and rigid, this style, for the woman no longer in her first

The round, rigid pompadour emphasizes fullness of the face and rotundity of figure even though it may add actual height. The softer broken pompadour is flattering to face and figure.

High coronet braids may be severe and trying or may, if they are slightly wider than the face, make a flattering background.

Hair curved over ears and cheeks lessens facial width; revealing ears adds to apparent width.

youth, is more becoming than the essentially youthful bobbed hair styles in which the hanging hair creates downward line direction and thereby emphasizes drooping lines of the face.

Curved over cheeks. If the hair is combed so that it covers the cheeks, lessening the amount of contrasting skin visible on the width of the face, the face seems longer and narrower. This device is more effective when the hair is of dark or medium value, since light hair does not break the line so decidedly. This is a softening, generally becoming, style that tends to minimize irregularities of feature. If the broad-faced woman is allowing her hair to grow long, she should be careful to train it forward over the cheeks and away from the neck, until it is long enough for more formal dressing.

Revealing tips of ears. If the hair is so arranged that the tips of the ears show, the face seems longer and less broad. This treatment gives the neck the longest possible line, without the added width across the face that results from showing both ears entirely.

Devices That Affect Apparent Size of Features

Close, loose, and exaggerated hairdresses. Just as the close, tight hairdress emphasizes and enlarges the face, so the large, loose arrangement that creates a large frame for the face makes it seem smaller by contrast. The small, thin face seems unduly small; it may seem narrower and longer. The too-broad face loses much of its appearance of undesirable width. The exaggerated hairdress, if unduly large, fails in its effect, as it makes the whole head seem larger and out of proportion. The hairdress that is long, giving a wide line low at the neck, fails completely to make the face seem smaller in contrast to the bulk of the hair.

Profile hairdress. When the hairdress follows the natural contours of the head, the features usually appear in best proportion, while the hairdress that alters the apparent shape of the head may exaggerate out-of-proportion features. A knot of hair placed at the same height as the nose makes its outlines more conspicuous. Similarly, one placed low at the neck emphasizes the chinline, and is to be avoided by women with chins too prominent, too numerous, or too receding. A small knot at the hairline, one that does not markedly change the contours of the head, is becoming to almost every type of woman.

Large, loose hairdress makes face seem smaller; close hairdress increases width.

Many small waves enlarge features. Many waves, especially small, fine waves, or many regular undulations in the hairdress, make the features seem large by contrast with the fine space divisions in the hair. If the features are irregular, small waves and numerous irregularities likewise emphasize this defect. A few large, loose waves, large indefinite curves in the outlines of the hair, are much more easily worn.

Straight simplicity refines features. Straight, simple lines tend to refine the features and give a slender aspect to the face. Straight or very soft natural lines are not to be confused with the close hairdress, in which style hair is brushed severely close to the head so that it provides no background for the features.

13

Hair combed across the back of the head reveals its true contour; hair combed up in two sections meeting at the center back breaks width and makes the head seem small; hair combed up loosely at the back increases the apparent curve and roundness of the head.

Hair combed high but forward on the head makes a large nose less apparent; hair masses on top of the head may seem to increase the length of the nose.

Stiff, sculptured curls having little relation to the shape of the head are less becoming than soft, natural-looking waves and curls arranged to add slight length to the face and figure.

Irregular Features

The recurring warnings in the previous sections that persons with irregular features should avoid this-and-that arrangement of the hair recommended for correcting various defects in proportion may seem less discouraging if massed for inspection.

Many small waves, which enlarge the features by contrast, also throw into relief any unduly large feature.

Any severe treatment brings the features into prominence. In particular, the broadening styles of the center part, the fully exposed ear, and the lengthening off-the-forehead arrangements are to be worn only by those with good features. It should be added that few women with good complexions and serene expressions need hesitate to reveal their faces.

Softening styles, however, are becoming to most women. Large, loose, natural-looking waves, framing the face in lines that approach the perfect oval, drawn over the cheeks unless the face is too long and thin, drawn over the forehead if the individual wears that style well, perhaps a low side parting—thus does a woman blend ill-assorted features into an attractive face.

CHAPTER II

Brooches, Clips, Necklaces, Earrings Change Apparent Contours of Face

THE LINES that may be introduced into the costume by means of costume jewelry materially affect the apparent shape of the face. They should not be worn thoughtlessly, but only after careful study before a mirror.

They should be chosen for their relationship to the face and neckline of the wearer, and to harmonize with the design of the costume.

Brooches and Clips Change Facial Picture

Carefully chosen and artfully placed pins, brooches, and clips effectively change the apparent contours of the face. Clips are especially useful, since they may be placed at the neckline in so many varied ways, and their position may be adjusted until the most becoming effect is achieved.

A clip worn at the center, front, has a slenderizing effect upon the face and neck. Two clips, one at each side of the neckline, draw the observer's eye in a horizontal movement across the wearer's face and neck, giving an impression of greatly increased width. A pair of clips, well placed, seem integrally a part of the costume design.

A single clip or a pair of clips placed at one side of the neck-line is more slenderizing than the pair divided, with one placed on each side.

A clip at each side of the neckline increases the apparent width of the face; a single clip worn low increases the apparent length of the face.

A pin or clip with greater length than width, especially when used to emphasize a *V* neckline, slenderizes the face and figure. A round pin or brooch adds rotundity.

Necklaces That Broaden

Choker necklaces increase the width and roundness of the face, at the same time adding fullness to the neck. If large, round beads are used, the effect is much more apparent; if the entire choker is made of large rather than graduated sizes, this is still more evident. The choker style of necklace, fitting close around the throat, is becoming to the thin face and neck, as it not only adds width and roundness, but also tends to hide the

Round, choker necklaces make face seem broader and rounder; longer, oval, graduated beads slenderize.

bony structure of the neck. This type of necklace is, it should be needless to say, trying for the full, broad face—yet many women with large faces wear them.

Necklaces made with a large, round front clasp coming high on the throat materially shorten and widen the face. This effect is increased if large, round beads as well as a round clasp are employed. A wide clasp may add still greater breadth. Many necklaces made in this fashion are more becoming if the clasp is worn at the back rather than the front. This style is becoming to the person with a thin neck, as it conceals the bones at the base of the neck and, at the same time, adds width to both neck and face.

Numerous short strands of beads, giving a heavy effect about the neck, increase the width of the face in proportion to the number of strands, their shortness, and the size and roundness of the beads used. They are especially efficient in covering the bones of the thin neck, but disastrous in their effect upon too-full faces and double or triple chins.

Heavy necklaces worn high about the throat make neck and face seem fuller; flat, triangular shapes, weighted into *V* by lengthening pendant, slenderize.

Necklaces That Slenderize

If oval or elongated shaped beads are used, especially if they are arranged in graduated sizes and if the necklace does not fit too closely about the throat but is slightly longer than the choker length, an oval shape is created that aids in emphasizing the oval contours of the face. A single strand of graduated pearls, long enough to give oval contours, is flattering to most faces. Knots between the beads make the string more flexible so that it hangs in a longer, less round line. The pearls themselves gain an illusion of slightly oval contours, the round line being broken by the introduction of the small knot separating the round beads. Since real pearls are almost always strung with knots to separate the pearls and prevent them chafing each other, the use of knots between imitation pearls makes them seem finer and closer to the genuine.

For the face that is neither too broad nor too narrow, the proportions of which do not need changing, this length may be becoming. The woman whose face is much too full will find it only slightly less trying than the choker, while those whose faces are either a trifle too narrow or too full will find models in this type of necklace that will improve the contours.

Necklaces made of flat, elongated shapes, with a long rather than a broad or round clasp or pendant at the front, add length and decrease the apparent breadth of the face, avoiding emphasis upon round or curving lines. Triangular shapes, with a larger triangle at the front weighting the necklace into a *V*-line, provide one effective means of adding to the length and decreasing the width of the face. Many other forms of necklace in which this principle is followed may be found.

Pronouncedly angular shapes may emphasize angular contours or, by contrast, make rotundity more evident. As a general rule, however, flat and somewhat geometric or angular shapes are more becoming to the too-full face than quick or curved shapes, while the thin, angular face finds them wearable.

A few longer strands of beads, one, two, or sometimes three, arranged so that they form a series of oval lines, may increase the apparent length of the face, decrease its width, and emphasize oval contours. Many women destroy the pleasing effect of long strands by winding them too many times and too closely about the throat. On the other hand, the woman who is too thin may make both her face and her figure appear fuller if she doubles or triples a long, slender necklace.

Earrings Almost Always Add Width

All earrings tend to increase the apparent width of the face, leading the observer's eye across the face from ear to ear rather than up and down.   For this reason they are becoming to many women, especially those whose faces are too thin or too narrow in structure.   Women of this type look their best with earrings and should affect them whenever they may consistently be

If earrings are not worn the face usually seems most slender; round button earrings add perceptible width and fullness; disks and hoops also give an impression of added roundness.

worn.   As they are made in designs suitable for all types of costumes, women to whom they are becoming may wear them at almost all times.

If earrings are becoming, they add interest to the face, giving it sparkle and animation.   The eyes especially may be flattered by earrings of becoming texture and color.

Large, round, button earrings add most to the width and roundness of the face, frequently giving a pleasing emphasis of curves to the too-thin face, but unduly emphasizing rotundity in one that is already too full.

Earrings, all earrings, are decidedly unbecoming to a large number of women, some of whom persistently lessen their attractiveness by wearing them, even though all semblance of oval contour in the face is destroyed. The face that may seem a pleasing oval in the absence of earrings may seem round or even square when they are worn.

Large, round disks and hoops add almost as much width as the round, button earrings. Although they add some length as well as width, they cause the eye to travel in circles, emphasizing the curves in the face. Therefore, they tend to add roundness to the face and neck. If too large and heavy they may make the extremely small, thin face seem smaller and more angular by contrast, but their more frequent effect is that of increasing the width and roundness of the face. They are, or should be, prohibited the woman whose face is originally too wide.

Earrings that are oval or rectangular in shape create a feeling of length as well as of width. Therefore, particularly if worn close to the face, they add little, if any, width. The person whose face is naturally of pleasing proportions, but who appears to disadvantage when material width is added by earrings with round lines, frequently finds that oval and rectangular shapes aid in emphasizing the already pleasing contours. The person whose face is slightly too full or a trifle narrow may frequently select becoming earrings from the oval and rectangular shapes.

Extremely long, massive, pendant earrings, reaching to the shoulder, hide the neck and thus add materially to the width of both face and figure. Massive earrings add breadth to the face, even if they are not exceptionally long, but the longer they are the more the neck is shortened, with resultant increased width of figure. The very tall, thin woman with long, thin neck may frequently affect large pendant earrings, but the great majority of women find them extremely unbecoming, if not ridiculous.

Heavy pendants are likely to pull the ear lobe out of shape, giving the entire face a distorted appearance. Earrings touch-

Small flat earrings add less width to the face than do long and massive pendants; earrings extending up above the lobe of the ear may add width from ear to ear but are less likely to make the chin and lower part of the face seem heavier.

ing the shoulder are especially unbecoming to the round-shouldered woman. The effect of long earrings should always be studied from front, side, and back views.

Long, slender earrings usually do not increase breadth and may create long, slender lines, adding to the length and lessening the width of the face. The extremely narrow face may find them very trying, while the person whose face already possesses sufficient breadth, or perhaps a trifle too much, may find them vastly slenderizing and becoming. Delicate, dainty, slender earrings will, however, make the heavy, very full, large face seem larger by contrast, no earrings being becoming to faces of this type.

CHAPTER III

Necklines Frame the Face

HE FRAME for the face provided by necklines and collars greatly influences the apparent shape of the face. Necklines should be chosen carefully with consideration of their becomingness, their effect upon the contours of the face, for probably no other detail of a garment is so important in its effect upon the appearance of the wearer. The correct neckline used with hats and costume jewelry of pleasing lines aids greatly in making the face seem an ideal oval and, likewise, in making it the center of interest of the costume. Unbecoming necklines may frequently be made less difficult to wear if they are used with necklaces, scarfs, flowers, or other accessories that alter their lines.

Necklines That Seem to Widen the Face

A high, close collar covering the neck, or a scarf wrapped in high, close effect, shortens the face and thereby increases its apparent width. This high line, especially if achieved by means of softer drapes and folds, is becoming to the too-thin or too-narrow face, but extremely difficult for one that is originally too broad and full. It is shockingly unbecoming to the woman with a double chin, as it centers attention on that undesirable feature and at the same time seems to force it into fuller, rounder lines. A straight, stiff line in a high collar may increase angularity in the thin face, soft-scarf effects being much more becoming. Scarfs have the added advantage that they may be arranged to give lower and more becoming lines to the too-broad face.

Horizontal lines leading the eye across the face and neck tend to increase their apparent width. Therefore, square necklines, as well as those that extend across from shoulder to shoulder, increase the appearance of width in the face, making it seem perceptibly wider than is actually the case. Scarfs draped in a horizontal line give this broadening effect, at the same time

High, close collar increases width; low line which supplies larger background, makes face seem smaller.

tending to be less severe, being less likely to accent angularity than straight or square-cut outlines.

The round neckline tends to carry the eye across the face and neck, increasing the apparent width and at the same time emphasizing curves in a manner that lends grace to the too-thin face but exaggerates the fullness in the too-broad face. The woman with a narrow face finds the round neckline becoming, adding to the attractiveness of both face and neck. The woman whose face is too wide finds that it gives an increased appearance of rotundity, and it should not be worn, except with accessories that break the round line and create long or V-shapes.

A round collar, fitting in close lines about the neck, shortens the neck, increases the apparent width of the face, and adds decidedly to its rotundity. It charmingly emphasizes youthful curves in the face that is nearly the ideal oval in shape and aids in making the too-thin face seem fuller, but it should be carefully selected for the very thin face, as its round lines may, by contrast, emphasize angularity. The person with too-full face,

Square line increases width; V neckline decreases apparent width.

especially one that has mature heavy curves, will always find this very round, youthful collar unbecoming.

Necklines That Add Apparent Length

The neckline that is cut low tends to make the face appear smaller in contrast to the amount of throat exposed. For this reason the face usually appears smaller when evening dress is worn, particularly if it is extremely décolleté. The low neckline is usually becoming to the woman with too-full face, but for the woman with a thin, narrow face its effect should be offset by lines that tend to add width.

The *V*-line, leading the eye down and inward, makes the face and throat appear longer, more slender than their true proportions. In this day, when slenderness of face and figure is so universally desired, the *V*-line is perennially in fashion, as

Round, high neckline broadens; lower, oval or *V*-line is more slenderizing.

Round, close collar increases width; pointed collar makes face seem longer.

it proves becoming to the majority of women. The woman with an extremely narrow face will frequently find that it makes her face appear too thin, although this effect can be largely overcome by the use of a round choker necklace, a

flower, or a round or broad pin placed so that it softens the
V-line. The too-broad face is frequently benefited by a necklace, a pin, or other accessory that accents the V-neckline.

A narrow oval line adds length to the face, giving an impression of oval facial contours. The long, slender oval, like the V,
is generally becoming. In fact, the oval is more becoming than
the V to the face inclined to be thin.

Pointed collars, especially if they fit around the neck with
a slight V, make the face seem longer and less full. A narrow
collar with long slender points, the points placed down at the
center rather than out at the sides, gives a decided slenderizing
effect. This type of collar, so appropriate for sportswear, is
trying to the thin, narrow face, but becoming to the broad one.

Irregular Features

Too many folds, curves, or other details tend to accentuate
irregularities in the features, to make the too-full face heavy
and the too-thin face sharp and angular. Of the two extremes,
the too-thin face can, however, wear minute and numerous details to better advantage. Many ruffles, frills, or pleatings near
the face may soften too-thin features, while they would make
the broad face seem heavier in contrast with their fine detail.

Soft, smoothly flowing, rhythmic lines, rather than those
that are harsh and rigid in outline, tend to conceal the contours
of the face. They are, therefore, becoming to the majority of
women, soft outlines of well-chosen shapes being more flattering than rigid lines following the same shape. Both the too-
full and the too-thin face find them pleasing, especially if the
features are irregular.

For this reason scarf necklines, which not only supply soft
flowing lines, but which may be draped to assume almost any

shape becoming to the wearer, are especially valuable. They conceal the defects of either the too-thin or the too-full face or neck.

Fur scarfs, combining the flattering softness of fur with sufficient flexibility so that furs may be arranged to assume the lines most becoming to the wearer, provide an important method of framing the face so that its apparent contours are improved.

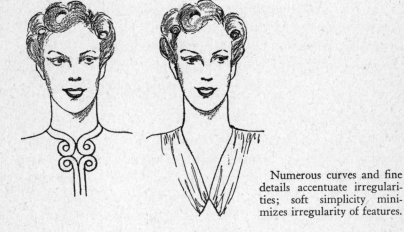

Numerous curves and fine details accentuate irregularities; soft simplicity minimizes irregularity of features.

Coat Collars

Collars open at the throat give length. High, close coat collars, or those with a scarf worn wrapped high and close around the neck, shorten or completely cover the neck and, by shortening the area of skin exposed, decrease the length and width of the face. This type of collar, particularly if of soft fur or fabric, or draped in soft lines, is becoming to the narrow, thin face. Stiff fabrics in harsh lines may be too severe for the thin, angular face. This type of collar tends to make the figure seem taller and more slender, therefore, if not too high and close, and may be recommended to the person with moderately full face and figure.

The collar or scarf that is draped low at the throat but high in the back gives a becoming background for the face, while, by revealing the throat, it makes the face seem longer and more slender. Many straight collars give this becoming effect when worn open; and scarfs may be draped so that this line is created.

If the collar is worn high at the neck and as low as possible at the throat in front, the line will be becoming to the broad face.

High collar, bow extending out at sides, gives breadth; scarf worn lower, with ends going up and down, increases length.

Ends may give length or breadth. Short scarfs or tab ends extending straight across the neck and out at the sides create a horizontal line that makes the face seem perceptibly broader. The figure is also made to seem wider. Many scarf effects may be arranged to form broad, horizontal lines, although the broadening may not be pronounced.

When a scarf or tie collar hangs down, creating a perpendicular line, the observer's eye is carried downward and the face is made to seem longer and less broad. The ascot tie, a smart way of wearing scarfs, gives a long line which, especially if tied low so that the throat is exposed, has slenderizing effects upon the face and upon the figure as well. Scarfs of a fabric that is soft and supple, rather than bulky, are most slenderizing, because they do not tend to cover all the neck.

Band or contrasting lapels. A band of contrasting trimming across the top of a collar gives apparent width to the face, even when the collar is worn open, as a horizontal line is created back of the face. The more pronounced this trimming, the

Contrasting band across top of collar increases width; fur extending down over lapels lengthens.

more decided the contrast between it and the body of the coat, the more evident is the broadening effect upon the face.

If the fur extends down over the lapels of the coat, carrying the observer's eye downward rather than straight across the collar, the face seems longer and more slender. An effect similar to that of a *V*-neckline has been created. This, of course, applies only to the coat that is worn open or, at least, turned back to display the long lines created by the fur.

Points may give length or width. Collars that are shaped so that a point comes low over each shoulder, extending far out at the sides, tend to make both the face and figure of the wearer seem broader, for the effect is much the same as that of a horizontal line at this point. Frequently, collars of this type may be arranged so that the broadening effect is less evident. The points may be folded over or made to seem less wide if the collar is standing up at the back and the points are away from the shoulder at the front.

Wide, low points at sides give width; narrow, high points form slenderizing background.

A collar cut so that the points are high and placed toward the back rather than the front of the shoulders, and cut narrow so that it does not extend across the shoulders, tends to lead the eye up and down rather than across the figure. The face and, likewise, the figure of the wearer therefore appear longer and more slender.

Lapels, wide or narrow. A collar made with wide, pointed lapels, the points extending up and outward, likewise carries the eye out across the figure, making the face and shoulders appear wider. It provides a youthful, boyish line that may be pertly becoming to slender faces and figures, but difficult for those that are full or heavy.

Slender, narrow, notched lapels lead the eye up and down, following the lines of a narrow *V*. The very thin woman finds the lines too long and too severe, accenting angularity and increasing the length of her face, neck, and figure. The woman

Wide, pointed lapels increase width; narrow, notched lapels decrease width.

whose face and neck need effects giving increased length and decreased width finds them much more becoming than wide lapels.

Big fur collars. A short, rather square or bulky collar, particularly if made of long-haired furs, tends to hide the neck and thus shorten the face, and at the same time to lead the observer's eye outward, making both the face and figure appear fuller. For the person with a thin face and neck, this is a graceful and becoming style, but for many persons it is extremely difficult.

The long shawl collar, forming an elongated *V-* or oval line, makes both the face and the figure seem longer and more slender.

High, bulky collar or long-haired fur increases width of face, neck and figure. Long, tuxedo collar of flat, short-haired fur, slenderizes.

This collar has an advantage for the face, in that, even when worn closed, it continues to form a *V*-line rather than a straight, high line. It has a disadvantage for the figure, particularly if long-haired furs are employed, in that, when closed, its several thicknesses of fur and fabric are usually concentrated over the bust, making the top of the figure appear heavy and mature.

The collar line that is formed with a band extending straight down the front or with a diagonal line reaching to the hem gives even greater height to the figure, at the same time making the face appear more slender. The shawl collar, ending in facings extending to the hem inside the coat, may give a similar effect.

CHAPTER IV

The Hat Is the Background for the Face

THE HAT can probably do more to alter the contours of the face than any other item of wearing apparel. It may form a frame softening the outlines of the face. Lacking sufficient size to form a frame, it may reveal the features frankly, to their advantage, perhaps, if they are good; to their disadvantage, if they are not perfect enough to be thrown into relief.

An interesting and becoming hat has a powerful influence in centering attention on the face. A hat should never, however, be so intricate in detail, so attention-compelling, that it, rather than the face, becomes the center of interest.

The tiny hat that makes no pretense of being a complete head covering or an adequate frame for the face has had a continuing favor for a number of years. This popularity indicates that, properly handled, it is more than an amusing "conversation piece," but a becoming ornament as well. The distinction between the pleasing and the ridiculous is often small, dependent sometimes on a hairdress that complements the hat, supplementing its lines and thus supplying a frame for the face that the hat alone fails to give. Sometimes a veil or well placed trimming accomplishes this purpose, and sometimes the hat violates all principles of good design and becomes audaciously amusing or downright ridiculous, according to the ability of the wearer to carry it. The hat that appears ludicrous when seen in old snapshots, or when tried on a season later than its purchase, is a hat of poor design. If the design is basically sound, it will seem flattering whether or not it is in fashion.

The Outlines of the Face

A small, close-fitting hat that is narrower than the widest part of the face gives the features undue prominence, making them seem large and out of proportion. Even the person with regular, delicate features finds the turban that is narrower than her features unbecoming, as it makes the top of her head seem unduly narrow and the cheek bones or widest part of the face too wide. Crowns of brimmed hats, also, should not appear narrower than the face.

A close-fitting hat should be slightly wider than the widest part of the face, making the features seem smaller and more delicate, and the face and entire head more pleasingly proportioned. In most instances the brimless hat should not be markedly wider than the face; the large hat makes the small face seem unduly small, and it makes most heads seem too large and out of proportion to the body.

The small close fitting calot or "beanie" almost exactly fitting the top or back of the head, often invisible from the front view, is as becoming as the hairdress which it should be selected to supplement. Trimming, often the only part of the part visible from the front, may be planned to give height or to emphasize width according to the basic principles of design discussed in this chapter. If the hairdress is truly flattering, the calot chosen to allow the hair, not the hat, to form the frame for the face, may be well advised. Careful study of profile and rear views is important, not only when the hat is selected but every time the hair and hat are rearranged.

Asymmetric trimming usually desirable. A small or brimless hat, particularly an off-the-forehead hat with trimming alike on both sides, relentlessly reveals irregularity. Contours

A straight, tight turban or a "pill box" narrower than the face materially increases width; softly draped lines, bows and feathers or flower hats with soft irregular contours are more slenderizing.

unlike on both sides of the face are particularly evident when the hat with bisymmetric trimming is worn.

Trimming alike on both sides of the hat emphasizes the sides of the face, leading the eye across and thereby increasing apparent width. This principle is applicable to both turbans and brimmed hats. Trimming placed exactly in the center also gives a bisymmetric division.

Soft transitional lines and asymmetric design (that which is not alike on both sides) hide facial defects, especially concealing the dissimilarity between features unlike on both sides. If the features are pronouncedly irregular, a brim shadowing the face will be most flattering. If only slightly irregular, softer lines in an asymmetric turban may be worn.

Trimming that is unlike on the two sides tends to decrease the width of the face and, at the same time, makes irregularities less conspicuous. Trimming should always be slightly to one side, never at the exact center, and should preferably be asymmetric in design and balance. Trimming placed at one side only provides the simplest method of producing an asymmetric effect.

Irregular lines most pleasing. A brim extending straight across the forehead cuts off the top of the head, thereby decreasing the length of the face and materially increasing its width. A straight brim extending far out at the sides and back is particularly trying, as it carries the width out beyond the face. The straight-brimmed sailor hat, worn on top of the head, rather than down over the forehead, cuts off little height; when worn at the back of the head, it gives background to the face without shortening it, although it shortens the apparent height of the figure from rear and side views.

A brim with an irregular line rather than one extending straight across the face causes no definite break in the length of the face. The eyebrow line, so smart some seasons, is particularly effective, in that it not only introduces no horizontal break, but carries the eye definitely upward, thereby increasing the apparent length of the face. The hat line extending upward on an oval line over the forehead aids in giving oval contours to the face.

A straight turban with a straight line across the forehead, especially if it is made with a band or cuff draped in predominantly horizontal lines, decreases the length of the face and increases the width in a manner that may be even more apparent than in the case of a straight brim, for the turban fails to give the large defects and make the background that may reduce the size of the face.

A straight, or nearly straight, sailor hat gives breadth to the face; an irregular horizontal line makes it seem more slender.

The turban draped with an irregular line, particularly with part of the forehead revealed, increases the apparent width of the face. The turban worn slanted in a diagonal line over the forehead, down at one side and up at the other, is more slenderizing than one worn straight, thus creating a horizontal line across the head.

Drooping brim widens face. The drooping brim hides the upper part of the face and decreases its length. As the drooping brim frequently has a horizontal line, which further increases the impression of width, it is particularly effective in making the too-long face look fuller, but unbecoming to the woman whose face is broad.

The hat coming low at the sides, hiding the neck and ears, carries the observer's eye downward, decreasing height. The face also looks shorter because the neck is hidden. If the long, drooping, shadowy brim partly covers the face, it may decrease width as well as length.

The turned-up brim, revealing the face and carrying the eye

A turned down brim hides the face, shortening and widening it; turned up brim adds length to face and to figure.

upward, gives long, slender contours. When part of the forehead is revealed, the line over the forehead curving high rather than extending straight across, the slenderizing effect of the hat with the upturned brim is further increased.

In this, as in other hats, soft textures, rhythmically flowing lines, rather than harsh, rigid ones, are much more easily worn and much more likely to emphasize a pleasing oval in the face. The turned-up brim may be very severe if textures and lines are stiff.

Shorter lines at the side, revealing the tips of the ears, make the face seem longer and more slender.

When fashion decrees hats coming down well over the head, it is wise to remember that styles are more flattering if they do not cover the entire ear but reveal its tip. Too short a line, revealing the entire ear and giving a horizontal effect extending from the forehead around the head, is much less becoming than the line that curves down, covering most of the ear but not its tip.

Lines that follow natural contours pleasing. Heavy lines and bulky folds make the face seem likewise heavy and solid,

A crown that seems too small for the head makes the wearer appear awkward; a crown that appears logically to fit the head gives the wearer more graceful proportions.

at the same time causing the entire head to seem bulky and large. Occasionally, a very small face will seem smaller by contrast with the massive type of hat, which is difficult for any woman to wear. It is this design so often used in matrons' hats that makes many women look older and more awkward than is actually the case. The woman of middle age so frequently betrays her years by the choice of a clumsy hat.

Hats that appear logically and structurally to fit the head are the most pleasing, giving the best proportions to the face and figure. Lines that follow the natural outlines of the head, with modifications planned to correct defects and make the face seem more nearly the ideal oval, are most becoming and artistically correct.

"A well-designed hat, suited to its wearer, should appear to be able to remain in place on the head without the aid of elastics or pins.   If it appears about to fall off it is not truly becoming." The author said this in earlier editions of this book.   She still finds the principle correct, yet in the past decade our eyes have become accustomed to small hats, obviously not designed as a head covering, but as a decoration to a well groomed head, as part of a becoming hairdress.   Many of these have charm and are truly flattering to their wearers.   Softly draped fabrics, bows, feathers, flowers, irregular in contour and offering a wide opportunity in the use of flattering textures and colors and an accent to the costume, have been used to form attractive head ornaments.   Those of irregular outline, with soft masses rather than rigid forms, have been most wearable.   The miniature or doll's hat, violating the principles of good design and obviously having no relation to the size of the wearer's head, has been successful only on those unusual women whose features are so flawless, their skin, their hair, their figure and carriage so perfect that they can unflinchingly bear the scrutiny that the fundamentally ridiculous hat calls forth.

High, heavy crowns; tall, pointed crowns; twisted, contorted shapes having no relation to the natural shape of the head— these are the "amusing" hats that appear grotesque on most women.   These are the hats that men ridicule and usually dislike.

Veils: Increase or Destroy Becomingness

When veils are the fashion they are entirely too widely and indiscriminately used. The smart woman, disgusted at the large number she sees which are unsuited to the hats upon which they are placed, and which are decidedly unbecoming to the wearer, rejects veils for herself. Then they are on the

A veil creates new lines; the veil partially covering the face introduces a horizontal line making the face seem shorter and wider. A small hat that is too stiff or too tiny for its wearer may be modified without bulk or heaviness by a skillfully draped veil.

way out of fashion. Yet veils, if rightly used, are flattering and are an effective means of modifying the lines of unbecoming hats and useful for freshening older ones.

May soften stiff hats. Hats which are becoming to the wearer, but which seem a little stiff or harsh, will have a softer and more flattering outline with a veil draped over them. A veil draped entirely over the hat and not over the face of the wearer may be made to give width where it is needed, or to give added height without introducing bulk.

Veil over face most becoming to slender women. When the veil covers or partly covers the face, it creates a horizontal break in line which makes the face seem fuller and, frequently, lessens the apparent height of the figure. Therefore, a veil extending down over the face may be very kind to the too-thin woman, partly because it both gives a suggestion of width and partially obscures and thus softens the contour. The woman with a broad face should either wear her veil thrown back or have it covering the entire face.

Flowing, loose veils which blow about the head with the slightest movement of air belong only on dainty, well-groomed, slender women. When flowing veils are worn, the rest of the costume should be free from floating ends.

The complexion when veiled seems clearer, because imperfections are hidden. If the veil is black or of a dark color, the skin seems whiter by contrast. Fragile, delicate veiling textures are most suitable for dainty women. Veils of heavier texture may give a well-groomed appearance to women of too pronounced a character to wear the fragile veiling suitable to petite women.

Defects May Be Corrected

"But if it weren't for my nose, my face would be all right," wails one woman. Another bemourns too much chin; another, the lack of it.

Frequently, the face approximates the ideal oval, is not markedly too narrow or too wide, but possesses one feature that is out of proportion, destroying harmony and beauty. The lines of the face may be noticeably irregular. Hats have a pronounced influence on the size and shape of the features.

Repetition emphasizes lines. If unpleasing lines in the face are repeated in the hat, they become much more evident. A drooping brim, the lines of which are similar to drooping lines of the face, makes the face seem older and more haggard, because the facial defects are emphasized, made more important

A drooping brim, repeating the drooping lines of the face makes them seem more evident; a brim turned upward at one or both sides seems to lift the face.

than more pleasing lines. Lines from nose to mouth are made especially conspicuous when a hat droops at the same angle.

Repetition will emphasize any line, whether pleasing or unpleasing. A hat, therefore, should always repeat pleasing lines, if it repeats any at all. The face with marked defects will, nevertheless, possess some pleasing lines. Although the mouth may droop, the chin may have a desirable oval line. If this is repeated in the curving line of the brim, the oval, not the drooping, line will be accented.

Contrast may also emphasize features. Lines at right angles to unpleasing lines in the face emphasize them in a very disagreeable manner. Drooping lines about the mouth will become much more evident when a hat brim turns upward in a line directly opposite to those of the mouth. Not only is the defect emphasized by lines in opposition to it, but it is caricatured.

Opposing lines may likewise emphasize pleasing lines in the face, accenting good features and ideal oval contours. A hat

A round crown and circular brim repeat the round lines in the face; broken and diagonal lines neither repeat nor oppose the round lines of the face and are therefore flattering to most women.

brim reversing the curve of the oval chin may accent the line of the chin as much as would the curve repeating it. In fact, the face appears more oval with an oval line at both the bottom and the top of the head.

Transitional lines are becoming. Straight, stiff lines, having little or no relation to the lines of the face, are harsh and severe, making the facial lines unduly prominent. Too-full curves are accented in contrast to the straight lines, and the face is made broader because straight lines in crown and brim cut off the top of the face. Angular lines appear more angular, partly because they have some relation to the straight lines of the hat, and partly because the straight type of brim reveals rather than shadows the face.

Lines that neither repeat nor oppose those of the face are becoming to the person with irregular features, as they distract attention from facial defects. A brim with a slanting, slightly curved line, higher at one side than at the other, becomingly

Off-the-face hat emphasizes turned-up nose; brim concealing the face minimizes turned-up nose.

shadows the face without calling attention to either good or bad facial characteristics. If the features are dissimilar on the two sides, as they are on the majority of faces, this type of hat is usually becoming.

Turned-up nose. Hats that have an upward-sweeping line at the front unduly emphasize the upward-curving line of the nose that is politely termed *retroussé*. A curving brim that appears to repeat exactly the profile line of the nose may give a truly ridiculous effect. A line that is directly opposite and that shows a curve exactly the reverse of that of the nose will, by its very contradiction, make the nose conspicuous. The brimless hat that reveals the profile without modification likewise accents the uptilted nose. A point or some other striking detail at the center of the hat is also undesirable.

A soft brim, one that droops rather than curves downward, shadows the face and conceals the curve of the upturned nose.

A large nose is made more prominent by tricorne; hat brim shadowing face conceals tilted nose.

A soft but only slightly irregular brim is most becoming. Either a severely straight or an extremely irregular line emphasizes the contours of the face.

Large nose. The large, prominent nose is made more so by repetition of its shape in the lines of a hat. The tricorne, with a point at the front similar to that of the nose, makes that feature unduly conspicuous. Sometimes there appear to be three noses on the hat and one on the face, an effect not only unbecoming but ludicrous as well. Small, brimless hats, and those with little or no brim at front and a longer one at the back, make the larger nose more prominent. Bisymmetric shapes or trimming placed exactly in the center also give emphasis to the nose.

The hat with a brim longer at the front than at the back, with trimming massed near the front, building out the forehead, gives balance to the large nose and makes it less conspicuous. Too-heavy masses at the front, destroying the balance of

A brim extending forward accentuates a receding chin; a brim and trimming sweeping upward center interest high on the head and make the chin less evident.

the head, would, of course, defeat their purpose, calling attention to the defect they are meant to conceal.

Receding chin. Trimming masses at the front, building out the front of the head, or brims longer at the front, make the receding chin even more insignificant than is naturally the case. If the hat repeats the slanting line of the profile, this effect is intensified.

A hat of moderate size, shadowing the forehead, making the upper part of the face less important, tends to bring the too-small lower part of the face into scale. The brim may be wide at the sides; it should, at least, extend beyond the widest part of the face, but should fit closely at the back, as a heavy line at this point makes the chin seem smaller by contrast.

The upturned brim revealing the upper part of the face and centering attention high on the head makes a receding chin less noticeable.

Forehead revealed exaggerates protruding chin; emphasis at front of hat minimizes protruding chin.

Protruding chin. When the chin protrudes, the profile assumes a backward slanting line that becomes most unpleasing when accentuated by a hat that slopes back from the forehead. This line is particularly disastrous in a turban or in a hat in which the brim turns abruptly away from the face, although a crown with these lines is unbecoming even when combined with a brimmed hat.

The protruding chin can be minimized by devices that build out the forehead, bringing the upper part of the face into scale with the lower part. Trimming placed near the front, brims that extend well forward rather than sloping back, and those extending beyond the chin line at front aid in reducing the chin. Unduly large, heavy effects over the forehead, those so massive that they do not appear to belong there, will only appear awkward and make the forehead seem smaller by compari-

Double chin emphasized by heavy folds and curves; interest centered high aids double chin.

son with their bulk, thereby making the protruding chin more obvious.

Double chin. Heavy bulges and folds, or numerous curves, repeat the drooping curves and lines of the double chin. The hat that curves down over the cheek and the one that is lower at the back repeat the line of the chin and by so doing call attention to a feature that every woman wishes to avoid emphasizing. Trimming placed low on the neck is unbecoming, especially if the neck as well as the chin is heavy. The turban and the very stiff, straight hat are likewise unbecoming, as they reveal contours.

The double chin is best concealed by a hat with a moderate brim, and by soft but not unduly curved or irregular lines in both brim and crown. Lines and trimming should be designed to center interest high on the head, preferably near the front.

Small and off-the-face hats reveal square corners of glasses; brimmed hat shadows glasses making them less conspicuous.

Brims that turn up at the back tend to lead the eye upward, away from the neck and chin.

Brimmed hat shadows glasses, concealing corners. Glasses, particularly heavy-rimmed spectacles, create an out-of-proportion feature, giving square corners to the face. A small hat, beyond which the square corners protrude, is decidedly unbecoming to any woman who must wear glasses on the street or at other times when a hat is worn. Brimless hats, extremely small brims, and those that turn up sharply away from the face should be avoided.

A hat with a brim that extends at least slightly beyond the corner formed by the glasses shadows them and prevents disturbing reflections of light that make the lenses more conspicuous. A soft, slightly drooping line is most becoming. A large brim tends further to minimize the glasses, but must, of course, be selected with discretion, after the consideration of other features of the face and figure of the wearer. When heavy, shell-rimmed spectacles are worn, sport or tailored styles of hats and other apparel designed with simplicity of detail are most appropriate.

CHAPTER V

Relating the Colors Worn to the Pigmentation of the Skin

ALTHOUGH one may make general classification of colors suited to types, specific recommendations of colors becoming to individuals should be based upon analysis of their skin, hair, and eyes.

The coloring of the skin is of chief importance, since the appearance of a glowing, healthful skin is most necessary to a pleasing and attractive appearance. The coloring of the hair is usually of secondary importance; that of the eyes, contrary to general opinion, should be the third consideration. This is because the areas of skin and hair are larger and, therefore, more conspicuous. When a hat is worn covering most of the hair, the eyes may gain priority, since their relative area has been increased.

Exceptions to this order may be made when either the hair or the eyes are particularly beautiful, and it is desirable to emphasize them above other features. Even when this is done, care should be taken in using colors that are becoming to the skin.

Since the skin ranks first in importance, the woman who wishes to increase her list of becoming colors should make every attempt to improve her complexion. Revision of one's opinion of wearable colors should be made frequently, according to changes in the skin produced by seasons or the state of health. Most women find that colors that are becoming in winter and early spring are not so flattering to the tanned or sunburned skin of late summer. The list likewise changes as one becomes older, sometimes increasing as the hair loses color. Discreet use of make-up intensifying natural color, occasional change from warm to cool coloring with the use of violet-red rather than orange-red rouge or vice versa, emphasis given to the eyes by discreetly applied mascara or shadow—all these increase the list of wearable and becoming colors.

Make-Up

Powder should match background color. Powder should be used, not to change the color of the skin, but to improve its texture, remove shine, and veil imperfections. Powder, therefore, should match the skin as closely as possible in hue, intensity, and value. Powders that are too light, too dark, too pink, or too yellow contrast unpleasantly with the natural color of the skin, revealing the presence of the powder, which should be an inconspicuous aid to beauty.

Powder foundations that actually change the color of the skin are useful to cover skin defects, scars, birthmarks, dark circles under the eyes. When used in this way they should match as closely as possible the natural color of the skin. These same foundations, if very skillfully applied and if completely covering all the visible skin of the face and neck so that there is no telltale contrast near the hairlines or eyes, or between the face and neck, may be used to improve the coloring of the unhealthy looking skin. It takes much skill and a sharp scrutiny with good eyesight to change the coloring to a perceptible degree. The average woman usually finds that a colored foundation that changes the actual color of her skin not only reveals its artifice, but that it has a mask-like quality that robs her of natural charm and facial expressiveness. If the skin is roughened or the pores enlarged, heavier concentrations of color are likely to emphasize these defects. A very light use of a color only slightly modifying the natural coloring is most likely to be successful.

Hue of rouge should match skin. The color of rouge and lipstick has great influence upon the apparent coloring of the individual. In most instances, rouge and lipstick should match the hue found in the wearer's skin. A person with orange-red coloring should use orange-red rouge; one with violet-red coloring should select rouge of that hue. In some instances, a slight change of hue may improve the individual's appearance. The person whose skin is extremely cool in coloring, the violet-red so subdued that the skin has an anemic, bluish cast, may find that rouge more nearly a true red, or even an orange-red, will lend an appearance of health and vitality that violet-red rouge would not supply. This is, however, an exception to the general rule, a method that should be used only after careful consideration and with discretion in the application of the make-up. A slight change in color, a more red tone to match red used in the costume, slightly orange-red or violet-red for wear with colors of these hues, is frequently advisable.

Make-up blends best with the coloring of the skin, giving it a softer, more transparent effect if it matches not only in hue but in value (lightness or darkness) and in intensity (purity, brightness, or grayness).

Since the natural coloring is most frequently of middle value (neither extremely light nor extremely dark), rouge should likewise be of medium value. A dark rouge can be made to appear lighter by using it lightly, but a too-pale rouge fails to give the depth of naturalness of color obtained from lower values.

Since nature softens or grays the natural coloring, a rouge of dulled, not too-vivid intensity is most natural. Vivid, bright-colored rouges stand out as spots of color no matter how carefully they are applied or how closely their hue approximates the natural hue of the lips and cheeks. They tend to coarsen the appearance of the skin. The physical condition of the wearer may change the color of rouge or lipstick. Colors sometimes become much more violet after they have been worn for several hours.

Placement changes size and shape of face. As a general rule, rouge should be placed where the natural color appears. Slight but not startling deviations from this rule may improve the contour of the face, making it appear more truly the ideal oval. If the face is broad the color should not extend too far out, the deepest color being near the nose, blended so that it fades out before the widest part of the face is reached. That placed slightly high tends to lengthen the face; that placed low or far out seems to add width. If the cheek bones are prominent, rouge should be placed below them, the color fading out softly over the high point of the bone, and being most definite below them and slightly nearer the nose. If the color is too far away, too sharply removed from the high or prominent cheek bones, they become more evident by means of the very device meant to conceal them. Rouge on the tips of the ears gives additional width to the face. Placed at the top of a receding chin it may give this feature greater prominence. At the tip of the chin it shortens the face. A slight amount under a double chin makes a shadow that helps to blot out that feature. This device is effective only under artificial lighting—and it must be done oh, so subtly!

Mouth changed by lipstick. The expression of the mouth may be greatly changed by the wise use of lipstick and totally eradicated by the unwise use of it. If spread on with a thick, waxy appearance, or extended beyond the actual outlines of the lips, it gives a hard, unnatural appearance to the entire face. Too-vivid color, or color dissimilar to the natural color of the lips, may also have this effect. Rouge so placed that the color is deepest at the center of the mouth, is blended out toward the edges, and is very faint at the ends will make the mouth seem smaller. It is usually best to carry the color out to the corners of the mouth, even though it be made more definite in the center. If the corners are left uncolored, the mouth and the entire face seem older; the effect is much the same as that of the drooping, sagging lines caused by the years, for they too obscure the corners of the mouth and make it seem smaller. Thin lips may be made to seem fuller if the color is deeper on the upper lip, and the division at the center is emphasized by a definite outline. Applying the color beyond the actual outline of the lips usually defeats its purpose, which becomes apparent, at the same time giving a harsh, unsympathetic appearance to the mouth.

Lipstick may be applied with a small brush, which is especially useful for obtaining a sharp clear outline. While a sharply pointed lipstick may be successfully used, a blunted point usually results in a smeared outline unless a finger tip or a brush is used to spread the color.

The color is more permanent as well as more natural if it is applied liberally, allowed to remain on about ten minutes, and then blotted with facial tissue to remove the excess. It may then be retouched slightly if necessary. If the basic color approximates the natural coloring, a more vivid lipstick may sometimes be successfully used for retouching.

Devices That Affect the Color of the Face

Emphasizing color in cheeks. The wearing of a color complementary to the flesh tints may increase the apparent amount of color in the face. The blue-greens complementary to orange-red and violet-red hues, therefore, are especially becoming to persons who need to increase the amount of color in their face and lips. The complementary colors bring out the color under the skin, giving a clear, transparent quality that is not to be obtained by the addition of rouge alone.

If the skin is too florid, or if too much rouge or rouge of an unbecoming color is worn, the use of the complementary blue-greens will increase and accentuate the color, coarsening the appearance of the skin.

High and low values. The use near the face of light colors in the flesh tints, pale orange-red or violet-red (the former most becoming to the majority of persons), increases, by means of reflection, the apparent amount of color in the face. Thus, of these flesh tints, the warmer off-white colors are especially becoming to the woman who needs to increase the apparent amount of color in her face, and difficult for the woman with a florid skin. They may be used either for the entire costume or as a transitional color worn near the face, relieving the trying effect of less flattering colors. Clear, smooth skins gain more apparent color by reflection than do those of rough, cloudy texture. The woman who tends to have too much color in her face may find the more neutralized effects in these same colors more easily worn—an orange-red of high value but neutralized enough so that the color is no longer definitely orange-red but a soft tan or beige.

White and other high values reflect light; therefore, they do not absorb or lessen the color of the face. All light colors tend to increase the color of the face, but not so markedly as do those in the flesh tints. Black and other low values absorb light, seeming to drain the color from the face. For this reason, they are particularly becoming to the florid complexion, but unbecoming to pale or yellow skins.

Vivid hues. The use of extremely vivid, intense colors lessens the appearance of color in the face, fading or neutralizing facial color tone by means of their greater strength. The person who is pale should be extremely cautious in the use of intense reds, violet-reds, or orange-reds and should accompany them with rouge of the right hue. Low and middle intensities will, in most instances, be more becoming.

The person whose skin is too yellow, having too little of the red coloring and too much yellow pigmentation, should, particularly if she is dark, avoid brilliant blues, which will make her skin seem flagrantly yellow.

The reflection from yellow worn near the face likewise increases the apparent amount of yellow in the skin. Vivid yellows are unbecoming to the person who has too much of this color in her skin, as they make this hue conspicuous both by repetition and reflection.

Minimizing yellow in the face. The use of colors analogous to yellow, especially orange and red-orange, lessens the apparent amount of yellow in the skin. The red in these colors reflects red into the face, while the yellow blends with the coloring of the skin, making the yellowness of the skin inconspicuous.

Persons with dark skin containing considerable yellow pigmentation find the red-orange range particularly becoming. Fairer persons with too much yellow in the skin sometimes find that the yellow-green and green range likewise lessens the amount of yellow in their skin. The further removed from yellow and the more green in the hue, the less conspicuous becomes the yellow in the skin.

Sallowness, which is an unhealthy yellow pigmentation in the skin, is increased in effect when neutral colors of value similar to the skin are worn. Light grays and tans, therefore, are particularly difficult for the person whose skin has too much yellow and too little red coloring. These neutral shades afford insufficient contrast, giving a monotonous appearance and emphasizing the lack of life in the skin.

Shadows in the face, circles under the eyes, and other unhealthy hues showing in the skin are emphasized by the use of complementary colors, sometimes by reflection of color. Frequently there is no actual discoloration of the skin, but the hollows take on the dark, usually violet color common to shadowed surfaces. Vivid greens, yellow-greens, and yellow are likely to cast violet or blue shadows, the complementary afterimage being thrown on the face. Reflection of color from vivid violets and blues, sometimes from green, may throw these colors into the face, particularly into hollows or lines in the face. Shiny-surfaced fabrics are more likely to produce this result.

Devices That Change Becomingness of Colors

Light values near face. The use of white, of off-whites, or of other light values near the face gives a relief from extremely vivid intensities or from hues that force yellow or other undesirable tinges in the skin. Pearl, ivory, or other light beads frequently give this value contrast. Soft flesh tints, subdued red-orange or red-violet, are particularly effective used as value contrasts near the face. Gray and beige and lighter tints of the color used in the body of the costume are likewise good. It is notable that light colors, which might be unbecoming if used in entirety for the costume, may make a most effective contrast if used as a relief from darker or more vivid colors.

Décolletage *softens unbecoming colors.* The expanse of flesh showing, when an evening gown with low-cut neckline and no sleeves is worn, separates the face from unbecoming colors. For this reason, many women are able to use colors for formal wear that would be exceedingly trying for more informal occasions, even under kindly artificial lights. Black, which may absorb the delicate color from the face when worn near it, may accent delicate coloring when used in a décolleté gown.

Dark value near face. A small note of black or other dark-value contrast used near the face may increase the becomingness of light colors. This is particularly true in the case of light neutral tones. Persons with rather light, drab coloring, with no decided value contrast, find the use of dark accents near the face especially helpful. A dark hat or a dark note in a necklace, earrings, a brooch, a flower, a collar, or a scarf may give the individual the emphasis needed to permit her to wear light, bright, or neutral colors. A fur scarf or cape may sometimes supply the dark accent necessary to make an otherwise difficult color becoming.

Color contrast near face lends vitality. No other factor is more effective than color contrast in making the face the center of interest in the composition created by the costume and the individual. Wisely chosen color accent will enhance the color-

ing of the wearer, making the eyes look darker and more colorful; the hair brighter; and the skin clearer, with more pleasing
flesh tints. The individual who wishes to wear a color that
she knows to be unbecoming may frequently use it effectively
by combining it with one of the colors that she knows to be
actively becoming. Earrings, necklaces, brooches, bracelets,
and other items of costume jewelry serve as most useful and
convenient methods of introducing becoming color accents near
the face. Flowers and scarfs are also recommended.

Many women who have learned to dress distinctively and becomingly choose simple clothes of good lines to serve as a background for jewelry or other accessories of colors that they know
to be flattering. They frequently invest a fairly large proportion of their clothing budget in accessories of more or less permanent value.

Textures change effect of colors. Textures have great influence on the becomingness of colors. Intense vivid colors are
more becoming, less likely to overshadow the personality of the
wearer, if they are used in soft, dull-surfaced fabrics. On the
other hand, dark colors—particularly black, which tends to
absorb color from the face—will be more becoming in a lustrous material like velvet. Extremely shiny fabrics like satin,
however, make almost all colors more difficult to wear, as they
reflect light into the face, showing up its imperfections much as
any strong light would. Satins are least trying when they
reflect a soft, warm light increasing the flesh tints. Rosy beiges
and warm off-whites are more becoming than most other colors
when in shiny-surfaced materials. As black absorbs light,
black satin reflects less than other satins. It is much less trying
than a dead white, which reflects all light.

Shiny textures, both by the light they reflect upon the skin and by contrast with their own smooth surfaces, emphasize imperfections in the skin. Shiny surfaces, therefore, should be relieved by the use of duller textures near the face, just as dark colors or those of vivid intensity are relieved by light values and more neutralized intensities.

Furs and velvets are usually flattering. Their lustrous, soft textures have life and animation, but do not reflect light on the face as do smooth, hard surfaces. Women who find both black and brown unbecoming in dull fabrics can usually wear one of these colors in furs.

Coloring changed by hats. Colors worn above the face, especially those worn in hats covering the hair, change the apparent coloring of the wearer in a most perceptible manner. A dark hat may give needed emphasis to an individual whose personal coloring is monotonous, too nearly one tone, and without decided value contrast between hair and skin. A hat in a warm color may increase the apparent warmth, reflecting warm lights into the skin. A hat of a cool color, reflecting its color into cool eyes, makes the eyes more prominent, thereby changing the individual's apparent coloring. It may at the same time intensify flesh tints by complementary contrast. No one should decide definitely that she can or cannot wear a color until she has tried it with light and dark hats, and until she has tried to wear the color itself in a hat.

Flattering Colors Best in Case of Doubt

The individual whose complexion is poor, and who is uncertain as to the effect of colors upon her appearance, does well to choose from a list of generally becoming colors. This includes largely dark and definitely grayed or softened colors, dark blue, especially a grayed blue, dark green, dark blue-green, dark red, violet-red and orange-red (the latter including browns, particularly so-called red-browns), dark warm gray or taupe, and black. Light tints, also in softened intensities, include white and more particularly warm off-whites, lighter blue-greens, and orange-reds.

Certain colors, most of them extremely vivid, are unbecoming to all but a few fortunate persons with flawless complexion and unusually pleasing coloring. Even to persons who can wear them they are seldom as flattering as less difficult colors. This list includes bright vivid blues, particularly in light or medium values; bright blue-violet, violet, and red-violet; and bright yellow and orange.

Colored nail polish or enamel should be definitely related to the color of the make-up. When bright fingernails are worn, they are almost always more successful if they match the lipstick. When paler, but definitely colored nail polish is worn, it may repeat the cheek rouge.

Magenta or violet-red fingernails will clash with red or orange-red lipstick. A coloring definitely unrelated to the natural coloring of finger tips or lips may occasionally be chosen to repeat some accent in the dress.

Brightly colored fingernails look well only on perfectly groomed, well-shaped hands. The tiniest flaw or chip in the enamel should not be permitted. It is said that long, conspicuous fingernails are worn to show the world that their owner belongs to the leisured class and has the time and money to keep them perfect. Whether or not this is a good reason for the fashion of brilliant fingernails is immaterial, as long as every woman wearing them makes certain that they are becoming to her hands, and that she can keep them in perfect repair, either by removing the bright polish when the tiniest flaw appears or by repairing the damage skillfully until the nails can be done over.

Unless the hands are beautiful in shape and in skin texture, the nails are well shaped and of smooth texture, colorless or very light rose polish is most becoming. Some well-groomed women have remained faithful to the simple natural polish obtained from a dry powder carefully rubbed to a polish with a buffer. Some beauty parlors report that this fashion is returning even among the less conservative women who have used the brighter polish for ten years.

Conspicuous fingernails may make the hands more noticeable than the face. This is seldom desirable, for the face should be the center of interest. A few women with beautiful hands and plain faces may deliberately wish to emphasize their hands so that they will attract attention to their best feature. If the individual has even a gleam of intelligence to give interest to her face, she need not feel that her hands are or should be more important. Bright nails matching bright lipstick may give interest to both face and hands.

CHAPTER VI

Relating the Colors Worn to the Pigmentation of the Hair and Eyes

THE EFFECT OF COLORS upon the hair and eyes should be carefully considered, even though these points should be subordinated to that of selecting colors becoming to the skin.

The person with a slender and well-proportioned figure, who need not fear increasing her size or emphasizing her silhouette and who has a clear, healthy complexion, can wear almost any beautiful color. She may consider her eyes and hair first, emphasizing whichever is the more attractive feature. Occasionally, persons with unusually beautiful hair or eyes can afford to wear colors enhancing their most distinctive feature, even at the expense of figure or complexion, although never if it pronouncedly magnifies a defect.

The Hair

Improved luster of hair emphasizes color. The actual color of the hair can best be enhanced by care, which increases its luster, the lights reflected by shining hair giving it added beauty of color. Massage and brushing, careful shampooing with complete rinsing out of the soap, the use of a mildly acid rinse—

such as lemon, vinegar, or tartaric acid, which restores the natural acidity of the hair—aids in achieving brilliance and luster.

Changing the actual color of the hair is likely to create unnatural contrasts with the coloring of eyes, eyelashes, and eyebrows; and with the skin, giving a harsh, coarsened appearance to the wearer. This is not always the case, the question being largely one of personal taste, together with the difficulty of altering the hair without seriously injuring its texture. Many dyes not only injure the hair but also affect the skin and general health of the individual. Bluing may safely be used to whiten the hair. Henna is not injurious, but usually produces an unnatural orange color.

Enhancing color of the hair. The hair may be made to appear brighter and more colorful if the opposite or complementary color is worn. Yellow hair will seem more golden, a more decided yellow, if a blue costume is worn. Yellow-orange hair will seem more colorful if the blue-greens are used as a foil. The so-called red hair, which is actually orange or red-orange, is frequently cheapened by the decided contrast with its complementary color, but brown hair, the darker value and more neutralized intensity in red-orange hued hair, may gain needed life and vitality. The entire range of cool colors— blue-violet, sometimes violet, blue, blue-greens and green—may be used to complement yellow and red-orange hair. The hue most becoming to the individual's skin, hair, and eyes should be chosen.

Intensity and value as well as hue should be carefully considered. A vivid intensity may coarsen the wearer's coloring; a neutralized intensity of the same color may greatly enhance it. A vivid blue may perceptibly brighten yellow hair, but, at the same time, make the skin unduly yellow, while blue eyes might appear faded by contrast.

Value contrasts give emphasis to hair. Particular care must be taken that the value is not so similar to the dominant values in the coloring of the wearer that a monotonous effect is created. Special care must be taken in the case of blondes, in which type the natural coloring is all of high value. If the dominant color of the costume is of light value, a dark value may be introduced as an accent.

If the value of the colors used in the costume are either lighter or darker than that of the hair, the latter gains in character and distinction. Values similar to that of the hair are likely to make it seem dull and insignificant. This is especially true when the same hue or one closely analogous to that of the hair is used. Attempting to match the hair is usually a mistake, unless one desires to subdue its color, as in the case of so-called red hair, which may look softer and more harmonious when blended in the color scheme by means of a matching or closely allied hue in a value similar to that of the hair.

Contrast in value is especially necessary with gray hair; it is imperative with hair that is turning gray and has assumed that greenish, muddy look, resulting from a mixture of gray and darker hairs.

Warm, vivid, analogous colors fade hair. Analogous colors that are slightly warmer in hue and more vivid in intensity make the hair seem faded by contrast. A bright yellow garment with hair less yellow and bright overshadows the yellow in the hair. In the same way, brown hair with brown apparel that is slightly more red, richer and more vivid in tone, loses by proximity to the more forceful color. This is particularly true if the texture is finer and more lustrous than that of the hair.

Fine furs with a warm reddish brown coloring frequently make the hair appear faded.

On the other hand, colors slightly less vivid, slightly less warm than the hair, enhance the color of the hair. Contrast of value will intensify this effect. A popular actress with colorful brown hair frequently wears a light dull brown, definitely several shades lighter and of a hue more neutralized and slightly less red than that of her hair. As a result, the beauty of her hair is accented.

The Eyes

Make-up alters size and color of eyes. Eye make-up may deepen the color of the eyes, increase their apparent size, and make them look more vital and alert; or it may make them look hard and coldly expressionless. Much more care is needed for the successful use of eye make-up in the daytime than for wear in the evening under artificial lights. Many experts advise that it be reserved entirely for evening use. Women who must wear glasses frequently find that eye make-up does much to counteract their unbecoming effect. When glasses are worn, make-up may be used in the daytime if it has been carefully applied and the results examined as it appears when the glasses are worn. Women who wear glasses may not have sufficiently good eyesight to apply eye make-up themselves, and for this reason may unknowingly wear splotched or too heavy mascara. Glasses of great magnification may make eye make-up appear heavier than it actually is.

Although darkening the eyelashes increases their effectiveness as a frame for the eyes, making the lashes seem thicker and longer and the color of the eyes deeper, they should not be made markedly darker than the color of the hair. Persons with blonde or light brown hair should use dark brown, not black, on their eyelashes. Many experts advise dark brown eye make-up for all except the person with inky, blue-black hair. Eye pencil may be used to give a faint outline at the base of the lashes as well as to darken the eyebrows. Care should be taken not to darken the skin, only the eyebrows.

Colored eye shadow, green in tone for green eyes, blue for blue, blue-green for those of this hue, dark brown for brown eyes, may be applied discreetly to the lids. If used so that it gives just a faint suggestion of color, it will deepen the apparent color of the eyes, making them seem larger and brighter. Violet eye-shadow, supplementing the color of nature's shadows, may give becoming depth to the eyes.

Eyes accented by matching hue. The color of the eyes may be greatly intensified by the repetition of their hue in the costume, the liquid depth of the eye acting as a mirror to reflect color. The color must be carefully controlled, however, and used either in small areas or with partially neutralized intensities. A dress in a vivid color of the same hue as the eyes, say, a bright blue dress, will make even very blue eyes seem pale, characterless, and dull by contrast; but a small area of this same vivid color would accent the blue of the eyes. A dress of soft grayed blue or one in a low value would not overpower the color of the eyes. The same is true of green. With brown, there is little danger of submerging the color of the eyes, as this color is naturally of a lower value and of a more neutralized intensity.

Often the apparent hue of the eyes may be changed by the colors worn. Gray eyes, which usually are not a totally neutral gray but green or blue, may be made to appear of a definite color, blue, green, or sometimes violet, by the use of these colors.

Intensifying color of the eyes. The use of a hue complementary to that of the eyes may also increase their apparent color. Yellow, orange, and red-orange, used either in the entire costume or in accents, may increase the coloring of eyes in the cool-color range as much as would a repetition of their coloring.

Blue-green apparel frequently makes blue eyes more green, or vice versa, giving a subtle, interesting hue to the eyes. Gold flecks in gray eyes may become apparent when orange is worn, while this hue in hazel eyes is very markedly accented. Hazel eyes frequently become gray when gray or cool colors are worn.

Since the skin is the first consideration in the selection of colors worn, and the hair of second importance, the eyes should be emphasized by the method most becoming to the skin and hair. Persons with skin of warm coloring and eyes of cool color may find that the orange tones are best, both for the skin and as a complement to the eyes. Persons with fair hair, cool skin, and brown or hazel eyes frequently find that the cool colors enhance hair, skin, and eyes.

CHAPTER VII

Critical Analysis of Individual Coloring

MOST WOMEN possess the happy faculty of overlooking the defects of face and figure that they see daily and never actually observe. This habit precludes their always appearing at their best. A periodical analysis of a woman's ever-changing coloring will permit her to choose costume colors wisely.

The hue of background and foreground should be noted, as this gives an indication of colors that should be avoided and those that are likely to prove becoming. Actual colors in variations of hue, value, and intensity should then be tried on, first, under a clear natural light, then under artificial lights, so that colors that are becoming under both conditions may be determined.

The effect of each color upon skin, hair, and eyes should be noted. One should not be content to say that blue is becoming, but to determine which blue is most becoming—blue, blue-green, or violet-blue. Whether light, middle, or low values of this blue do most to enhance the coloring of the individual should also be determined. Likewise, can the individual wear all intensities? Which does she wear best? These questions should be asked with regard to every hue, value, and intensity, and in relation to shiny and dull surfaces, which reflect color upon the skin or absorb color reflected from it.

A list of the colors most becoming in daytime, those most pleasing in street shades, for general daytime or afternoon wear, should be made. The most flattering colors, those that are wearable but do not greatly enhance the appearance of the individual, and those that should not be worn because they detract from the charm of the individual or emphasize her defects, should all be noted. Color combinations as well as separate hues should be considered. A woman having such a list of colors, the result of an analysis made by other persons, should be able to select colors for herself almost as well as another person could do it, for the list gives her the eyes of the critical observer.

The rating scale for color readings. The chart, pages 78, 79, for color readings has been planned so that little if any writing is required. Checks should serve to indicate both the coloring of the individual and the colors that may and may not be worn. This rating scale necessarily has those limitations imposed by black-and-white print. For this reason, it should be used in conjunction with the color plate showing the basic hues found in lips and cheeks and in the background skin tones, and the major hues that should be considered in their relation to the costume.

If possible, color readings should always be given with actual samples of colored material. It is desirable that fabrics of each hue be used in three values and in three intensities of each value. This means that a set of samples for professional or classroom use should include 9 variations of each of the 18 hues listed. For personal use, a woman may experiment, first, among those colors suggested in the chapters on color types as usually most becoming to her own type. Colored papers, obtainable at any school or artist's supply store, will give basic colors and their scientific color names.

Skin tones. The hue of the lips and cheeks may be determined by holding the color plate directly against the face, comparing the coloring of the cheeks and lips, first, with orange-red, then with red, then with violet-red. In many instances, the hue will be found to be between two of these hues, in which case a check may be placed between them rather than directly after them. If the coloring is naturally vivid, a check will be made under definite; if it is faint, the check will be under subdued; while average coloring will be indicated under medium. This point may likewise be made more flexible by placing the checks at intermediate points rather than definitely under one of the three.

The colors shown on the color plate may be held against either the forehead or the neck, the hue of the background skin tones being most evident at these points. The amount of yellow in the skin is particularly important, since a predominance of yellow gives an unhealthy tone. Sometimes yellow is sufficiently grayed to appear almost green-yellow, in which case a check might be made above yellow where green-yellow would appear if included on this chart (it has been omitted because the skin is not actually green-yellow, but, rather, a grayed-yellow).

Color-and-line analysis should be severely honest, uncomplimentary in case of doubt, rather than flattering. If the skin is rated as having slightly more yellow than it actually possesses, it will be easier not to prescribe colors that will accent the yellow in the skin.

Persons unused to analyzing the skin may at first have some difficulty in distinguishing between clearness and transparency.

RATING SCALE FOR COLOR READING

LIPS AND CHEEKS

Hues	Definite	Medium	Subdued
Orange-red...............			
Red.......................			
Violet-red................			

BACKGROUND SKIN TONES

Hues	Light	Medium	Dark
Yellow....................			
Orange-yellow.............			
Yellow-orange.............			
Orange....................			
Red-orange................			

TEXTURE OF SKIN

Clear	Medium	Cloudy
Transparent	Medium	Opaque

HAIR

Hues	VALUE OF COLOR			INTENSITY OF COLOR			TEXTURE		
	Light	Medium	Dark	Vivid	Medium	Grayed	Bright	Medium	Dull
Green-yellow...........									
Yellow.................									
Orange-yellow..........									
Orange.................									
Red-orange.............									
Gray...................									
White..................									
Mixed..................									
Blue-black.............									
Brown-black............									

EYES

Hues	VALUE OF COLOR			INTENSITY OF COLOR			LUSTER		
	Light	Medium	Dark	Vivid	Medium	Grayed	Bright	Medium	Dull
Violet-blue.............									
Blue...................									
Green-blue.............									
Blue-green.............									
Green..................									
Brown..................									

78

HUES IN RELATION TO NATURAL COLORING OF INDIVIDUAL

Hues	VALUE OF COLOR			INTENSITY OF COLOR			RATING OF COLOR		
	Light	Medium	Dark	Bright	Medium	Grayed	Becoming	Wearable	Unbecoming
Yellow...............									
Orange-yellow...........									
Yellow-orange...........									
Orange.................									
Red-orange.............									
Orange-red.............									
Red....									
Violet-red.............									
Red-violet.............									
Violet.................									
Blue-violet.............									
Violet-blue.............									
Blue..................									
Green-blue.............									
Blue-green.............									
Green.................									
Yellow-green...........									
Green-yellow...........									

The terms *clear, medium,* and *cloudy* are used here to indicate skins that are free from blemishes, scars, or similar imperfections, while the terms *transparent, medium,* and *opaque* relate to the thickness of the skin; to the extent to which undertones of bright color seem to show through the outer skin. Skin, obviously, may be clear or free from imperfections and yet not be transparent.

Color and texture of hair. When analyzing the hair, it is necessary to distinguish between the color of the hair and its texture. After determining the actual hue, one must judge, first, whether it is light or dark, which is easy to determine; then the intensity, whether it is bright, medium, or grayed, which is somewhat more difficult, since many people are prone to judge the hair as bright when there is definitely a bright colorful sheen. The hair might be what we usually call *brown,* yet have colorful high lights. We would check the brown hair as red-orange, but we must not make the mistake of checking it as bright, which would indicate that the hair was so-called red rather than brown. Brown hair of this character would actually be of medium intensity. Its texture would unquestionably be bright. A so-called red head might have red-orange or, perhaps, orange hair of bright intensity. Its texture might be dull, medium, or bright.

Eyes. Eyes must likewise be judged according to their hue, value, intensity, and natural brilliance.

Cautions. When giving color readings, it is desirable to analyze the coloring, first, in its natural state without any make-up whatsoever, then to experiment with make-up until the most pleasing effect has been obtained. Rouge of the natural hue should be applied; but, since slight differences in hue sometimes make vast differences in becomingness, it is often worth while to apply and then remove several different rouges until the most becoming one has been found. A powder blended to match the natural background hue of the skin should likewise be applied before the samples of color are tried on. Unless the individual is intending to adopt new make-up permanently, it is best to try the colors on her as she usually appears. It is very unsatisfactory to use a larger quantity of make-up or more vivid coloring than the individual will herself adopt.

When studying one's own coloring, it is well to remember that a mirror tends to neutralize coloring, by adding a bluish tinge, thus making the coloring appear slightly colder or more violet than it actually is. Study of the color in the finger tips aids in determining the actual color of the cheeks, since the two are closely akin. The color inside the wrist and of the back of the hand gives an indication of the background coloring of the neck and forehead. Personal analysis made by the aid of mirrors and inspection of the hands should be checked with a careful study made by another person.

A Few Becoming Hues Preferable to Many Dubious Colors

Many persons are discouraged by the fact that a careful color reading seems to limit their list of truly becoming colors. For this reason, colors are classified as *becoming, wearable,* and *unbecoming.* If the color reading is made with strict honesty, the individual should find the colors listed as *becoming* very definitely flattering. These are the colors that should form the basis of the wardrobe and that should be worn, not only on those occasions when the individual is making a special effort to appear at her best, but when she is tired, ill, or otherwise in need of colors that will improve her appearance. Wearable colors may be worn when she is physically at her best and has less need of flattering colors, or when she definitely feels the necessity of wearing a color not usually included in her wardrobe.

CHAPTER VIII

Colors Becoming to Individuals of Cool Coloring

FROM ANALYSES of the colors becoming to a large number of individuals, general rules pertaining to the colors becoming to types may be formed. These rules are helpful as an indication of colors that may be tried on the individual, but should be used in conjunction with personal analysis and critical judgment of each color and its effect upon the appearance.

Hue of skin determines colors. Much more helpful than classifying persons as blondes or brunettes, which takes into consideration only the value of the hair, sometimes of the skin, is that of terming them of either cool or warm coloring, according to the actual hue of their skin. Those with violet-red in cheeks and lips are said to have cool coloring, and those with orange-red to have warm coloring. This classification aids in selecting colors. As a general rule, persons with cool coloring wear cool colors to best advantage—blues, greens, blue-greens, blue-violets, violet, and red-violet; persons with warm hues appear best in warm colors—reds, oranges, and yellows.

Drab or Neutral Blonde Needs Color Accent

The pale, colorless blonde, sometimes spoken of as the drab blonde because her coloring is neutral and uninteresting, needs the aid of color in her costume, yet her choice is limited by the weakness of her own coloring. Her complexion is dull, neutral, dead-looking, lifeless, even when carefully made up. Skin and hair of the pale or sallow blonde are of nearly the same value and hue; her eyes, while showing contrast of hue, are frequently similar in value. She should wear colors that are slightly stronger, more forceful, than her own coloring, but should avoid those that are so much more characterful that they overpower her coloring. She must seek colors that will bring out flesh tints without emphasizing the yellow in her skin, that will reflect color into her eyes and give life to her hair. She usually finds the cool hues—green, blue-green, blue, blue-violet—her most becoming colors. Sometimes, if there are no dark tinges in her skin, she may wear violet and red-violet. Even the cool colors must be of lower intensity, as vivid ones increase the yellow in her skin and contrast unfavorably with her neutral coloring. Medium and dark values, or those that are very light, higher in value than her own light coloring, are best, for the pale blonde needs value contrast. If light colors are worn, a dark accent near the face may supply sufficient contrast to make them interesting. A dark hat may so change the apparent coloring of the individual that she may wear more definite and forceful color than she could without it. Too much dark color, as a dark dress and hat, will drain all color from the face unless used in conjunction with a light color worn near the face.

While the drab blonde should avoid neutral colors, she may occasionally find a neutral accented with a small vivid note of cool color wearable. Grays, though difficult if her complexion is muddy, are preferable to tans, which too closely approximate both the hue and the value of her hair.

If the pale blonde wears warm colors, they should be greatly

COOL TYPES

	Drab or Neutral Blonde	Vivid or Colorful Blonde	Dark and Light Contrast
DESCRIPTION OF PERSONAL COLORING OF EACH TYPE	Hair and skin of dull neutralized yellow of light and nearly same values. Pale lips and cheeks of grayed violet-red. Eyes of cool, frequently pale, colors, blue, green, gray.	Vivid yellow or yellow-orange hair, fair skin with clear violet-red coloring in lips and cheeks. Cool, blue, green or gray coloring in eyes, usually deeper in tone than in drab blonde.	Blue-black hair, fair skin with violet-red coloring, cool dark blue, green or gray eyes. Contrast of dark hair and fair skin most striking characteristic.
MAKE-UP MOST EFFECTIVE WITH PERSONAL COLORING	Violet-red rouge, slightly more intense and darker than natural coloring usually best. Occasionally a soft dull red or orange-red may be recommended. Dark brown mascara. Eye shadow, to match eyes, may be used at night.	Violet-red rouge and lipstick as nearly as possible matching hue and value of natural coloring. Dark brown, not black mascara. Faint eye shadow in hue of eyes possible at night.	Violet-red rouge of comparatively dark value, darker than that worn by cool blonde types, may be fairly vivid in intensity. Frequently absence of rouge on a pale skin pleasingly emphasizes fairness.
ACTIVELY BECOMING COLORS ENHANCING PERSONAL COLORING	Colors of soft grayed character, just slightly more vivid than that of the wearer, most becoming. Cool colors, soft pale and fairly dark grayed greens, blue-greens, blue, and blue-violet excellent. Much neutralized reds, red-orange, in pale, middle, or dark val-	Colors of light to dark values more vivid than those of the drab blonde, but grayed or softened should be worn. Cool colors are best, blue-violet, blue, blue-greens, and greens. Red-violet, red and red-orange are good. Yellow, if exactly matching	More vivid cool colors than are permitted blonde and partially neutralized warm colors both successful. Vivid greens, blue-greens, blue, and all violets are good especially in middle and darker values. Red, red-orange, orange, and yellow, neither too vivid nor too dull,

84

	ues good. Dark accent near face needed with light colors.	the hair, is excellent. Yellow-green good. Black and off-whites recommended.	good. Black and white, singly or in combination. Value contrasts in color likewise becoming.
PASSIVELY BECOMING COLORS THAT NEITHER ADD NOR DETRACT	Violet and red-violet in soft coloring are wearable. Lustrous black possible, especially with color accent.	Definitely cool blue-gray or warm rosy gray wearable, especially with accent of cool or warm color. Very light or deep neutralized orange is permissible.	Neutrals, grays, and beiges add nothing to coloring but may be worn. Very much grayed dull colors likewise contribute little.
ACTIVELY UNBECOMING COLORS THAT IMPAIR PERSONAL COLORING	All intense colors submerge the wearer. Dead white, dull black, and gray difficult. Yellow and orange, especially in tan and beige tones near color of hair, should be avoided. Yellow-green is exceedingly trying.	Yellow and orange tones more vivid than those of the hair must be avoided. Exceedingly bright colors either cold or warm as well as totally neutral colors are poor.	Pale delicate colors unless used with contrast detract from coloring of wearer.

subdued or cooled. Soft rose shades, red, and orange-red may serve to give her some of the warmth she lacks, reflecting some of the color into her face. Dark, warm colors, as dark red, may be becoming, especially if white is used near the face. The pale blonde, however, usually finds that the cool colors do the most for her, giving warmth to her hair and skin, while intensifying the color of her eyes.

Colorful Blonde Permitted More Colors

The blonde with golden hair and more vivid coloring in her cheeks, less yellow or neutral-colored skin, has a much more simple problem than has the drab blonde. She has fewer defects to overcome, more points to emphasize. There is less danger of colors overshadowing her own coloring and further subduing her personality. She should, however, strive for colors that will emphasize her delicacy of coloring—too strong, too vivid colors will destroy this quality, her greatest charm. She also finds the cool colors most becoming, but she may wear them in less subdued intensities. She finds dark values, even black, contrasting favorably with her vivid, golden, blonde coloring and emphasizing her charm. Blondes with warm coloring wear the warm colors more successfully than the colorless blondes; they may even wear fairly vivid reds without totally submerging their personality, but usually they will find the cooler colors more flattering. The violet-reds, being cooler than red or orange-red, are frequently more becoming than the latter hues.

There is, of course, no sharp division between the drab and the vivid blonde, there being many variations of the two broad classifications. Some individuals might even change from one to another, according to their health, age, or make-up. The dictum that the more definite the coloring of the blonde the more vivid and the more warm the colors she may wear successfully should serve merely as an indication of the colors each individual may wear.

Cool, Dark Type Wears More Forceful Colors

The cool, dark type, the so-called brunette who has blue-black hair, a fair skin with violet-red coloring, and eyes of cool color, possesses an attractive contrast of coloring, which permits her far greater freedom in her choice of colors than that enjoyed by either the drab or the vivid blonde. She, too, however, appears best in cool colors, which make her eyes appear deeper and emphasize the blue lights in her hair and the coolness of her skin. She may, however, wear cool colors in vivid intensities, colors so forceful that they would destroy the delicate coloring of the blonde. Vivid greens and blues, as well as those of lower value, are vastly becoming. Pale, delicate colors, on the other hand, coarsen the coloring of the individual. The violet range is particularly becoming to women of this type. Warm colors neutralized to some degree are more becoming to the cool, dark type than to the blonde; but the cool colors emphasize her distinctive coloring, accenting the difference between her type and that of the warm-colored brunette.

The person with cool, dark coloring wears neutral colors well, both the tans and grays being becoming, particularly if used with accent of vivid color. Black and white, repeating the light-and-dark value contrast of her hair and skin, are particularly effective. Other value contrasts, particularly those formed of cool colors, are flattering to this type.

CHAPTER IX

Colors Becoming to Individuals of Warm Coloring

As A GENERAL RULE, persons with warm coloring should wear warm colors in their costumes. Warm colors will be more becoming than cool colors, warm beiges more becoming than those of cooler appearance, warm grays more pleasing than cool ones. If cool colors are used they should be neutralized or grayed, so that their coldness is softened, made less strikingly cool, and given a suggestion of warmth. Low values, further submerging the cool character, will also make them more becoming to persons of warm coloring.

The use of warm colors as accents, especially if placed near the face, will aid in making cool colors becoming and will increase the effectiveness of black and neutrals.

As with other types, greater liberty in the use of color is permitted if the skin is clear and healthy in appearance.

These general rules must be used in conjunction with analysis of the individual's coloring: consideration of her type of warm coloring as well as study of her specific color problems.

There are two decidedly different groups of women with warm coloring. Those with so-called red hair comprise one group, their vivid red-orange hair; light, but creamy-yellow skin background; and the orange-red in their lips and cheeks making their coloring predominantly warm, whether their eyes are cool or warm. Persons whose hair is termed *brown* (in reality a more subdued or neutralized red-orange), with flesh tints of orange-red, and an orange or yellow-orange background coloring give an impression of warmth that is intensified if the eyes are brown. The latter group may be again divided into those types with vivid coloring—the vivid brunette—and those with soft olive skins.

Colors for the Red-Haired Types

Red-haired types are the most definitely warm in coloring, because their coloring is of purer intensity. Because of the very vividness of their own coloring, they have a limited range of becoming colors. Warm colors, unless greatly subdued, clash violently with the red-orange hair, cheapening its hue. Red-violet is particularly difficult, and reds are almost equally disastrous, although occasionally neutralized intensities in very light or very dark values may be permissible, if not advisable. Red-orange, orange, yellow-orange, and yellow, which range, of course, includes the beiges and browns that are neutralized intensities of these hues, blend and harmonize with the coloring of the red-headed individual. Well-chosen colors of this range, in darker values and duller intensities, enrich the color of the hair, making it seem brighter by contrast, but at the same time making it less strikingly conspicuous, more a part of the color composition created by the costume and the coloring of the wearer. The too-florid or too-yellow skin may also be subdued, made to seem clearer and of a more pleasing color, by the use of hues analogous to those of the skin and hair.

When the wearer desires to accentuate the red-orange coloring of her hair, she may actually increase its apparent redness

WARM TYPES

	"Red-Headed" Types	Vivid Brunette	Olive Skin Brunette
Description of Personal Coloring of Each Type	Red-orange hair, skin fair and creamy with orange-red, red, or slightly violet-red flesh tones. Eyes cool blue, green, gray, or warm hazel or brown, but coloring predominantly warm and vivid.	Dark, subdued red-orange hair. Warm skin with deep orange-red coloring. Warm brown or sometimes dark eyes of cool color. Effect predominantly warm.	Subdued grayed orange-yellow coloring has a definitely yellow-green cast. Cheeks pale with a suggestion of grayed orange-red coloring. Hair is dark with subdued red-orange lights. Eyes usually dark and warm.
Make-up Most Effective with Personal Coloring	Orange-red rouge and lipstick of medium or low value in softened grayed rather than intense color. Dark brown mascara may be used. Eye shadow the color of the eyes is sometimes effective at night.	Dark, subdued orange-red rouge and lipstick. Dark brown, sometimes black, mascara. Eye shadow may be used with eyes of cool color.	Dark, orange-red lipstick of subdued intensity with little if any rouge is most effective. The use of both changes the type to more nearly that of the vivid brunette. Dark brown or black mascara if needed.
Actively Becoming Colors Enhancing Personal Coloring	Red-orange, orange, and yellow range in grayed intensities, less vivid than the color of the hair, particularly harmonious. Dull metallic gold, beiges, and medium and dark browns included in above. Subdued, cool colors, green, blue-green, blue, and	Strong, forceful colors, particularly fairly vivid, warm colors in low values, red, red-orange, orange, yellow, warm beiges, brown, wine especially becoming. Black, especially with color accent, is good. Warm off-whites, if slightly darker than the skin,	Warm colors neutralized to a touch of coolness are first choice. Cool colors grayed to give them a suggestion of warmth are also effective. Dark reds, red-oranges, red-violets, including the more colorful browns and beiges

	combinations of warm and cool colors effective. Black and warm off-whites excellent.	are flattering. Bright and dull golds if the texture of the skin is good.	and deep wines, are excellent.
Passively Becoming Colors That Neither Add Nor Detract	Gray and silver possible, unless skin is poor. Blue-violet possible, but not so effective as blues and greens or oranges.	Warm, rosy gray and darker taupe may be worn. Red-violet and medium values in softened blues, dark navy, medium and dark green, especially a warm yellow-green or bronze green, are possible.	Black especially with color accent may be used. Warm off-whites permissible. Orange and lighter red-orange and rose shades wearable. Dark and medium green, yellow-green, and dull blue are possibilities.
Actively Unbecoming Colors That Impair Personal Coloring	Red and red-violet both too similar and too much in contrast to the vivid tones of personal coloring. Violet seldom successful. Dead white also difficult.	Violet usually conflicts with the definite red-orange coloring of the wearer. Light cool grays and dead white are trying. Delicate, pale colors coarsen the individual's coloring.	Intense vivid cool colors, particularly blue, blue-violet, dead white, gray, especially cold gray, are difficult. Light colors, lighter than the skin, are most trying, especially in cold tints.

and, at the same time, add to the effect of color in her cheeks by the use of blues, blue-greens, and greens, which are opposite in character and complementary to her own coloring. Very bright, vivid red hair usually becomes harsh and ordinary in color when intensified by complementary contrasts. Dull, drab red hair and pale skin may, on the other hand, gain life and sparkle from complementary contrasts. If the skin is inclined to be yellow, intense cool colors, particularly blue, should be avoided.

A combination of warm and cool colors, as a dress of brown with an accent of blue-green, or a dress of a cool color with an accent of warm color, as blue with a yellow or orange accent, is likely to be particularly becoming to the blue-eyed, red-haired person.

Black, which absorbs color, may be effectively used to subdue the too florid coloring that sometimes accompanies red hair. It, at the same time, emphasizes the red hair, the contrast throwing it into relief but tending to make it appear more golden than red.

Off-whites, as creamy-yellow white, are much more becoming than pure white to persons with definitely warm coloring, as these shades blend with the warm tones of the skin and hair. The warmer off-white shades, those with subdued orange and red-orange coloring, may be especially becoming to persons with so-called red hair. An accent of deeper and more vivid warm color, or a cooler color, may be combined with the off-white shades.

Neutral colors are becoming to the more vivid red-haired types. Warm grays and beiges tend to be most easily worn, although women with fair, clear skin and cool eyes may frequently wear cool grays to advantage. A touch of accent in either warm or cool color usually adds to the wearability of neutral colors.

Color Selections for the Vivid Brunette

The brunette with warm, vivid coloring; dark, but distinctly colorful hair, with coppery or red-orange lights; dark skin, with warm, orange and orange-red hues; and, frequently, with brown eyes possesses such strong forceful coloring that there is little danger of overpowering her personality by clothing of too-forceful coloring. On the other hand, her coloring, though vivid and forceful, is both darker and more subdued than that of the red-haired type and does not clash as easily with other colors. The vivid brunette can in fact wear a wider range of strong color than any other type, provided, of course, that her skin is fairly clear with no unhealthy appearing pigmentation. She should, however, avoid delicate pastel colors, which may make her own coloring appear coarse by contrast. When high values or light colors are worn, they should be warm in hue. The warm off-whites, especially those in orange and red-orange, may form an effective contrast with her dark coloring, without making her skin appear yellow, as dead white or pale, cool colors would do.

Warm colors of low values (the vivid brunette may wear intense colors if the value is low); rich dark reds; dark browns; deep, warm tans and beige; dark brownish or rosy grays; and, sometimes, red-violet and violet are usually the most becoming colors for the vivid brunette. Black, particularly with an accent of warm colors, is usually becoming. Black and other dark, neutral colors are flattering to the florid brunette.

The Latin Type

The brunette so often called the Latin type, with very dark brown, almost black hair, dark skin that seems to have almost yellow-green tinge, usually with brown or black eyes, possesses a subdued warmth. Her olive skin is not basically yellow-green, but rather an orange that is neutralized enough so that it has a slightly yellow-green appearance.

Warm colors neutralized or grayed until they have a dusty, slightly greenish quality are particularly effective with the olive skin, emphasizing the distinctive coloring of the individual. Vivid warm colors are also effective with coloring of this type, which is sufficiently forceful not to be overpowered by strong colors, yet is not in itself so vivid that it will tend to clash with other definite hues.

Intense, vivid, cool colors should be avoided; but neutralized, softened, cool colors, which have obtained a slight feeling of warmth in the neutralization, may be becoming. Intense, cold colors will force the yellow and yellow-green in the skin, making it look dark and muddy. Blue and blue-violet, especially in vivid intensities, should be avoided for the same reason. A very dark navy blue with a warm color accent may be worn; but a subdued and dark value of a warm color, or a black with a warm accent, would be more becoming.

Green, especially the middle and low values, sometimes fairly high values, frequently makes the skin appear clearer and whiter, the more decided green of the costume blending with the greenish tinge in the skin, but overshadowing it, making it seem less greenish. Accents of a warm color will make most cool colors much more becoming.

Warm beiges and browns, containing more orange and red-orange than yellow, are much more becoming than the yellow-ish colors, which make the skin appear dull and brownish. Warm taupe or warm gray may sometimes be used if the skin is clear. Cool, bluish grays should be avoided. Red-violet, red, and red-orange are, in most instances, the most becoming colors and should be used as the foundation of the wardrobe.

CHAPTER X

Intermediate Type Selects Colors to Emphasize Best Features

IN THE COURSE of trying colors on large numbers of individuals, the author has become convinced that persons whose coloring is cool appear to best advantage in costumes of cool coloring, while those whose coloring is warm find warm colors most becoming. If we accept this general rule, we can readily appreciate that those persons whose coloring is a combination of warmth and coolness may select from a wide color range.

In America, where there is a fusion of Northern and Southern peoples, we find that large numbers of persons have a mixture of warm and cool coloring rather than being definitely either warm or cool. There are many combinations of color that may be classified as intermediate: the hair may be warm, the eyes may be definitely cool, and the skin may range between the two; or the hair and skin may be cool and the eyes warm.

It is the individual of the intermediate type who most frequently fails to wear the most becoming colors, because she has failed to recognize the true character of her coloring. A number are at a loss as to whether they should be classed as blondes or brunettes, knowing only these two broad classifications. Others definitely class themselves as one or another, wearing the colors traditionally becoming to that group, without appreciation of the effect upon individual coloring.

Combining some of the traits of cool and warm types, possessing some of the characteristics of both blonde and brunette, the intermediate type may wear colors becoming to both of these groups. While she may have more variety in her dress than individuals whose coloring is definitely warm or cool, she is wisest if she carefully analyzes the effect of various values and hues upon her skin, hair, and eyes and wears the colors that do the most to improve her appearance, even though many other colors may be fairly becoming. She is free to emphasize her best characteristics. If her eyes are a clear, deep blue and of good size and shape, they may be still further enhanced by selection of blue apparel. The skin and hair of intermediate types usually look well with either cool or warm colors, provided the intensity is not too great. Hence her choice is not limited by giving first consideration to skin and hair, as is that of the person with a more clearly defined, and therefore limited, type of coloring.

Yellow Hair, Cool Skin, and Brown Eyes

One of the most distinctive combinations of warm and cool coloring is that in which the skin is fair and cool, red-violet in coloring; the hair yellow, usually light and not too vivid so that the feeling of warmth is present but not striking; and the eyes brown and definitely warm. Golden tans and browns, which enhance the color of the eyes and at the same time emphasize the color of the hair, are frequently becoming to this type. However, care must be taken to avoid using tans near the value of the hair, or it will appear drab and uninteresting. If the skin is sallow as well as fair, accents of contrasting color will increase the becomingness of the tan-brown range. Blue-green and green may be used as a cool accent, while orange and red-orange are frequently becoming, if a vivid, warm color is to be used in this way.

Blues, greens, and violets contrast with the hair, increase its golden color, and are pleasing with the fair cool skin. Reds, oranges, and yellows, if not too intense for the delicate coloring of the skin and hair, harmonize with the brown eyes and give warmth to the skin.

Make-up important for dark-eyed type. Light eyelashes and eyebrows frequently detract from the beauty of brown eyes and make the individual seem lacking in emphasis. Darkening of eyebrows and lashes, using a dark brown, not a black, mascara will darken and increase the size of the eyes, markedly improving their appearance. When the natural coloring is faint, either orange-red or violet-red rouge may be used, according to the colors worn. With reds and oranges the orange-red is preferable. Sometimes it may be chosen for wear with blue and blue-greens, which are complementary to red-orange. Usually, however, the red-violet rouge is preferable with cool colors. With violet, blue-greens, greens, and blues, violet-red rouge seems most natural. The person who has appreciable natural coloring should match it in rouge and lipstick if she finds it necessary to use artificial color.

Brown Hair, Brown Eyes, Medium or Fair Skin

Warmer in color than the type just studied, wearing much the same colors, but finding the warm colors preferable in most instances, is the person whose hair, instead of being fair, is definitely brown and fairly dark, or at least of middle value. Her skin, however, is fair and red-violet in coloring, differentiating her from the warm-skinned brunette. The violet and red-violet shades, usually so difficult to wear, are becoming to her. Wine reds, deep red, red-orange (especially warm browns and tans), and soft yellows emphasize her eyes much more than do the violet shades. They are likewise pleasing with her hair.

Creamy white or the warm off-white shades in flesh or orange tones are preferable to dead white. Black accented with color is preferable to all-black, except on florid women of this type.

Green and blue may emphasize dark tinges in the skin and should be avoided if the skin is not clear and healthy. They are, however, especially in low and middle values, frequently becoming to this intermediate type, if the skin is clear and definitely cool.

Brown Hair; Gray, Green, or Blue Eyes; Fair Skin

The type with cool eyes, blue, green, or gray, which frequently assume the hue of cool colors worn, and with fair, cool skin with red-violet flesh tints possesses both positive coolness and warmth, the latter supplied by brown hair with red-orange lights.

This prevalent intermediate type, possessing both definite warmth and coolness in her coloring, has, particularly if her skin is clear, the widest color range from which to select her costume. She may wear either warm or cool colors; but frequently she finds the latter more becoming, as they blend with cool skin and eyes and, at the same time, may increase the color of the hair by means of complementary contrast. It is true that the person with predominantly warm coloring may wear more vivid warm colors than can this intermediate type, and that those with predominantly cool coloring may wear more vivid cool colors; but the intermediate, with about evenly bal-

INTERMEDIATE TYPES

	Fair Hair and Skin, Dark Eyes	Dark Hair and Eyes, Fair Skin	Cool Skin and Eyes, Warm Hair
DESCRIPTION OF PERSONAL COLORING OF EACH TYPE	Light-yellow hair, fair skin, usually with violet-red coloring in lips and cheeks. Eyes brown and definitely warm, giving a distinctive combination of warm and cool coloring.	Dark brown hair and eyes having warmth of subdued orange-red, but with fair skin with definite violet-red coloring. Warmer than light-haired intermediate type but having mixture of warm and cool coloring.	Cool, fair skin with violet-red coloring; cool blue, green, or gray eyes with brown hair gives contrast of cool and warm coloring with coolness predominating. Hair may also be brighter red-orange.
MAKE-UP MOST EFFECTIVE WITH PERSONAL COLORING	If natural coloring is faint, either orange-red or violet-red rouge may be used, according to the colors being worn. The use of dark-brown mascara aids in emphasizing the large eyes.	Violet-red rouge in comparatively dark value, of fairly vivid intensity, may be used. May be varied with more grayed violet-red color. Very dark-brown or black mascara may be used.	Violet-red rouge and lipstick are most becoming, especially if personal coloring is distinct. If pale, orange-red may be occasionally used, especially with warm colors.
ACTIVELY BECOMING COLORS ENHANCING PERSONAL COLORING	Red-orange, orange, and yellows, including golden browns and the darker rosy beiges, those darker than the hair, emphasize warm coloring. Reds and red-violets may be worn in light, medium, and dark values, particularly if somewhat softened, although this type may wear fairly clear colors.	Warm colors are most becoming; red-violet, red, and red-orange may be worn in slightly or much grayed intensities and in most values, although more vivid colors should be fairly dark. Dark subdued blue and green, rich black and warm off-whites	Cool colors most becoming; green, blue-green, blue, blue-violet, and cool grays are especially becoming if slightly grayed. They may be worn in most values. Red-violet and violet flattering if not vivid, especially in very light or dark values. Red-orange and orange in softened color are especially

	Violets, blue-violets, blues, and greens are good if subdued, especially with accent of warm color. Black and warm off-whites are usually becoming, especially with accent or in combination.	are good, especially with accent of warm color. Warm beiges are good, as are browns, particularly with contrast of lighter values.	good with accent of green or blue. Rich black, white and black, and white are good. Contrasts of dark and light colors likewise good.
PASSIVELY BECOMING Colors That Neither Add Nor Detract	Not too neutral grays, either warm or cold, are possible, especially when used with color accent. Yellow-green may be worn.	Violet may be worn. Dark warm taupe gray is likewise possible.	Red may be worn but is seldom the individual's most becoming color. Rose shades and the slightly red-orange casts best, better than pure red or pink. Yellow and gold sometimes possible.
ACTIVELY UNBECOMING Colors That Impair Personal Coloring	Tans near the value of the hair and yellows more vivid than the hair should be avoided. Extremely vivid, cold colors very difficult.	Light grays and grayed beiges should be avoided. Vivid and light blues and greens are particularly trying.	Browns and tans matching either the hair or the color of the skin and gray beiges should be avoided. Extremely vivid colors are bad.

anced warm and cool coloring, may wear in greater variety modulated intensities of either warm or cool colors.

Being able to wear either warm or cool colors, it is particularly easy for this type to emphasize the best features. If the eyes are large and well shaped, they may be made to seem more so by the color in the apparel worn. If the eyes are blue, a large area of soft blue or a small area of intense blue will intensify their blueness. Likewise, blue-green, green, or gray may improve the apparent coloring of the eyes, blue-green intensifying either the blue or green hue, giving them an interesting subtle color, while gray may increase the cool, thoughtful air that eyes of this color lend to the countenance. As a general rule, middle and low values of soft, grayed, cool colors both increase the color of the eyes and make them appear darker and with more depth.

Violet, red-violet, and blue-violet are becoming to this type, more so than to any other coloring. Blue-violet and violet may likewise increase the color in the eyes. Red-violet is particularly becoming to the complexion, especially in subdued intensities. Both light and dark values of red-violet are becoming. Red may usually be worn, although it is seldom the individual's most becoming color. The intensity of red is best when subdued; low values tend to be better than high. Red-orange and orange tones may enhance the color of the hair and may be especially becoming if used either as an accent to cool colors or with an accent of cool color. Browns and tans near the color of the hair should be studiously avoided, for matching hue, intensity, and value make the hair look drab and uninteresting and give the individual a monotone appearance. Warm, rosy beiges are more becoming than those with a gray or yellow cast.

Black, with white or color—if the individual's flesh tints are weak—is usually becoming, especially in more lustrous textures, as satin or velvet. Gray, either cool or warm, the former in medium or low values, the latter in light values, is becoming, especially when accented by a touch of vivid blue, blue-green, green, or sometimes violet, red-violet, or red-orange, the latter in a coral shade.

Color contrast, a background or large area of a cool color of softened intensity with an accent of warm color or vivid intensity, or vice versa, makes a particularly pleasing color scheme for the person whose own coloring is composed of contrasting warmth and coolness. Value contrasts, or contrasts of light and dark values, are also becoming. Medium values, in which there is definite contrast of hue, are becoming, but should be avoided when the hue is near that of the wearer's hair.

CHAPTER XI

Colors Vitalize Women with Gray or White Hair

THE WOMAN whose hair has lost its original coloring and has turned gray or white is handicapped more by tradition, which designates black and lavender as suitable colors for her to wear, than by actual unbecomingness of colors themselves. In fact, snowy white hair may increase the list of becoming colors, softening, as it does, the individual's coloring and giving a becoming frame to the face.

The wise woman, when her hair has become white, capitalizes this feature, wearing colors to accent its snowy whiteness. In return it gives her an air of distinction, an appearance of sophistication.

Women whose hair is in that trying stage of turning gray, or whose hair is still definitely gray, lack the advantage of the white-haired woman, but they may minimize this disadvantage by choosing colors carefully, avoiding those that emphasize yellow or brownish tinges in their hair and choosing those that make their skin and eyes appear to best advantage. They should attempt to emphasize the blue-gray or blue-whiteness of their hair. They must also consider changes in the skin, which may have become yellow and darkened or florid or pale, or which time and the becoming frame of gray hair may have softened and improved.

Mixed Dark and Gray Hair Difficult Problem

The individual whose hair is in the process of turning gray, partly dark and partly light, presenting a salt-and-pepper effect if the hair was originally very dark, has difficulty in selecting becoming colors. She must avoid colors that will emphasize the mixture of color in her hair. White and black mixtures, or mixed light and dark colors, may emphasize the feature that she wishes to conceal. She must likewise avoid colors that will make her hair assume a greenish cast, for the mixture of color in her hair frequently makes it seem a muddy green. She will find many colors becoming when a hat is worn concealing the greenish hair.

Brown and tans, especially yellow tans, should be avoided. Black should be worn with a hat or with color accent. Soft, grayed colors will be more becoming than vivid ones. Dark values are likely to be more becoming than light ones, the latter making the hair look greenish gray. Medium values may be becoming if they are of soft warm colors; in cool colors they are likely to be too similar to the greenish tone of the hair. Dark red, violet-red and, if the skin is not yellow, violet, blue-violet, and blue will be becoming. Dark blue-green is usually effective. Dark green is frequently becoming. Light greens and yellow-greens emphasize disagreeable tones in the hair. Soft, medium values in red, orange-red, rose, and henna shades are becoming to the hair and to all but the florid complexion.

Wider Color Range for Definitely Gray Hair

The person whose hair is definitely gray finds it less difficult to select becoming colors. Her coloring has now become decidedly cooler than it was before her hair lost its pigment, and the disagreeable greenish cast of the transitional stage has largely disappeared. The hair now has or should have a bluish-gray cast. This bluish character should be intensified by the colors worn, as the blue tinge is much more pleasing than brownish casts.

Grayed, warm colors in nearly all values—the reds, red-violet, and red-orange—will usually be becoming. The cool colors, violet, blue-violet, blue, blue-green, and green, preferably in soft grayed colors, are becoming to gray-haired women who have cool eyes and skin. Blue-green and green are especially flattering. Tans, browns, and black are the only colors that need especially be avoided, and the latter is permissible if used with accents of color. White is also difficult to wear unless it is combined with color, as white alone may make the hair seem too definitely dark and cold.

Grays may be worn, but they should be chosen with care, attention being given to their effect upon both the skin and the hair. Grays slightly darker than the hair and of a slightly bluish cast, but not bluer than the hair, will make the hair seem lighter, a desirable blue-whiteness. Grays lighter than the hair are likely to make it appear dark and dingy. Warm grays sometimes emphasize the cool, bluish grayness of the hair, but they must be chosen only after careful consideration, for sometimes they emphasize brown or yellowish casts in the hair or contrast unpleasantly with it. Cool grays, or those that are truly neutral, are, in most instances, more becoming, particularly if used with a color accent, rose or coral, turquoise or other soft blues and blue-greens, jade greens, or one of the violets or red-violets in soft, fairly light values.

As warm grays tend to be trying, so do beiges in the more definitely warm neutral effects. If beige is to be worn, it should be decidedly warm, rosy, and less neutral in cast than those that approach gray.

White Hair Permits More Vivid Colors

As the hair becomes whiter, more silvery in tone, it becomes increasingly beautiful in itself, forming a softening and becoming frame for the face. The woman whose hair has turned completely white, therefore, may wear more colors, nearly all hues, vivid as well as more neutralized intensities, and all values from light to dark. Many women, especially youthful women whose hair has turned prematurely white but whose skin remains clear with good coloring, find that colors that were not becoming when the hair was dark are extremely pleasing with white hair.

The woman possessing white hair and a good complexion may wear vivid red, while the woman whose skin is more faded finds the softer more neutralized reds, usually in higher values, as soft rose, even flesh tints, more becoming, as they do not overshadow her more delicate coloring. Red-violets are becoming, especially in grayed intensities. Violet and blue-violet must be even more neutralized or they will give unpleasant greenish or yellowish tinges to hair and complexion. Blue is likewise best subdued, but very flattering in soft shades, especially if the eyes are blue. Blue-green and green are definitely flattering, but yellow-green as well as yellow is distinctly difficult. Shades of brown and tan likewise do nothing to enhance the appearance of the individual, although they are not so disastrous to the white-haired woman as to the one whose hair is just beginning to turn gray.

Black is becoming, as it accents the whiteness of the hair. White or colors used with black frequently make it more be-

GRAY- AND WHITE-HAIRED TYPES

	Mixed Dark and Gray Hair	Definitely Gray Hair	White, Silvery Hair
DESCRIPTION OF PERSONAL COLORING OF EACH TYPE	Hair that is beginning to lose its pigmentation has a definitely greenish cast that should be rendered inconspicuous by the colors worn. The general coloring appears cooler. Skin may have become yellow or florid but is more frequently paler in lips and cheeks. Eyes may be either warm or cool, but the hair and skin become the most important considerations.	Hair that has turned definitely gray loses its trying greenish cast, becoming bluish gray, which tone should be intensified by colors worn. This type appears definitely cooler, particularly if flesh tints are not too vivid. If the eyes are cool, the type is definitely cool, but gray eyelashes may make brown eyes look cool.	Much cooler and much more becoming than mixed or gray hair is silvery-white hair, which softens the features and clears the skin.
MAKE-UP MOST EFFECTIVE WITH PERSONAL COLORING	Fairly dark and definitely grayed or softened rouge, in orange-red or violet-red matching natural coloring, should be discreetly applied. Too much color emphasizes aging skin. If natural color is pale or subdued, violet-red rouge is likely to be best, regardless of original youthful coloring. Mascara usually too harsh; if used, should be dark brown.	Except on very fresh, youthful, clear skin, a very much softened medium or dark rouge should be used. Violet-red is usually more becoming. The youthful person may wear somewhat more vivid rouge. Persons whose skin remains definitely warm may wear a dark orange-red rouge. In most instances it is best to let the eyelashes and brows remain gray. If darkened, a dull, dark-brown mascara should be used.	A light or medium soft violet-red rouge is usually best on this type. It should be delicately applied. Eye make-up should usually be omitted.

ACTIVELY BECOMING Colors Enhancing Personal Coloring	Dark values, especially in cool colors, are likely to be most becoming. Warm colors may be worn in medium and light values as well as dark ones, but intensities must be definitely grayed. Dark red, soft rose, red-violet in similar dark and medium shades, and dark blue-green, blue-violet, and blue, and black are becoming. Creamy white is good, excellent near the face when dark colors are worn.	Grayed warm colors in all values, reds, red-violets, and red-orange, are favorable. Cool colors, also grayed, best for gray hair with cool eyes. Light and middle values with accent of dark color pleasing. Gray darker than hair, especially if combined with color or, is excellent. Black good if in lustrous texture or combined with color accent.	Increased color range, delicate pastel tints, medium and dark values may be worn; light colors preferably with darker accent. Red from soft flesh and rose to deep dark tones is best when partially neutralized. Red-violet and red-orange are also good. Blue, blue-green, and green in middle and darker values flattering. Black accents the hair.
PASSIVELY BECOMING Colors That Neither Add Nor Detract	Dark green may sometimes be worn. Violet is likewise a possibility. Gray, if darker than the general tone of the hair, is fairly becoming.	Warm grays, with a definite rosy, pinkish cast, may sometimes be worn. Likewise a very rosy beige or a much neutralized rose. When the hair is covered by a hat, tan and brown shades may be permissible, especially on brown-eyed women.	Violet may be worn. Creamy whites may be used with color accents. Grays are better than on gray-haired women and should be darker than the hair; cool if skin is fair, warm if skin is warm.
ACTIVELY UNBECOMING Colors That Impair Personal Coloring	Black-and-white or dark-and-light mixtures, tans and browns, yellow-green, light green, light blues, light and medium greens and blues, and all bright colors should be avoided.	Tans, brown, and dull, dead blacks, should be avoided. White and light grays, lighter than the hair, are likewise poor.	Tan and brown shades extremely difficult unless the hair is covered. Dead white is poor. Yellow-green should be avoided.

coming to the complexion. White and very light pastel colors are usually becoming, creamy white being preferable to dead white, especially if the skin is dark or yellow. Very light values, with hair of light value, give the individual a dainty, fragile appearance, which is decidedly becoming to many white-haired women, but is lacking in character and force on others. This can be remedied by using accents of dark value, thus supplying the value contrast that no longer exists in the individual's coloring.

Grays are more becoming to the white-haired woman than to the one whose hair is gray. Lighter grays may be worn, but they should be a shade darker than the hair or they will make it appear dark and gray rather than white. Cool grays, bluish grays, are preferable for the woman with clear skin having no yellow tinge; warm grays are preferable if the skin is not beautiful. If the skin is definitely aged and yellow, it is best to avoid grays entirely. Blue-gray with an accent of blue or blue-green is an especially charming color scheme for the older woman with white hair, blue eyes, and skin of delicate coloring. Rose and coral shades with warm gray are becoming to many women, especially those with brown eyes.

CHAPTER XII

Harmonious Combinations of Color

Color Interest

COMBINATIONS OF COLORS, the use of two or more colors, make the costume more interesting than one alone. The use of a second accent color may make an otherwise unbecoming color wearable or even actively becoming. An interesting combination of colors will make an otherwise ordinary costume distinctive and highly individual.

Color harmonies, arranged so that the dominant contrast or accent is near the face, make it the center of interest. Costume jewelry, collars, scarfs, hats, or hat trimming may supply color contrast, which gives accent near the face.

It must not be forgotten that the coloring of the face itself, of the skin, hair, and eyes, forms the basis of the color scheme. The colors of the wearer are added to any combination of colors that she adopts in a costume. If her costume is at one with herself in hue, value, and intensity, or perhaps in value alone, the whole effect will be monotonous. Her personal coloring may add a jarring note to an unwisely chosen costume that is harmonious in itself.

There are three forms of color harmony, as follows:

Contrast of hues. A contrast of hue, a combination of two or more colors containing different pigmentation, is the most obvious form. Such a harmony might be formed by a combination of yellow and blue, yellow and green, or by two closely related colors, as yellow and orange. The various ways in which contrasts of hue may be made pleasing will be discussed later.

Contrast of value. A second form of color harmony, one equally effective in costume design, is that produced by contrast of light and dark colors, termed a contrast of value. Since value contrast is necessary to avoid monotony, contrasts of light and dark colors are especially becoming to those persons who do not have a contrast of light and dark in their personal coloring. It is effective and interesting on all types.

Black and white form the most decided contrast, one that may be extremely dramatic. Less sharp contrasts might be formed by black and gray or by white and gray. The three gradations of value might be used together. Light and dark grays might be incorporated.

Visualizing these contrasts of value alone will aid in understanding those harmonies formed by contrasts of light and dark values of the same hue. A light green may be combined with a dark green, a light red (pink) with a dark red. In order to achieve true harmony, these contrasts should be in exactly the same hue. A light violet-red used with a dark red or orange-red will be far less pleasing than two violet-reds. A contrast of decidedly different hues together with a contrast of value, as pale yellow used with dark blue, is also correct. The most important point to remember is that there should be a decided contrast so that the appearance of an intended matching of hue is avoided.

It is likewise important that for cases in which only two or three values are employed there be a decided contrast between them. If a number of variations of value are used, they should show regular gradations from light to dark. It is possible to combine a large number of similar values, the slight changes from one to another progressing in regular order, thereby producing a pleasant feeling of rhythm. Thus a dress might shade form a dark violet at the hemline to a pale violet at the neckline.

Since dark colors appear heavier than light ones, they should be at the bottom of the costume or small accents on a light costume, when not used as the basis of the costume itself.

Contrast of intensity. Contrast of pure bright colors with those of grayed or neutralized intensity provide a third means of color harmony. Since vivid colors are less suitable for an entire costume, yet may be effective and becoming in small areas, harmonies formed by the addition of accents of vivid color to otherwise neutral or grayed costumes are important in costume design. A bright blue-green might be used as an accent to a grayed blue-green, or it might be used with black or white, or with a soft grayed red-orange. Thus a contrast of intensities of the same hue supplies a color harmony, or differing intensities may be used with a contrast of value or one of hue.

Matching Hues

Harmonies composed of one hue with variations of value and intensity are known as monochromatic or one-color harmonies. These are easily combined as used in costumes, although it is sometimes difficult to find the required variations. However, in the past few years, manufacturers and retailers have attempted to concentrate on a few basic hues, showing light and dark, bright and grayed colors of exactly the same hue. Thus all greens for one season are a true green, not a blue-green or a yellow-green. Another season they might be blue-greens, but it is planned not to use two slightly different hues during the same period. Individuality and variety are possible through accent colors as well as from a choice of the most becoming of the season's basic colors.

When it is impossible to match exactly the color of two items, as a dress and a hat, a decided contrast is preferable to the use of two closely similar colors. If the hue is the same, a slight contrast of value or of intensity is less serious than a slight contrast of hue.

A slight difference between two supposedly matching colors may frequently be made less apparent if the two colors are separated by a contrasting color. Thus a coat and hat may seem to match exactly if they are separated by a large fur collar.

Related or Analogous Colors

Hues that, though different, have something in common are combined in harmonies of related or analogous colors. All cool colors or all warm colors would be used together in this form of harmony. Blue, blue-green, green-blue, and green might be effectively employed together, the slight differences between the hues producing an attractive rhythm. The differences may be less pronounced when a series of slightly varying hues are combined, rather than when only two colors are used. The ranges of colors, as seen on the color plate, between blue and violet, between violet and red, or from red to yellow, from yellow to green are all effective analogous harmonies.

The yellow, orange, and red-orange color scheme, with its variations of beige, tan, and brown as well as the more vivid intensities, is particularly effective both in harmonies of slightly varying related hues and in those formed of one hue in different intensities of values.

Decided Contrast of Hue

More decided contrast than that produced by two closely related colors is sometimes needed to give emphasis to the costume or to give a pleasing balance of warm and cool colors. Combinations of two hues are more easily used in costumes than a greater number of hues. When a number of colors are used, they are most effective in a fabric having a design in several colors or one in which a number of colors are grouped to accent a fairly dark or neutral foundation color. Black, gray, white, dark brown, dark blue, or any soft, grayed color might thus be accented with several more definite colors used in conjunction.

Warm and cool colors combined. Two decidedly different hues, one a warm color, one a cool color, form a sharp and striking contrast. If both are bright, the effect may be too bold for a becoming costume, but if the basic color is somewhat grayed, the accent color may be vivid. Green-blue might be accented by orange, blue by yellow, red by blue-green, green by violet. The colors on opposite sides of the color circle (shown in the color plate, frontispiece) are opposite in their characteristics. One supplies what the other lacks. They, therefore, form harmonious combinations when used together. A monochromatic or an analogous combination may likewise be accented by an opposite color. Thus a series of blues might be accented by yellow.

Accents of opposite colors enable many persons to wear otherwise unbecoming colors. Those women who do not appear at their best in cool colors may find that the violet, violet-blue, blue, and blue-green range is becoming if accented by yellow, orange, or red-orange used near the face. Those to whom cool colors are becoming may likewise wear warm colors accented by blue-green, blue, or violet-blue.

Those persons to whom warm colors are most becoming may very wisely purchase accessories and costume jewelry in these becoming hues, using them with neutral and cool colors as well as with costumes of warm hues. Amber, carnelian, coral, and semiprecious stones of warm hues are excellent choices for accessories of permanent value.

Turquoise, jade, and lapis lazuli are among the semiprecious stones of cool colors that form becoming accents for persons with cool colors. They are excellent with subdued warm colors, yellows, oranges, red-orange (including the beiges and browns). They may likewise be used with grayer, lighter, or darker colors of the same hue as their own coloring.

It should not be forgotten that warm coloring in the skin or hair may give a warm contrast to a costume of cool color.

Three or four widely diverse colors. When three or four colors are used together they should, unless they are neighboring or analogous colors, be widely different, so that each supplies the quality that the other lacks, all together achieving a balance of warmth and coolness. Orange, blue-green, and blue-violet achieve harmony in this way. This type of harmony is more difficult to apply to costumes, not only because it requires a better-trained eye and a more expert knowledge of color, but because a great diversity of color in a costume, unless very skillfully designed, prevents the costume from appearing as a unified whole. Fabrics woven or printed in several colors, with the color broken in small areas and blended by skillful placement, are the wisest choice for all, except expert designers, who wish to incorporate more than two hues or closely related hues in the same costume.

Using Color as a Basis for Wardrobe Selection

Some women would like to wear more interesting and individual colors but feel that it is more economical to confine their selections to black or some other single color.

It may be just as economical to have a wide variety of colors in the wardrobe, if they are all selected with a definite, planned color scheme in mind. If economy must be a constant consideration it is advisable to select one basic dark color as an accessory color. This makes it possible to use the same shoes, handbag, hat, gloves, and hosiery with a number of different costumes.

If black is becoming, especially in a hat, it makes a good accessory and background color, for, with it, almost all colors, except possibly brown and navy blue, are smart. However, black and brown may also be combined in certain textures—brown furs, for instance, may look very well with black. Black hats and black shoes, however, are seldom advisable with brown. Navy blue is not especially good with black, but almost all other shades of blue are excellent with black—pale blues, gray blues, bright blues, violet blues, and green blues are all extremely effective with black.

The black basic costume, with touches of either pale or bright color, is chic and may be made becoming to almost every woman if the proper accent is chosen. Black and white or off-white is likewise widely becoming. If black is chosen as the basic color, one need wear very little actual black, except in accessories; and one need never wear unrelieved black. Yet one is more likely to have a harmonious costume if black is decided on as the basic color before a single purchase is made.

Women who wear many outdoor clothes, particularly of the

tweed and more rugged types, do well to provide brown accessories for these sport clothes. Tannish-brown leather not only makes flat-heeled shoes seem smart when, otherwise, they would be merely dowdy in black, but it is a practical leather color that does not show wear and scuffing, and it blends with almost all outdoor colors—not only with tannish and brownish tweeds, but with the greens and blues that frequently look so well in outdoor clothes. It likewise goes well with yellows and reddish tones, in fact, with almost all colors except black.

If economy must be considered, a coat in the chosen basic color will be most satisfactory.

Black. Black is probably the most satisfactory of all colors since, with different accessories, it may appear very simple or sophisticatedly dressy. It is especially important that black be well cut and well fitted, for black may be either dowdy or distinguished.

With a black coat, dresses and hats of almost any becoming colors may be worn, and the wardrobe is really less limited as to color interest than if a more definitely colored coat were chosen. Black has the almost unique advantage of looking well in every season of the year.

Navy blue. Navy blue is an excellent spring and summer coat color which may appear more youthful and more flattering than black. While it permits many interesting color harmonies, it presents difficulties which black does not, as there is the difficulty of matching blues themselves. Navy-blue shoes tend to have purplish casts and seldom exactly match the coat. For this reason black is often preferable for the shoes to be worn with a navy-blue coat.

It is also difficult to get navy-blue hats, particularly straw hats, which look well with the navy-blue coat. Unless the blue hat is of exactly the same hue, it is usually better to wear a contrasting hat, perhaps of natural-colored straw or of a bright color—possibly violet, red, or green.

In considering a black coat, a contrast of texture, apparently giving a difference of color, tends only to add interest to the black costume, but the blue costume, having apparently different blues, appears poorly chosen and cheapened as a result.

In the fall, a blue, spring coat still looks like a spring coat, while the same model in black appears suitable for fall and early winter. This is partly because the blue does not blend well with fur colors; it looks better with gray fur rather than black or brown fur, and, for this reason, has customarily been endorsed by fashion largely as a spring color. Blue being a "cool" color looks fresh and cool for spring and summer, but chilly for fall and winter.

Brown. Brown, a warm color, which is largely used in fall and winter is also effective for spring and summer. Because brown is less widely used as a spring color its unusualness among the predominately blue- and black-clad crowd gives it added distinction.

Browns are more easily combined than navy blues, for browns of varying hues and values harmonize readily. Brown leathers, brown furs, and brown fabrics may be harmonized easily. More care should be used in selecting brown hats and dress and coat fabrics. If the hat does not match exactly, it should be either definitely darker or definitely lighter, giving a deliberate contrast. The brown dress worn under a brown coat should likewise be either a good match or one showing pronounced contrast.

Brown fur coats, especially the more luxurious brown minks, are universally accepted as proper for wear with almost every color and texture. The richness of their coloring and their luster make them look well with black; but a brown, cloth coat of similar coloring is usually unsuccessful with black.

Beige. Beige is not becoming to all women, nor is it always in fashion, but it is a highly practical color, which, for this reason, makes it an economical coat color. Beige combines well with almost every color except gray of the same value. A beige coat may be worn with almost any shoe colors—with black, brown, navy blue, tan, or beige. Hats of definite colors not only look well with beige but usually improve the appearance of a beige coat. While beige itself is not universally becoming, beige with the proper accents of brighter or darker colors is quite widely wearable. The large woman should not forget that light colors tend to make her look larger and that the light beige coat will tend to increase the size of the figure. The silhouette, however, may be less evident in unobtrusive, neutral beige.

Gray. Gray combines with all colors. A bluish gray, a pinkish gray, some variation of gray may be found for every color. Some women to whom beige is unbecoming, because it is too much like their skin and hair tones, may look well in gray, especially light, bluish grays. Women with white hair, who frequently find that beige makes their hair look yellowish, may wear carefully chosen gray, preferably gray a shade darker than their hair, so that their hair looks more silvery by contrast.

Gray or beige looks best with decided accents of contrasting color. Both hue and value should contrast with this light, neutral color.

Dark green. The woman who plans her costume carefully may find green as useful and as economical as a more neutral color. A dark green coat may be worn with dark brown or black accessories, or with those that are carefully matched. Dark green combines well with definite blues, especially slightly violet blues. The woman to whom blues and green are especially flattering can work out sufficient variety with dresses and accessories in those colors. She may also wear dresses of brown, beige, gray, or black with her green coat. A combination of yellow and green is especially effective and may often be more becoming than yellow alone. Soft oranges may likewise be used with green, and light greens combine effectively. Red and green are likely to give a Christmas-tree effect, yet, if the green is dark, red and green may be extremely effective.

Wine color. Dark, wine color, which is flattering to almost all women except those with red hair, makes a becoming coat color, but one of which many women tire quickly. It should, therefore, be chosen only by women who have several coats or who like the color so much that they are sure they will not become tired of it. While it limits the number of colors that may be worn in dress and hat, careful harmonizing will give considerable variety to the wardrobe.

Lighter reds in the same violet-red cast, down to rosy tones and pale, dusty pinks, are effective. Greens and beiges are good. Some wine reds look well with brown; others, with black. Yellows, oranges, and orange-reds should be avoided. Greens must be very carefully chosen and should usually be very dark or very dull, if they are to be used with wine red.

PART II

Silhouettes and Sizes

Silhouettes and Sizes

ASK ALMOST ANY WOMAN engaged in shopping for clothes how she plans to choose them. She will usually answer by naming the season and the occasion—something suitable for the street, for formal wear, for sports, for hot afternoons. She may say she wants something new and different; more likely she will assume that you know that. She probably knows the effect she wants to achieve—tailored but not too severe, or something striking or very feminine. If there is something about her person that particularly pleases or annoys her, she is likely to take that into consideration from the first.

"I want a blue that just exactly matches my eyes."

"It's awfully hard to find anything, because I'm so short."

"I can't wear anything that will make my neck look any longer and skinnier than it is."

And she may add wistfully, "I'll never have another outfit as becoming as that green sport suit I had last year."

Few women realize enough of the reasons for a successful costume to be able to apply the same principles to a different one.

The cardinal principle underlying the achievement of beauty of figure, without changing actual measurements, is that proportion and not dimension is significant. A small foot or a small waistline is no credit to the large-framed woman. Her appearance will be improved when she ceases to pride herself on such smallness and brings it into scale. The slender woman with spreading hips must sacrifice some of her appearance of slenderness to bring her whole body into scale with their circumference. The short woman must avoid broadening effects, and the tall woman must seek to broaden her figure. In this way each approaches the proportions, though not the dimensions, of the normal figure.

In designing a costume, it is well to remember that conflicting centers of interest, too many details, make a costume intricate and confusing. A well-designed costume has a major center of interest near the face and not more than two or three minor or subordinate accents. More than these give a spotty appearance, causing the observer's eyes to jump from accent to accent with a restless movement, and give a decidedly unpleasing appearance to the costume. Secondary centers of interest may be on the hands or arms in the form of bracelets, rings, or interesting cuff details; at the waist or hipline; or, if repeated in a subdued manner, the accent used near the face may be at hemline or feet.

The principles of beautiful proportion are, of course, quite independent of style and mode. Unfortunately, styles and modes are often quite independent of beautiful proportion. As the eye becomes accustomed to seeing them, poor proportions may seem more beautiful than they really are. Thus, low beltlines encircling the hips create a proportion difficult for many figures, yet, when they were the rule, others seemed awkward. The same is true of fads, such as extremely short skirts, light-colored hosiery, and hats having no relation to the size and shape of the head.

As a part of the crowd, it is sometimes good policy to sacrifice some individual beauty of line. Yet in every mode there are degrees, and every woman profits by knowing what devices display her figure to best advantage.

With the figure, as with the face, the aim in design should be to emphasize pleasing features and to center interest away from unattractive ones.

CHAPTER XIII

Optical Illusions Affecting the Figure

THE STUDY OF DEVICES for changing the apparent contours of the face has made familiar the principle that slenderness may be gained either by adding length or by decreasing width, and that long thinness may be minimized by lines that shorten or by those that broaden. In the treatment of the figure, however, it is not possible to list, without qualification, certain devices that will give height and certain others that, by adding width, seem to make the figure shorter. In practically every case, it is necessary to say that, if wisely used, certain lines will give a certain effect, and to point out how unskillful variations will often produce an opposite effect.

Critical Analysis of the Figure

Proportion of head to body. The actual size of the figure is less important than its proportions. It is not alone the actual height of the figure that makes an individual appear tall, but rather the proportion of the head to that of the body. A small head makes its owner appear much taller than an individual of the same height with a large head. The height of the figure is sometimes measured in terms of heads (the measurement from crown to chin). Seven and one-half heads is considered average height. Some persons also regard this as ideal height while others prefer eight heads. Most professional mannikins have small heads and elongated bodies, sometimes being as much as nine heads in height.

The width of the head should obviously be less than the length, if the head is to have the oval contour that is considered ideal. Styles of hairdress and of millinery may be used to alter its apparent proportions.

Weight. The normal weight for an individual's height gives another basis for determining the costume lines needed. The late Dr. Lulu Hunt Peters, authority on weight control, recommended that the ideal weight be estimated at 110 lbs. for 5 feet and 5½ lbs. for every inch beyond that stature. Fashion authorities generally feel that this weight, while probably ideal from a physician's point of view, is somewhat too high to give a perfect foundation for the costume. Since Dr. Peters allowed for 10 per cent variation, according to the size of the body frame, and since her table was for both men and women, 5 lbs. per inch rather than 5½ is probably a safe basis for figuring ideal weight. Even when using this figure, one must consider whether the frame is small, medium, or large. A person of small frame may be overweight at a much lower figure than a person of large frame, yet may not appear so large, even though more rotund. Persons of large frame may need slenderizing lines whatever their weight.

Posture. Posture influences the actual everyday height of the individual, for most people stand as erect as possible when being measured, but frequently fail to do so at other times. This must be considered when judging height and when prescribing lines. It is not sufficient to note whether or not the individual stands at her greatest height; we should also note what part of the body droops or sags. In one case only the neck and head may be stooped and in another the loss of height may be near the waistline where the trunk is allowed to sag. This may make a difference of several inches in the height, and it likewise makes a great difference in the contours of the body. Protruding diaphragm and abdomen, hollow back, and the protrusion below are caused by sagging of the trunk.

Proportion of shoulders, bustline, and hips. The artist's ideal of a perfectly proportioned woman's figure is usually that of shoulders and hips of the same width. In that of young girls the hips are narrower. If the shoulders are wider than the hips, or if they are made to seem wider, a more youthful looking figure results, and therefore the fashionable ideal figure has shoulders at least slightly wider than that of the hips.

If the shoulders are narrow, or the hips wider than the ideal, carefully placed shoulder pads should be used to increase shoulder width to the desired proportions. Too heavy padding and padding that extends too far out over the arm should be avoided, as it gives a heavy, muscular effect that is unfeminine and unattractive. Individual adjustment of shoulder pads, moving them in or out perhaps only a fraction of an inch, and adding or subtracting padding to make the shoulders higher or lower and to make both shoulders appear the same are most important means of making the figure seem to have ideal proportions.

The hip measurement should also be the same or slightly less than the bust circumference. A well-fitting brassiere that raises the breasts to the naturally high line of the youthful figure usually increases the bust measurement, making both waist and hips seem smaller in comparison. The extreme uplift that forces the breasts into an extremely high line defeats its purpose by attracting attention to the problem figure. Only the very thin girl or woman with no natural breast development finds it desirable to pad the breasts to increase their actual bulk; it is better to employ lines that decrease the apparent size of the hips.

The arm. In a person of normal weight the arm tapers from the wrist to the elbow without becoming perceptibly wider above the elbow; in the person who is below normal weight, the arm is smaller above than below the elbow; and in a person heavier than normal weight it is much larger above the elbow, the arm curving outward farther than the natural shoulder. A shoulder pad widening the shoulderline sufficiently so that the sleeve hangs straight without revealing the bulging arm hides this defect and makes the entire figure seem in better proportion. The apparent size of the hands is frequently dependent not only upon their actual size but upon that of the arm and of the amount and the length of hand revealed by the dress. Sleeves tightly fitted below the elbow make the hands seem larger; loosely fitting sleeves and cuffs wider than the hands reduce the apparent size of the hands.

Waistline. The waistline ten inches smaller than the bust and hip measurement is the ideal for the trim slender figure; that which is eight inches smaller than these dimensions may still give pleasing and graceful proportions. If the difference is more than ten inches, either hips or bust is likely to seem too large; if the difference is less than eight inches, the waistline is likely to appear thick and heavy, the figure matronly. The waistline would be judged when a carefully fitted foundation garment is worn, provided of course that this garment is necessary.

A well-fitted brassiere, eliminating sagging breasts and the resultant roll of flesh underneath them, reduces the actual waist measurement much more effectively than a tight constriction at the waistline. If heavy hips are too tightly girdled, the flesh of hips or abdomen may be pushed upward, making the waist larger than its actual measurement. The waistline as it appears on the clothed figure is important in determining the lines that should be worn and the placement and use of the belt.

Legs and feet. In the figure of average proportions, the thigh is about the same width as the hips. If it is perceptibly narrow or heavier, this point must be considered in choosing becoming lines.

The calves, ankles, and feet can best be judged in proportion to other parts of the figure, since, if they are perceptibly smaller, they will make the figure appear unduly heavy. Small lower limbs seem to give an inadequate support to the large body. They frequently remain small when weight is put on in middle age. Effort should then be made to increase their apparent size, thereby increasing the apparent grace of the entire figure.

One cannot judge the feet without considering whether or not the arches are erect or fallen. Frequently one must compromise beauty of line and prescribe shoes that will give adequate support to sagging arches. The feet themselves and the lines of the figure will be improved.

Perpendicular Lines

As nearly everyone knows, but sometimes fails to remember, straight perpendicular lines tend to increase the apparent height of the wearer. Not everyone knows, however, that not all straight perpendicular lines give "long lines" to the figure. A large number of evenly spaced perpendicular lines lead the

Wide panels give breadth; narrower ones give slender effect.

A narrow, perpendicular line formed by a zipper, trimming or a row of buttons tends to divide the figure in halves; usually emphasizing true proportions; while becoming to the slender figure, it makes the heavier figure seem wider.

eye across the figure, from one stripe to the next, emphasizing width, not length. A broad panel may likewise cause either a horizontal movement or one of vertical feeling.

Center panels. A panel extending the full length of the figure may be especially effective in increasing the apparent height of the wearer. Its width must, however, be proportioned with due regard to the size of the wearer. An extremely wide panel, one extending almost the width of the figure, tends to lead the eye of the observer across the figure, thus increasing its apparent width and minimizing its height. A narrower panel will cause the eye of the observer to travel up and down the figure, in perpendicular movement, thereby increasing the height of the figure. A slight adjustment in the width of a panel may add greatly to the apparent grace of the wearer. The extremely thin, short woman will wish to avoid the severely straight, long, narrow panel, which makes her appear appreciably thinner as well as taller. Panels in contrasting color, pleated panels, and similar means of obtaining softer lines than those of the severely straight panel are desirable.

Narrow center line. A row of buttons, a band of trimming, or other perpendicular effect placed in the center of the figure divides the figure in two in such a manner as to place emphasis on width rather than on height. Several perpendicular lines grouped to give an effect similar to that produced by a panel are usually much more becoming than a single narrow perpendicular trimming used in the center. When a single line is employed, it is frequently more easily worn when placed at one side instead of in the exact center.

Side panels. When they are in fashion, side panels may be used to modify the figure; carefully placed, they may either reduce or add to apparent height. If placed too far out over

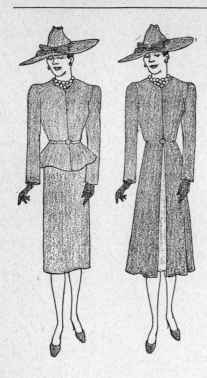

A short tunic, especially if it is opened at the front, giving the effect of side panels, materially shortens and widens the figure; the same over-dress carried the full length of the skirt, as in a redingote, lengthens the figure.

To give long line, entire length of diagonal should be visible from the front.

the hips, they tend to add width and shorten the figure. If they are shorter than the dress, they perceptibly lessen apparent height. Panels of contrasting color, which are shorter than the dress and are placed far out over the hips, leaving a wide panel of the dress revealed, are especially difficult for the short woman to wear.

Panels at least slightly longer than the dress tend to increase apparent height. If they are placed carefully, so that a pleasing space division, a panel of correct width, is formed in the center of the figure, panels or drapes at the side of the skirt are especially graceful on the short, thin figure. Pointed panels further add to the apparent height of the wearer. A slight adjustment in length or width of panels may perceptibly change the apparent proportions of the figure.

Diagonals

A diagonal line, being longer than a perpendicular line, placed lengthwise of the figure tends to increase the apparent height of the figure. Not only does it lead the eye up and down, but it leads it over the longest path. A surplice closing, a diagonal line extending from the shoulder at one side to the hem at the other, therefore gives an appearance of height to the figure. The entire length of the diagonal should be visible from the front view, but should not extend too far out at each side or it may tend to carry the eye outward.

Points. A pointed line likewise leads the eye up and down, increasing the apparent length of the figure. It has an added advantage, in that the converging diagonals lead the eye inward, decreasing apparent width and giving height and slenderness. A pointed drape that has not wide, diverging lines is especially slenderizing. Pointed hemlines not only prevent

A V-shaped neckline and pointed seaming at the waist makes the figure seem taller than the square neckline and horizontal lines at the waist.

Horizontals may lead the eye either up and down or across the figure.

a horizontal break in the figure but give a perpendicular movement. However, since they are striking, they call attention to the figure, especially to the legs and feet, and are therefore difficult for the woman with a problem figure. They are suitable only for evening dress, and they are less slenderizing than long, full-length skirts, which are flattering to all figures.

A *V*-shaped or pointed neckline and *V*- or pointed seaming at the waist and hipline are effective devices for increasing apparent height and avoiding the break created by horizontal seamings. As the *V*-shaped neckline may make the thin face too long, it should usually be combined with soft fabrics or with accessories having a softening influence upon the face. As slenderness of face and figure are fashionable, however, the *V*- or pointed lines in a softened, not too-severe or geometric, interpretation are usually becoming, even to the short, thin woman. When she wears square or horizontal lines at the neck, at the waist and hips, and in the hemline, her height is greatly reduced and her width is exaggerated until even the thin figure may appear square and squat.

Horizontals

Horizontal lines are a well-known device for decreasing the apparent height of the figure; but few persons realize that, if incorrectly placed, these horizontals may lead the eye up and down the figure from one horizontal to the next and give an impression of increased rather than lessened height. Evenly spaced horizontal lines are most likely to lead the eye up and down; tucks, seamings, or folds at regular intervals actually add height to the figure. Unevenly spaced horizontals, particularly if used in conjunction with color contrast, lead the observer's eye across the figure, increasing its apparent width and minimizing its height. As horizontal contrasts may be introduced in scarfs and belts, in contrasting jackets or blouses, or in the color of dresses showing beneath seven-eighth or three-quarter length coats, they are a means of lessening the height of the figure that can be applied to most costumes.

Wide sleeves and heavy cuffs add width at the hipline; close fitting sleeves give a longer, more slenderizing line.

Short sleeves add to width of figure; lessening height; bare arms give a long line.

Details

Sleeves. A long, narrow sleeve gives a perpendicular feeling, while a wide sleeve produces a horizontal movement, which adds width and breaks the height of the figure. If the sleeve is wide and even, the short, thin woman may appear to have wide, heavy hips and too great width. Her height, of course, will be seriously broken. A close-fitting sleeve, emphasizing the slender line of the arm, but not fitting too tightly if the arm is extremely thin, removes all bulk from the width of the figure and carries the eye of the observer up and down rather than across the figure.

If the sleeve is of one color, rather than with contrasting cuff or other trimming, the length of the arm is increased, while undue emphasis of width is avoided. Contrasting cuffs, which cause the eye of the observer to travel across the figure from one wrist to the other, add width and thereby shorten the height. If the cuff or sleeve trimming is bulky as well as contrasting, the effect is still more disastrous to the short woman. Fur of self-color and of close, sleek character is more easily worn as a sleeve trimming, but it is less slenderizing than the fabric sleeve.

Gloves of contrasting color have an effect similar to that of color contrast used in the sleeves.

Short sleeves, especially when in a dark color contrasting with the skin, break the length of the arm and place emphasis upon the width of the shoulders and of the entire figure. The very short sleeve, especially that formed by the extended shoulder-line, may make the figure as a whole seem more slender in comparison with the broad shoulders. A sleeveless dress permitting the entire length of the arm to be seen may place emphasis upon length and make the entire figure appear taller and more slender.

Collars and capes. The short, heavy woman must use great discrimination when selecting dresses with collars. Wisely chosen, they may add grace to her figure and give lengthened and softened lines to her face. Contrasting collars are especially difficult and should usually be rather small, since a large collar of contrasting color is almost certain to cut the figure horizontally. Large cape collars are most becoming if they are pointed or *V*-shaped, since they give long lines, which lead

In a bolero the figure seems taller than in a hip-length jacket.

A full length coat gives greater height than a three-quarter length one.

the eye to the center of the figure rather than toward the sides. When double points are used, they must not be placed so far apart as to lead the eye outward rather than lengthwise. Round or square collars, obviously unsuited to the short, heavy figure, are often a pleasing contrast to slenderness. Collars of self-fabric without pronounced or conspicuous trimming at the outer edge are most easily worn. A contrasting trimming on a self-color collar is likely to break the length of the figure as much as would a collar of entirely contrasting color.

Length of coat or jacket. A jacket ending near the center of the figure markedly decreases height, the horizontal line of the jacket cutting the length of the figure. The length of the legs is materially decreased, the figure seeming not only shorter but in many cases poorly proportioned.

A bolero jacket, ending at or slightly above the waistline, gives greater length of limb, making the entire figure seem taller and more slender.

Coats of three-quarter or seven-eighth length are usually less becoming than those of full length, as they break the line of the costume and leave too short a line underneath to be in pleasing proportion with the length of the coat. This is especially true if the dress or skirt worn underneath the coat is of a contrasting color, which gives a border that breaks the length of the costume and makes the figure seem perceptibly shorter and heavier. A flaring, swagger cut, or a short length with a wide, full hem, shortens the figure more than does a close-fitting, straight line.

Lines of hat. The effect of hats on the figure is much the same as the effect of the caps placed on the top of the perpendicular lines shown in the accompanying illustration (p. 142). The lower down on the head the hat is worn, the more pronounced becomes its effect upon the figure. If a small, close-

The shape of the hat influences the apparent height of the figure, just as the cap at the top of the perpendicular lines influence their apparent length. All the figures on this page are of the same height.

fitting turban is worn, there is no horizontal break in line to arrest the eye, and it will continue to travel upward, beyond the actual length of the figure, making the wearer seem taller, in the same manner that the straight line without a cap seems longer than the line next to it.

A hat with a wide brim, creating a straight horizontal line, makes the figure seem shorter than it actually is, for the eye is not allowed to travel the full length of the figure, but is arrested before it actually reaches the top of the figure. Thus the figure wearing a straight-brimmed hat loses even more apparent height than does the straight line with the straight horizontal cap.

The drooping hat brim not only arrests the upward movement of the observer's eye but actually causes a downward movement, making the wearer's figure seem perceptibly shorter. This can, to some extent, be overcome by placing striking trimming above the brim, which, particularly if high on the crown, may aid in retaining an upward movement.

The upturned brim, even though it is worn well down on the head, encourages the observer's eye to travel upward, beyond the actual limits of the figure, thereby increasing apparent height. When the line of the upturned brim begins high on the head, its height-giving characteristic is even more evident.

A slanting diagonal line in the brim may lead the eye up at one side, adding to the apparent height of the wearer. Trimming placed high at one side has a similar effect, while that placed at the lower edge of the brim, accenting downward movement, tends to make the wearer appear shorter. The slanting trim that is widest on the upswept side adds to apparent height, while that which is larger on the side that dips down shortens the appearance of the figure.

CHAPTER XIV

Texture and Color Affect Silhouette and Size

GREAT AS WE KNOW the effect of line to be upon the appearance of the figure, the effect of color and texture is also so powerful that several dresses of identical design, but in fabrics of different color and texture, may produce widely different effects upon the figure of a woman wearing them.

Shiny Textures Increase Size and Reveal Silhouette

Shiny surfaces reflect light, thereby increasing the apparent size of the person wearing them. They likewise reveal the silhouette as the high lights on the shiny surface reveal contours. A person with a large bust, large arms, or large hips finds shiny-surfaced fabrics particularly difficult to wear, as they not only increase the apparent size of the entire figure, but accentuate the poorly proportioned features, the high lights upon them compelling attention. Only the slender, well-proportioned woman should wear satins and other shiny-surfaced fabrics. The too-thin, angular woman finds them as trying as does the stout, rotund woman.

Dull Textures Decrease Size and Conceal Silhouette

Dull textures absorb light, thereby decreasing the apparent size of the wearer and tending to conceal the silhouette. Fab-

Shiny textures high light curves and increase rotundity; dull-surfaced fabrics are more slenderizing.

Stiff fabrics increase actual size of silhouette and apparent size of the wearer; softer fabrics are more slenderizing.

rics with dull surfaces, therefore, aid in decreasing the apparent size of the woman wearing them, by promoting an appearance of slenderness, at the same time adding grace to the figure by minimizing irregularities of silhouette. Dull-surface fabrics are becoming to nearly all types of women, there being no type of figure that cannot wear them in some interpretation.

Stiff Fabrics Increase Size but Conceal Silhouette

Stiff fabrics stand out from the figure, increasing its apparent size while concealing the actual outlines, the silhouette. Therefore, while a stiff fabric, such as taffeta, usually makes the wearer appear larger than she actually is, the woman who is only slightly larger than she desires to be may sometimes conceal excess weight by a dress of stiff fabric so designed that it conceals the real outlines of the figure, leaving the observer with the impression that it is the dress and not the wearer that possesses actual breadth. This device is particularly helpful in concealing irregularities of figure. For instance, the fairly slender woman with large hips may find that a taffeta gown with molded bodice, revealing the slenderness of the upper part of the figure, and a bouffant skirt, conceals the actual outlines of the too-heavy hips.

Stiff fabrics, unless carefully handled, give harsh angular lines and may accentuate an appearance of angularity in the too-thin figure. However, if used so that they stand out from the figure, not fitting closely, this is not likely to occur, since stiff fabrics, as a general rule, are best suited to the slender woman. They should, under most circumstances, be studiously avoided by the stout woman, and used with discretion by the slightly heavy woman attempting to disguise actual contours.

Heavy Fabrics Also Increase Size and Conceal Silhouette

Like stiff fabrics, heavy, bulky fabrics increase the size of the wearer and, at the same time, conceal the actual contours of the figure. They tend, however, to make the figure seem

Heavy, bulky fabrics add to the actual size of the silhouette; smooth, light-weight fabrics are more slenderizing.

Transparent fabrics reveal the actual contours and are difficult for the imperfect figure; soft, opaque fabrics are more wearable.

square and awkward, to emphasize angularity in figures that possess it, and actually to create that effect even upon the rotund figure. Thick, heavy fabrics must be very carefully handled, as extremely heavy fabrics are seldom becoming. For this reason, the development of sheer velvets and lightweight sheer

147

woolens has made these fabrics becoming to the larger woman who formerly could not wear them because they markedly increased her size.

Heavy fabrics should be avoided by all except the tall, well-built woman who is neither too thin nor too fat, only the athletic figure and carriage being consistent with them. Moderately heavy fabrics of soft pliable character can be worn by the person of average figure, who will, however, usually find the lightweight fabrics of this type, such as the sheer or very lightweight tweeds, more becoming than heavy tweeds. A lightweight velvet is also more becoming to this type than heavy, deep-piled fabrics.

Transparent Fabrics Reveal Silhouette

While transparent fabrics neither increase nor decrease the size of the figure, they reveal its contours mercilessly so that the stout, rotund figure appears more so, while the thin, angular body is likewise accentuated, revealed in its lack of grace. Therefore, only the person near ideal proportions finds extremely transparent materials becoming; opaque, or at most slightly translucent, fabrics are more becoming to women who have imperfections to conceal.

It is true that a transparent material made over a carefully constructed opaque slip may be becoming to the woman whose figure is far from perfect, but only if the shoulders and arms it reveals have graceful contours and are not out of proportion to the rest of the body. A transparent costume over a straight, tight slip, which in itself reveals either rotundity or angularity in the wearer and also bad proportions, such as the too-large bust or hips, is especially unbecoming. Likewise a transparent dress worn over a slip with a straight top and straps may be unbecoming because the straight top of the slip creates a horizontal break in the figure. This is especially evident if the dress and slip are of dark material or conspicuous color contrasting with the flesh. A rounded line at the top of the slip, preferably with the slip following the outlines employed at the neckline of the dress, is much more becoming.

Transparent fabrics, especially in loose, floating draperies may give a very becoming, light, airy, graceful effect. Several thicknesses of transparent material used together conceal the contours, yet give a light elusive quality to the costume. Two or more layers of sheer fabric of the same color are more slenderizing than several layers of contrasting color.

Clinging fabrics reveal the silhouette and emphasize bulk. Fabrics that cling closely, especially knitted fabrics, emphasize the silhouette and reveal even minor irregularities and figure defects. They are becoming only to the slender of almost perfect proportions. The woman who is even slightly overweight should either avoid them entirely or should be sure that they are fitted very loosely and worn over suitable foundation garments, and slips which counteract their clinging tendencies.

The young girl with a perfect figure or the slender older woman with good figure and posture may find clinging fabrics very becoming, because they reveal and emphasize true contours of the figure.

When selecting apparel made of clinging fabrics, one should always be sure that they are becoming from all angles, especially from the back view. One should also consider whether or not the fabric is going to hold its shape well. Many knitted and clinging fabrics stretch, losing their proportions, tending to bag out at the seat, the knees, and the elbows. Very often the pressing and reblocking necessary to keep them in shape totally offsets their proposed advantages of not crushing or wrinkling easily.

Printed fabrics, or prints as they are generally referred to, break silhouette, give color, life, and animation. They may be very flattering as testified by the facts that they have been approved by fashion creators for the past dozen years, and that they have seldom, if ever, since machine printing developed, been entirely absent from the fashion picture. This continued use of prints means that women like them because they are becoming, and because they are practical, not showing spots or wrinkles readily.

But not all prints are becoming to all women. Unsuitable prints are so unpleasant in appearance that they sometimes make it seem safer to avoid printed fabrics entirely.

A few simple principles make it easy to select prints that are wearable and becoming. When one looks at some prints, one finds that one's eyes jump from spot to spot. This is especially true when the designs are bold in outline and widely spaced, without connecting lines between the individual designs. Other prints carry the eye up and down, giving an impression of added height to the wearer. The opposite effect is obtained when the line direction of the print is horizontal, carrying the observer's eye across the figure. Some prints have a swirling-'round feeling, increasing the apparent rotundity of the wearer. Angular, geometric designs may make the figure seem stiff and more angular than it is; these prints, difficult for the too-thin figure, are too conspicuous for the heavy figure.

Prints Should Be Scaled to Size of Wearer

Dainty, fragile-appearing designs are becoming to petite women, but appear too delicate for heavy figures, making the

Large, spotty prints increase apparent size of the wearer; small, all-over designs give an indefinite outline to the silhouette which is flattering to the out-of-proportion figure.

Striped effects may be created by printed designs as well as by the more obvious geometric stripes; some stripes lead the eye across the figure while others have an up-and-down line direction; the former makes the figure seem wider; the latter more slender.

figure seem larger by contrast. Large, sprawling patterns may also make the large figure appear heavier, while they seem too big for the small figure to carry. Moderate designs of moderate size, or allover patterns of indefinite outlines are the most easily worn. Striking color contrasts, brilliant colors which command attention, are difficult for all but perfect figures, and there is always danger that they will overshadow the personality of the wearer.

Light Colors Increase Size and Conceal Silhouette

Light colors reflect light, making the surfaces they cover seem larger than they actually are. At the same time they tend to conceal the silhouette, as there is little contrast between the light color and the average background, particularly the background of space. A light dress worn by a person on the stage against a black backdrop would of course reveal the outlines of the figure, but in most instances conditions are the reverse.

Therefore, light colors, even though they increase the apparent size, may be becoming to even fairly stout women, as they make the silhouette inconspicuous. This is partly due to the fact that light colors appear actually to possess less weight, so that the woman in a light dress appears lighter and, therefore, less conspicuously stout, even though she may appear somewhat larger upon close inspection. The thin woman finds light colors particularly becoming, as they both increase her size and lessen angularity by concealing contours. The figure that is badly proportioned frequently appears at its best in light colors, which always tend to make the silhouette inconspicuous.

Dark Colors Decrease Size and Reveal Silhouette

Dark colors are quite opposite in their effect, as might be expected. They decrease the size of the wearer but emphasize the silhouette. The stout woman finds that they make her appear more slender but reveal uneven proportions, as in the hips or the bust. They may also call attention to her size by throwing her massive figure into relief against a light background. For street wear, against fairly dark backgrounds, a dark costume will make the silhouette less conspicuous.

Dark colors also tend to make the figure appear heavier in actual weight, even though dimensions may be less. Therefore, while dark colors decrease the apparent size and are becoming to most stout women of well-proportioned figure, they should be used advisedly, as they will not always have the traditional slenderizing effect. On the other hand, dark colors are distinctive upon the ideal figure, emphasizing its pleasing contours and making it appear even more slender than it really is. The too-thin woman, more than any other type, must avoid dark colors, for they will make her appear thinner and reveal her angular outlines.

Bright Colors Increase Size and Reveal Silhouette

Bright colors, vivid colors of full intensity, reflect light and increase the size of the surfaces they cover. At the same time, vivid colors make the silhouette conspicuous. Therefore, vivid, intense, bright colors are most becoming to the slender woman of good proportions. They may be used with care in fabrics and lines that conceal angularity of the too-thin woman, so that she profits by seeming larger without having her silhouette accented. Stout women, no matter what their proportions, should avoid bright colors.

Dull Colors Decrease Size and Conceal Silhouette

Dull, neutralized, or grayed colors decrease the apparent size of the wearer and make the silhouette inconspicuous. Therefore, while a bright blue or a bright red dress would make a woman seem larger, a dull, soft, gray blue or a dull, soft, subdued red makes her seem smaller and does not emphasize the outlines of the figure.

Warm Colors Are Difficult to Wear

Like vivid colors, warm colors (red, orange, yellow, red-violet), colors which give an impression of warmth, increase the apparent size of the figure. A warm color is advancing, aggressive; seems nearer to the observer; and, therefore, makes surfaces that it covers seem larger. A warm, bright color most decidedly increases apparent size. Stout women of warm coloring, to whom warm colors are naturally suited, are greatly limited in choice of color, if they are to make the most of both face and figure. Warm colors, except in very subdued or grayed intensities, should be avoided by all stout women. They are best on the well-proportioned slender woman, as the angular woman also finds them trying because they reveal her silhouette.

Cool Colors Flatter All Figures

Cool colors are receding, seem farther away from the eye, and, therefore, make surfaces they cover seem smaller. This is especially true if the color is neutralized or grayed, although any cool color—blue, green, blue-green, blue-violet—tends to make the figure seem smaller. No type of figure needs to avoid them. Stout women find cool colors much more becoming than warm colors. Those whose proportions are not perfect also find cool colors preferable to warm. The thin woman can wear them even though they may decrease size, because they soften the outlines, but never accentuate them.

CHAPTER XV

Devices That Make Large Hips Less Evident

DISPROPORTIONATELY LARGE HIPS are a frequent figure defect. Girls and women who have given little thought to their figures begin complaining that dresses are made too tight over the hips, until suddenly they discover that it is their figures that have become wider across the hips, thighs, and lower back. If they are wise, they keep this defect a secret from the world. They will avoid those models apparently designed to emphasize the hips (becoming only to the slim almost hipless figure). They will hide large hips under carefully chosen lines that minimize the width of the hip and center attention elsewhere.

Broad base triangle. A sleek, close coiffure or a small, close-fitting hat; trim, narrow shoulder lines; and a slim bodice, gradually widening into wider hips and flaring skirt, create a silhouette narrow at the top and broad at the base, a triangle that lacks grace and balance and, therefore, emphasizes the figure defect.

A wide-brimmed hat, a collar giving a broad line at the shoulders, or a shoulder and sleeve cut to give breadth will give balance to the figure and make the hips seem narrower. Shoulder pads aid in broadening the shoulderline so that it balances wide hips.

A coat cut with slightly flaring lines, a flare beginning above the widest part of the hips, thus concealing them, may be balanced by width at the top of the figure. Sometimes both shoulder and hat width are needed, at other times one will be sufficient. A coat cut with swagger lines, the flare beginning at the shoulders, may effectively conceal heavy hips. Care must be taken, particularly when heavy fabrics are employed, to supply the necessary balance at the top of the figure.

The straight coat should hang sufficiently loose to hide the actual contours of the hips. A coat of the princess type, if expertly fitted, the waistline slightly large and high enough to avoid a break at the small of the back, with an easy looseness over the hips, gives maximum slenderness and length to the figure and at the same time minimizes large hips.

Skirt fullness may conceal hips. A wide, full skirt commencing sufficiently high above broad hips may conceal their actual outlines, making it appear that the garment, not the figure, possesses the actual width. If the bodice is slender, emphasizing slim lines above the waist, the illusion of an entirely slender figure may be created. A bertha or scarf giving a wide shoulder line, or a neckline cut with horizontal lines, may be needed to give balance to the figure. A wide hat could, of course, also supply it. The concealing full skirt combined with slender close-fitting lines on the upper part of the figure is successful only when the hips alone are over size. The woman who is even slightly too plump all over, or at any point other than the hips and thighs, will find that these lines make her seem much heavier.

Horizontal lines to be avoided. Horizontal lines employed in the skirt, particularly at the hips, lead the observer's eye across the figure, giving an impression of greater width than actually

Broad-base, triangular silhouette emphasizes hips;
broad-shoulder-line balances
wide hips.

Closely fitting hipline with
flare below it reveals faulty
proportions; when the flare
begins above the largest part
of the hips it may conceal
their actual contours.

exists. Every effort, therefore, should be made to avoid horizontal details at the hips or in the skirt when the hips are at all broad and out of proportion. Horizontal lines in the bodice, particularly high on the shoulders, or in the full-bloused waist aid in making the upper part of the figure balance the lower.

Closely fitted waistlines and swathed hips reveal size; a loosely fitting belt and bloused bodice make the hips seem smaller.

Horizontal lines created by belts, yokes, and pockets all tend to emphasize width of the hips; perpendicular lines created by seams or pleats minimize their width.

Bloused bodice minimizes large hips. A full bodice, bloused above the hips, makes large hips seem smaller by contrast with the wider lines above them. Therefore, garments made with moderately close fitting but not tight skirts and a loose, bloused bodice are especially to be recommended to the tall, or at least the slender, woman, for they make the entire figure seem wider and shorter; they minimize the hips by balancing them with greater bulk above.

The most unbecoming and difficult style for women with large hips is that with draped or swathed hip, that wrapped with a girdle or sash. These devices make the hips seem larger in three ways—by adding actual bulk of fabric at the hipline, by centering attention upon this portion of the figure, and by creating horizontal lines that lead the eye of the observer across the figure, thus giving the illusion of greater width than actually exists. This style seems obviously unsuited to all whose hips are less than ideally slender, yet, when it is the fashion, it is made and sold in large sizes and worn by many women who thus call attention to a serious figure defect. The swathed hipline may make even the woman with an almost ideal figure seem to have too-full hips. The very slender, flat-hipped woman may find swathed hips becoming because they accent her slenderness, at the same time giving her a suggestion of soft roundness.

Perpendicular lines, leading the eye up and down rather than across the figure, not only add height but decrease apparent width. Perpendicular lines may be introduced to overcome the trying effect of other details, such as the swathed hipline or the meeting of skirt and blouse. Pleats may be arranged so that they give this perpendicular movement, if spacings are chosen that, instead of leading the eye across the figure, put emphasis upon the length of the pleats. Panels and drapes or the ends of a sash may also supply perpendicular movement.

Joining of skirt and bodice. The horizontal line created by a belt or by the joining of skirt and bodice enlarges the hips.

This is especially true when the belt, the end of the overblouse, or the seaming of skirt and bodice comes at the widest place on the hips. A contrasting belt, like other horizontal trimming, very markedly enlarges the hips.

The broadening effect of horizontal lines at the seaming of skirt and bodice may be avoided by the use of broken, curved, or oblique lines that carry the observer's eye up and down rather than directly across the figure. There are many of these devices to be found in present-day fashions, for the designers of the day are well aware of the flattering effect they have upon the figure. Therefore, garments employing these methods of reducing the hips may always be chosen for women with large hips.

Sometimes curved or oblique lines, which, if correctly employed, decrease the size of the hips, will lead the eye outward to the largest part of the figure, high lighting its defects. When selecting garments for the woman with large hips, one should study every line, and determine where it leads the eye whether it carries the eye outward beyond the figure, or whether it accentuates a figure defect.

V- and U-shapes helpful. Pointed and oval shapes, V- and U-lines, lead the eye toward the center of the figure, rather than accentuate the too-wide outlines. These shapes, therefore, may be advantageously used to decrease the apparent size of too-large hips. They are especially effective if they point downward, the narrowest point coming at or just below the widest portion of the hips. If they point upward, there is danger that the wide end of the V will lead the eye outward, the diverging lines centering attention on width rather than length. A V arranged with the wide portion at the shoulders, increasing the apparent width of the upper part of the body, the point at the

Definite horizontal joining enlarges hips; pointed, broken, curving or oblique lines minimize hips.

Lines leading to the largest part of the hips increase their apparent size; V-lines leading eye toward center over widest part of figure and out to increase size at the waist make the hips seem smaller.

hips decreasing their width, is extremely effective in equalizing the figure with too-large hips. A jacket may either conceal large hips or make them seem larger according to its length; one ending just at the largest part of the hips tends to call attention to them, while one ending above the hips may, particularly if it is full or is worn open to give a loose line, make the hips seem smaller by contrast. The jacket ending below the hips may likewise conceal them. Long jackets, however, definitely tend to shorten the figure.

CHAPTER XVI

Lines Minimizing Enlarged Diaphragm and Abdomen

*P*OOR POSTURE, relaxed, sagging muscles, and excess fat that accumulates in bunches on the least-exercised parts of the anatomy cause enlarged diaphragms and abdomens. These defects may occur separately or together. Pregnancy brings a similar but more exaggerated problem. While it is difficult entirely to conceal too-great enlargements at this point, the apparent grace and proportions of the figure may be greatly improved by carefully planned costumes carefully adjusted when worn.

Garments with soft, concealing folds that build out the figure above and below the protruding curves will be found becoming to the woman with either a large diaphragm or abdomen. The long *V* or surplice closing, which is effective in centering interest away from the circumference of the large-hipped figure, is often the worst possible design.

Foundation garments. A well-fitting brassiere, whether a separate garment or part of a one-piece foundation, is the first step toward improving the figure with enlarged diaphragm and abdomen. It should not compress the breasts, but allow them to assume the raised position natural to the youthful figure. A well-fitting brassiere makes the lines beneath the breast less full, first, by preventing the roll of flesh caused when the breasts sag, and secondly by contrast with the larger bustline. When the breasts are held in normal position, good posture is much more easily maintained and the bulging, protruding abdomen and diaphragm become smaller in fact as well as in appearance.

A roll of flesh over the diaphragm may be caused by a too-tight corset, which pushes the flesh up. A one-piece or combination foundation garment is frequently the wisest choice. Not all one-piece garments are suitable, however. One that is designed to give restraint over the diaphragm, to flatten out this area, should be chosen. Sometimes light, flexible boning may extend over the diaphragm. Under no circumstances should the foundation garment be tight at the waist, as constriction there pushes the flesh up, thus enlarging the diaphragm. It is difficult to fit a separate corset so that it will not exaggerate the diaphragm. If one is chosen, it should be loose at the waist, fairly high in front and worn with a well-fitting brassiere that extends well down over the corset, holding the two garments together so that they create the effect of a one-piece foundation.

For the woman with a large abdomen, a separate corset with a long brassiere is frequently preferable to the one-piece restraining garment, although the latter, with special abdominal support, may be satisfactory on some figures, especially those having a large diaphragm as well as a large abdomen.

Lingerie that is clinging or slight in quantity may permit the dress to fit too closely over the rounded diaphragm and abdomen.

Weight of dress. Unless the dress is constructed so that its weight is distributed, it will have a tendency to hang in a strained, tight line over the protruding abdomen or diaphragm,

The weight of a one-piece dress pulls the material tightly over the abdomen; a two-piece dress distributes the weight and hangs in more slender lines over the abdomen.

The short bolero makes the diaphragm more conspicuous; a longer one balances the figure and tends to conceal its defects.

making these badly proportioned parts of the figure unduly prominent.

A two-piece dress, made with the skirt hanging on a bodice or lining, the blouse hanging free from the weight of the skirt, is frequently preferable. In a dress so constructed, the weight of the skirt does not pull the blouse smooth and close over the protruding diaphragm. In many one-piece dresses, particularly those that are made with a heavy skirt, a full skirt, or one that is heavily trimmed, the dress is drawn down the length of the front, every bulge in the figure being made apparent. An inner belt to which the outer garment is tacked so that it is held in its most flattering position, with fullness and blousing carefully controlled, is a helpful device for fitting dresses so that they conceal the large diaphragm and abdomen.

Boleros and jackets. A long, straight bolero, long enough to hang below the large diaphragm, may successfully disguise it. The bolero, like the separate blouse in the two-piece dress, hangs below the protruding diaphragm and, being free from the weight of the skirt, does not cling too closely to the figure.

A short bolero—one that does not completely cover the diaphragm, but ends so that it reveals this figure defect—is extremely unbecoming to the woman whose figure is large at this point. The bolero that hangs open at the front likewise reveals the bulging line. The most unbecoming bolero of all is the one that curves away from the opening, the repetition of the curves emphasizing the protruding curves of the figure.

A long, well-fitting jacket, one that fits easily though not too loosely, may be even more becoming than the long bolero, in that it gives longer lines, carrying the eye of the observer well below the protruding curves. If the abdomen as well as the diaphragm is large, the longer jacket is obviously much more becoming. Like the blouse of the two-piece dress, the jacket is not drawn close to the figure by the weight of the skirt. As the jacket usually fits more loosely than the blouse, because it laps over, forming at least two folds of material over the front, the garment is further prevented from clinging and thus revealing the rounded diaphragm. Too many folds of the material should be avoided lest they give bulk and so increase the size of the diaphragm.

A jacket that is worn open tends to draw attention to the figure revealed inside its opening. This is especially true if a blouse of contrasting color is worn under the open jacket.

Cut of bodice. A loose, easy line over the bust and a loose armscye are necessary to prevent making the upper part of the figure appear unduly small in comparison with the large diaphragm, thus emphasizing the latter. Dresses that are too closely fitted at the top, those with tight narrow lines, make the middle of the figure appear grotesquely large and badly proportioned, high lighting defects that might be concealed by looser lines at the shoulders and bust. Sometimes lines that definitely increase the size of the upper part of the figure may be chosen. More frequently, however, a loose-fitting garment is preferable to one that has actively broadening lines. But care must be taken that the garment fits. A too-large garment, one with a too-long shoulder line, destroys the line of the entire figure.

Plain, unrelieved dress fronts reveal bulging curves and awkward proportions. Beads or other decorations over the protruding curves likewise accentuate them. A long jabot or a scarf arranged to fall in soft lines at the front aids in concealing the too-large abdomen. Discretion, however, must accompany its use. A scarf of conspicuous color or a jabot of bulky pro-

The diaphragm is unusually prominent when the jacket is worn open; concealed by jacket worn closed.

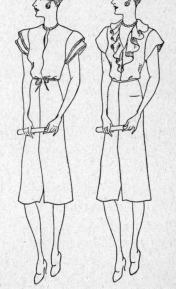

A jabot enlarging silhouette at the upper part of the figure makes the diaphragm less conspicuous; flat, close lines at the neck reveal the diaphragm and abdomen.

portions might emphasize the abdomen by making that part of the figure the center of interest or by increasing the size of the silhouette at a point where it is already too large. Likewise, care must be taken that the scarf or jabot does not end just above the prominent part of the figure, thus centering attention near it and revealing rather than concealing it. In many cases, a dress must actually be tried on before one can be sure whether

The low, bloused line conceals the diaphragm; diaphragm is accentuated by surplice closing which reveals its curve. Draped lines over the diaphragm are more likely to accentuate than to conceal bulges.

it will conceal the defect or tend to exaggerate it. Sometimes a slight adjustment, perhaps tacking a fold so that it will always fall in the most pleasing line, may be necessary to make a dress becoming to the woman whose figure is too full over the abdomen and diaphragm.

A dress made with a full waist, bloused low over the hips, is effective in concealing the large diaphragm and, correctly placed, aids in concealing the large abdomen. The full waist, bloused so that it stands out from the figure above the waist, covers the bulge, enlarges the entire waistline, and, in this manner, equalizes the unevenly distributed flesh. If the waistline is placed too high, rather than over the hips, the curve of the diaphragm and the heavy waistline are revealed; but with the low bloused line, a straight, smooth effect is gained at this point.

Garments cut with a curve over the diaphragm, as are some surplice dresses that assume a curve at this point, serve to rivet attention on this too-round part of the figure, thereby exaggerating an unlovely line.

Hemline and beltline. Too frequently one's attention is first centered on the large abdomen or diaphragm by a poorly fitted dress that rides up at the waist and hemline, disclosing the fact that the large abdomen "takes up" more material, causing the dress to be short in front. When the line is drawn up by the large abdomen, the hang of the skirt is also spoiled, frequently clinging close at the sides and flaring out abruptly in front in a manner which high lights the figure defect. Careful adjustment of the belt and hemline may make a very unbecoming dress suitable for the woman with this figure defect. Frequently the alteration may best be made by shortening the waist at the sides and back, thus giving the necessary additional length at the front and correcting both belt and hemline difficulties. At other times, the adjustment must be made at the hemline or at both points. Sometimes the girdle or belt may be lowered without an actual change in the length of the waist.

Decorative details over abdomen accent it. Obvious as their unbecoming effect usually seems to the discriminating observer, many dresses intended for large women, who so frequently have too large an abdomen, are made with buckles or conspicuous decoration or ornamentation placed at the center of the belt or directly over the abdomen. Frequently radiating lines focus interest on the already too-conspicuous part of the anatomy. While it is bad design for the center of interest of any costume to be so far removed from the face, this is especially serious when interest is centered upon a figure defect. Decoration placed near the face may, if sufficiently interesting, distract attention from the figure defect.

A bulky belt or girdle, or draped effects at the front of the skirt, increase the apparent size of the diaphragm and abdomen more often than they conceal them. The inspired designer and the accomplished fitter, however, may sometimes use folds or drapes of material to minimize the enlarged diaphragm and abdomen.

V-line at waist. A *V*-line at the waist is frequently much more becoming than a straight line, but it will accent rather than conceal the large abdomen if it is incorrectly placed. While a *V*-line that dips down in the front may give a slender waist and hipline, which aids in concealing the enlarged abdomen, the inverted *V*-line tends to accent the large abdomen, making it seem still more conspicuous. Straight *V*-lines are preferable to those formed by curves, as a curved line tends to exaggerate the too-great curve of the abdomen.

Maternity Wear

Becoming maternity wear should first lay emphasis upon flattering lines, colors near the face, and youthfulness, for the average mother-to-be would rather look like a young woman who is pregnant than a matronly woman who has grown heavy and too large over her entire figure. Costume jewelry or other accessories worn at the shoulder or neckline, a color accent at the neckline, bows or ruffles near the neckline, all center attention near the face and thus make the middle section of the figure less evident.

Flaring jacket, slim skirt. Lines that hide the actual contours of the figure and at the same time center interest near the face are found in the over-blouse or jacket with an interesting collar or neckline, the jacket cut with a flare both front and back. The back flare balances the necessary loose line in front, and the collar interest centers attention near the face. When this flaring jacket is worn with a relatively slim skirt, the loose coat seemingly tops a slender figure. The skirt worn under this should be supported by an underbodice, periodically altered so the skirt always hangs well, and straight at the bottom. One successful skirt model for this maternity costume is cut over the abdomen so that the skirt hangs straight and close to the legs.

The fabric of the jacket should be neither stiff nor bulky, but should have sufficient body so that it does not cling to the figure. Tall girls may wear it in contrasting colors, but the average woman will find it most successful when the skirt and jacket match. For evening wear with long skirts, contrast is more easily worn. Rich fabrics and decoration used for the jacket aid in centering attention near the face.

Wrapover models. Dresses made in coat lines wrapping over at the front may be either extremely becoming and satisfactory, or they may be the worst possible choice for maternity wear. Those models that emphasize the enlarged contours usually have a curving surplice line, which emphasizes the large curve over the abdomen. A surplice line that ends at the waist or hipline is less becoming than one that begins at the shoulder and ends at the hem and gives a long line, which increases the apparent height of the figure without placing any emphasis upon its circumference. Conspicuous buckles or bows used as fastenings of wrapover models further accentuate the lines that the wearer wishes to conceal.

Plain surfaces. Large areas of plain, unbroken surfaces are usually unbecoming, especially so if the color is bright or the texture shiny and conspicuous. Seamings or folds of the material, which break up the surface without making it either bulky or fussy, make the full contours of the figure less evident. Plain surfaces are even more difficult when the material is stretched tightly over the figure.

Contrasts of color and texture. Pronounced contrasts of color or of texture make the figure more conspicuous and, in so doing, make its defects more apparent. A contrast between skirt and blouse obviously must be avoided. Contrasts creating a perpendicular panel, such as a blouse showing at the front of an open coat or jacket, may be equally disastrous, as they concentrate attention upon the front of the figure. For this reason, jackets, unless large enough to be worn closed, are not becoming models for maternity wear.

Loose, shapeless garments. The garment should not be loose and shapeless, merely large enough without being interesting or of good design. Loose dresses, which hang from the shoulders to the hem, cling closely to the front of the figure and make its outlines more apparent. A belt adjusted in fairly low, loose lines may make an unbecoming dress of this character becoming. Two-piece dresses, with the skirt hung on a bodice and an overblouse or tunic hung loosely over it, offer an effective means of distributing the weight of the garment so that the weight of the skirt does not pull the blouse close and tight against the abdomen. Underwear of soft, non-bulky but not unduly clinging character is helpful.

Foundation garments. A maternity corset must be expertly fitted for comfort and protection. One of its chief services is so to distribute the weight of the abdomen that part of it is borne by the broad lower back. It should permit adjustments that continue to give smooth lines over which outer garments may be worn becomingly.

Jabots and revers may gracefully conceal figure. Jabots with long, loose folds that end below the largest part of the figure are among the most becoming lines possible for maternity wear. The jabot beginning high about the neck and filling out the shoulders, which may seem too small for the enlarged body, is usually becoming. It conceals the lines of the bust as well as of the abdomen, thus making the figure appear more normal.

More tailored revers may, if long enough, also aid in hiding the contours of the figure. Long scarf ends on coats or dresses may be at once modish and becoming. However, a scarf tied near the waistline may add bulk to the abdomen without hiding it in the least. As this is usually more a matter of adjustment than of the original design of the garment, it is possible for the wearer to adjust the scarf becomingly.

Low fullness equalizes silhouette. A skirt that is full enough at the bottom to give width to the lower part of the silhouette equalizes the outlines of the figure and makes its enlargement less apparent. If a skirt is narrow, clinging close to the knees and legs, the middle of the figure will seem much larger than the bottom. Bulky fullness near the hips or waistline must be avoided. Flaring lines, cut to avoid bulk near the waistline and releasing fullness at the bottom of the skirt, are usually a becoming choice.

During the earlier months of pregnancy the dirndl skirt, together with full peasant-style blouses, preferably of matching color, are sometimes successful, especially on the very young "junior" type bride who is proud of her new status and doesn't wish to conceal it, but does wish to wear youthful styles not too different from those to which she is accustomed. After the waistline is greatly enlarged, this style is not to be recommended. The accommodating fullness of the skirt, topped by the restriction of the waist band, ceases to be becoming even if the waistband is elastic or otherwise constructed to permit expansion.

Belt should not curve up at front. Special attention should be given to adjustment of the belt, so that it will not pull the dress up in front. A slightly uneven hemline, provided it is by design and not an ill-adjustment caused by the enlargement of the figure, may be graceful in relieving the awkwardness of maternity wear. The excessively uneven hemline with long trailing ends usually requires more poise and bearing than is natural to the pregnant woman. Beltlines designed to curve upward are awkward for maternity wear, because the upward-curving line enlarges the apparent size of the abdomen.

Entire figure demands larger sizes. In choosing garments to be adapted to maternity wear, it is well to realize that the entire figure, not just the abdomen, becomes larger. The general enlargement makes fitting easier, rather than more difficult, as a size giving ample room at waist and hips may be used without requiring great alteration. It is usually advisable, however, to alter the lines of the shoulders, taking care that the armscye is well placed, as a trim sleeve and shoulder line adds to the grace and shapeliness of the entire figure. The armscye should not be placed high enough to make the shoulders appear narrow, for moderate width of shoulder aids in giving balance to a wide hipline. Shoulder pads should be used to alter the apparent width of the shoulder and to give them an upright, erect appearance.

CHAPTER XVII

Lines Modifying the Large Bust

THE DISPROPORTIONATELY LARGE BUST, which gives the individual an awkward and decidedly mature appearance, may be greatly modified by the lines of the apparel worn. In fact, during the last few years fewer women possess extremely large busts, for modern methods of dressing, particularly modern corseting, minimize the too-generous proportions.

A corset or other restraining garment that is tight and stiff at the waist, particularly over the abdomen and diaphragm, pushes the flesh upward, increasing the actual size of the bust and, at the same time, making it appear larger by contrast with the constricted waist and hipline. One can readily demonstrate this by pressing the hands over the abdomen and diaphragm, pushing them in, and noticing the resulting increase in the size of the bust.

The correctly fitted restraining garment molds the figure into unbroken lines, smooth, flowing curves. It allows the flesh to assume a nearly normal position, but it restrains it to smooth, firm contours.

Uplift brassieres with a divided bust line give the high line occurring naturally in youth, but the extreme uplift may make the large bust much more conspicuous, sometimes making it several inches larger than its natural bust measurement. Pronounced bust lines are at present the fashionable and accepted ideal for the feminine figure, yet only a decade ago the extremely flat, boyish figure was the desired and required line. For this reason many women who failed to achieve a totally breastless effect when the boyish figure was in may still feel that their breasts are larger and more conspicuous than they should be. Sometimes they are mistaken in their desire to create a bustless effect. This chapter is, of course, intended for women who really should minimize and conceal the size of their bust line.

Narrow skirt emphasizes upper part of figure. A narrow skirt and close-fitting lines at hips and waist make the upper part of the figure appear larger in comparison with the slender lines below. A high belt, tight enough to accent the curve of the normal waistline, is extremely unbecoming, as it makes the large bust much more apparent.

Width at the lower part of the figure makes the bust appear smaller by lessening the contrast. Wide, flaring skirts and those with horizontal lines, which make the hips appear broader, tend to bring the upper part of the figure into proportion, giving balance to the entire figure and minimizing its defects.

Closely fitted neck and shoulder ungraceful. Severe, close lines at the neck and shoulder make the bust appear larger by contrast. The dress or coat that is darted to make it narrow at the shoulders and wider at the bust will, in most instances, tend to increase the curve of the bust. An expert tailor may use this device successfully when fitting the woman with the large bust, but the effect is usually unbecoming to the figure of this type. Plain, close-fitting necklines, particularly those without collars or with high collars, are very difficult to wear.

Soft, loose, graceful collars and long, draped jabots are par-

Narrow skirt empha-
sizes upper part of figure;
flaring skirt and low belt
equalize figure.

Horizontal lines in
waist increase width; perpendicular lines give
length.

178

ticularly becoming to the figure with the large bust. The loose, soft collars tend to bring the neck and shoulders into proportion with the bust, while the jabot conceals the actual outlines and thus minimizes the size of the bust. Jabots beginning above the largest part of the figure, hanging to the waist or below, are most becoming. Self-color jabots are more becoming than those of a contrasting color, which have a tendency to attract attention to the figure.

Perpendicular lines give length. A principle, seemingly so obvious that it would not be worthy of mention were it not so frequently violated, is that horizontal lines increase the apparent size of the upper part of the figure, at the same time accenting the large bust. Yokes, square necklines, and shorter bolero effects create horizontal movement.

Perpendicular lines not only give length, thereby decreasing apparent width, but, if well spaced, break up the surface, making the breadth seem much less than it actually is. It is, however, important that the placing of perpendicular lines be carefully controlled, for too many of them, particularly if evenly spaced, may lead the eye across the figure, rather than up and down, thus increasing its width rather than its length.

V-line reduces apparent size. Rounded and curved lines used in the waist tend to accentuate the too-full bust. This tendency is apparent whatever direction the rounded lines assume, but is particularly evident when they are combined with horizontal effects. Oval or *U*-shaped necklines, beads ending in a wide curve, particularly if the beads are large and round, are unbecoming, especially if the curve comes at the largest part of the figure.

V-necklines, deeper *V*-shapes with vestee fronts, *V*-seamings, and similar lines, which lead the eye toward the center of the figure, reduce its apparent size. Care must always be taken that the wide part of the *V*, the diverging rather than the converging lines, does not come at the largest point of the bust. Instead, the point of the *V* should come just below the fullest

Curved lines in waist accentuate bust; V-line reduces apparent size.

Closely fitted neck and shoulder contrast with large bust; soft collars and jabots give graceful concealment.

part of the figure, as this aids in focusing attention in toward the center of the figure without accenting the fullest part.

Loose folds tend to conceal contours. Garments that fit closely reveal contours and emphasize rather than decrease size. A dress fitting tightly, with a strained line across the bust, ac-

centuates its curves unduly and makes it appear even larger
than its actual dimensions. An ill-fitting sleeve and too small
armscye may give a tight appearance to the entire blouse.
Shiny surfaces, which in themselves tend to increase size and
to high light undesirable curves, further accentuate the unbecoming effect of tight-fitting bodices. Transparent materials,
especially when worn over tight-fitting slips, likewise emphasize the too-large bust.

Light-colored blouse makes
upper part of figure seem
larger and heavier; solid colors tend to equalize the figure.

The large, loose blouse, hanging straight above slim hips,
may effectively conceal the actual lines of the upper part of the
figure, giving the impression that the entire figure is slender.
A waist that is bloused at the hips so that it hangs almost
straight from shoulders to hips, or a loose jacket or long-bolero
effect, will frequently accomplish this result. Actual bulk over
the bust should, of course, be avoided. Heavy fur facings in

coats, bulk owing to cumbersome double-breasted effects, should also be avoided.

Light-Colored Blouse Makes Upper Figure Heavy

A light-colored blouse in contrast with a dark skirt makes the upper part of the figure seem larger, heavier, than the lower, thus accentuating the out-of-proportion bust line. If the colors are vivid as well as bright, this effect is further increased. A light satin blouse still further reveals the too-full line of the bust.

An entire dress or coat of one color tends to equalize the proportions of the figure and, therefore, is most becoming to the woman with any irregular proportion, particularly a large bust. A solid color is likewise usually better than figured material, especially if the design is large or the pattern conspicuous.

CHAPTER XVIII

Costume Lines That Improve Round Shoulders

ROUND SHOULDERS, due either to structural deformity or to poor posture, may be made less evident by means of costumes selected and fitted to minimize the defect.

Armscye and set-in sleeve becoming. Raglan and kimono sleeves exaggerate round shoulder lines, making them appear even more ungraceful than their actual contours. Even persons with normal shoulders may appear stooped and round-shouldered when wearing garments cut with these types of sleeves. This is particularly true of stout women who have a roll of flesh at the back of the neck and between the shoulder blades. Women who have even a slight tendency to stooped or rounded shoulders, who carry their heads too far forward, should avoid both kimono and raglan sleeves and shoulder lines.

Peasant blouses with gathered and smocked necklines are usually disastrous to the round-shouldered figure, tending as they do to make any figure appear stooped. Sometimes for this reason, however, they may give the appearance that the costume, not the figure, is at fault.

A carefully fitted shoulder line, with an armscye carefully cut to come at the structural point of the joining of shoulder and arm, is most becoming to the round-shouldered woman. An armscye coming too high on the shoulder may call attention to the shoulders, while one that is too wide or too low down on the arm gives much the effect of the kimono sleeve, exaggerating the rounded shoulders. A normal, easy-fitting, set-in-sleeve,

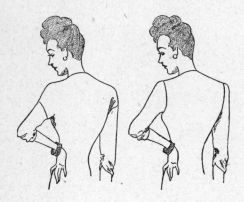

Kimono and raglan sleeves greatly emphasize round shoulders; carefully placed armscye and set-it sleeves lessen round-shouldered appearance.

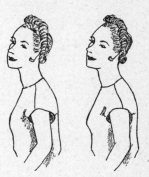

Shoulder seam slanting forward unbecoming; shoulder seam slanting back very helpful.

therefore, should be the unvarying choice of the stoop-shouldered woman.

Shoulder pads carefully chosen and adjusted to add just the right amount of width and to raise the shoulderline in exactly the right place may straighten the round line of the shoulders and make them appear almost entirely normal.

Shoulder seam slanting back imperative. A shoulder seam placed too-far forward, in front of the natural center of the figure, makes the back seem much larger and more prominent, and round shoulders much more conspicuous. If the shoulder seam slants forward, its line further increases the curve of the shoulders. Even a shoulder line placed in normal position, on the high or center point of the shoulders, gives a round-shoul-dered effect, if it slants forward.

A shoulder seam placed slightly back of the normal center line, particularly one that slants gently back, possesses an almost miraculous power of making the shoulders appear thrown back in a straight, erect attitude. So important is the effect of the correctly placed shoulder seam and armscye that a special fitting and alteration is advisable for every woman whose beauty of figure is lost because of a rounded-shoulder line.

Correctly placed mass at back becoming. Massive, heavy details at the front of the neck and shoulders appear actually to pull the body forward, making the shoulders more stooped. A scarf with longer ends in the front, a bow, a flower, or other conspicuous trimming details placed at the front, or long, heavy beads, make the shoulders assume a more stooped appearance.

Longer scarf ends at the back of the neck, or similar detail correctly placed to give slightly greater weight at the back, may appear to pull the shoulders back, giving them apparently straighter lines, and thus making round shoulders much less evident. Placement becomes largely a matter of individual study, observing the effect of each line upon the individual. As a general rule, the lines should be long and the weight placed low, so that attention is centered below the rounded-shoulder blades. Masses placed high in the back may be effective in filling out the too-great curve above the rounded shoulders, but will sometimes, if too heavy or poorly placed, act much as do masses at the front of the shoulders, appearing to weigh the shoulders down to more stooped and rounded contours.

Heavy details in front unbecoming; collar or other detail at back becoming.

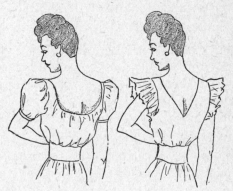

Low, round neckline unbecoming; square or pointed line better.

Low, round neckline accentuates defect. Low, round necklines repeat the curve of the shoulders, thereby making them much more apparent. An evening dress cut with a low curved line outlining the round shoulders at once reveals and accentuates their defects. If there is decided contrast in color and texture between the dress and skin of the shoulders, the unbecoming effect will be especially marked.

A square or pointed neckline does much to overcome the rounded contours of the shoulders. These lines should be carefully studied, and placed so that they come at the most pleasing point. The square neckline, in particular, must be carefully handled, for its lines are in decided opposition to the too-great curves of the shoulders and may accent them by contrast. The point on a *V*-line should come well below the curve of the shoulders, otherwise it may center attention on the defect, its converging lines leading the observer's eye to the curved spine of the wearer.

Collar aids in concealing defect. Collarless necklines too frequently reveal the unpleasing curves at the back of the neck and shoulders. When tucks are used to narrow the garment at the back of the neck, they often call further attention to awkward shoulder lines. As a collarless neckline in a daytime dress must be rounded in order to be high, its curves serve to accent defects of posture.

If a collarless neckline is to be worn at all, it must be carefully adjusted so that its outlines come at the least unbecoming position in the round shoulders. It is frequently possible so to adjust it that its line breaks the most pronounced curve of the stooped shoulders.

A collar, if well shaped and correctly placed, may correct the too-great curve of shoulders and may fill out the back of the neck, giving a straight line. A soft, crushed collar or scarf; a straight collar rolling up and away from the back of the neck, points or straight ends hanging down in the back may all be becoming. A flat, round collar, like round necklines, is exceedingly unbecoming.

Long, pointed cape is wearable. Round, circular capes add to the round lines of the shoulders, producing a bunchy, awkward figure. Short, round capelets, those that are flared and circular over the shoulders, are much more unbecoming than longer ones, although all circular capes give much the effect of

Circular cape exaggerates defect; long pointed cape more wearable.

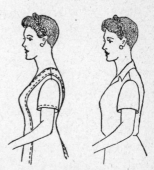

Definite waistline reveals round shoulders; loose hanging or bloused waist conceals round shoulders.

kimono sleeves. They should, therefore, be avoided by all women possessing stooped shoulders.

Long, well-fitted capes, particularly those with long, pointed or slender, oval lines, may conceal the defective shape of the figure. They may, therefore, be actively becoming rather than unbecoming as are the circular capes. Some capes have lines so graceful that they almost entirely conceal the defects of even the hunchbacked. Long, loose, back panels, having much the effect of a slender cape, are also frequently becoming.

Straight hanging waist conceals round shoulders. A definite waistline, revealing the curve of the figure, makes rounded shoulders more apparent. A belt worn at the normal waist-line, dresses or coats fitting in close princess lines, or fabrics that cling, revealing the contours of the body, are especially unbecoming to the woman with round shoulders.

A bloused waist; a long, unbelted overblouse; a jacket; bolero; or other device for supplying a waist that hangs loose

Drooping brim emphasizes round shoulders; brim turning up at back is becoming.

and free from the figure aids in concealing the curve of the spine and, thus, makes stooped shoulders less apparent. Full-length, one-piece garments, even though lines are not fitted to the figure, are more likely to cling, because of their weight.

Hat may minimize shoulder defects. A drooping hat brim, especially a wide drooping brim, gives unwelcome emphasis to stooped shoulders. If the hat is larger in the front, its drooping brim seems to pull the shoulders further forward, while, if there is a brim in the back also, it repeats the rounded lines of the shoulders and, by so doing, accentuates them. Even a small hat drooping greatly at the sides will make the shoulders appear more stooped.

A hat carefully selected to overcome individual defects may give balance to the figure and distract attention from its short-comings. A hat of moderate size, rather than the extremely close-fitting, brimless hat, or the hat with large, drooping brim, is preferable. The brim that turns at least slightly upward is preferable, although one that turns up abruptly, creating a close-turban effect, is trying, if the shoulders are markedly stooped. A coat collar filling in the curve at the back of the neck and thus making the back appear straight will simplify the problem of hat lines. A small turban may be very becoming when worn with a coat collar or with a fur scarf, but most trying without them.

If the hair is worn in a loosely waved mass at the back of the neck, it tends to make round shoulders less evident. Conspicuous hair styles should, however, be avoided lest they center attention at the back of the neck.

CHAPTER XIX

Methods of Hiding Large Upper Arm

THE LARGER UPPER ARM makes the fitting of dresses and coats difficult and requires a size or even two sizes larger than necessary for the body itself. When the necessary material is available, a gusset or insert in the sleeve provides the best means of altering garments to fit the woman with a large upper arm.

Correctly placed armscye with loose sleeve. In attempting to obtain slim lines, the shoulder is frequently fitted too narrow, the armscye too high and too tight, and the sleeve too narrow. This type of too-small dress emphasizes rather than minimizes the too-great size of the arm. The tight sleeve reveals its actual contours, while the tight armscye and narrow shoulderline make the arm appear to stand out from the body, to seem larger in proportion to the figure.

A dress with a correctly placed armscye, one that is sufficiently large to avoid constriction of the upper arm and that is placed at the edge of the shoulder, or slightly lower, so that it does not make the arm stand out from the body as does the too-high shoulder line, does much to minimize the too-large upper arm. A correctly fitting armscye will require a sleeve sufficiently loose to conceal the actual outlines of the arm. The shoulder pad should be so placed that the sleeve hangs straight from a point slightly wider than the widest part of the arm.

While the dress that is obviously several sizes too big, except in sleeve width, makes the wearer appear awkward and shapeless (although it may hide the too-large arm), a loose, carefully fitted dress may hide the defective proportions of the arm and, at the same time, give symmetry to the entire figure.

A high armscye in a tight sleeve makes a large upper arm more conspicuous, a shoulder cut wide enough so that loose sleeve hangs straight conceals bulge.

Loose bodice makes arms less large in contrast. A loose, bloused bodice, hanging in soft, loose lines, makes the arms seem relatively smaller and their outlines less definite. On the other hand, a close, tightly fitting bodice makes the arms seem larger in relation to the comparatively slimmer lines of the torso. The severe, close lines of the bodice also make the outlines of both the sleeves and the bodice clear-cut and distinct. Severe, tailored lines will likewise make the outlines more definite, even if the garment is not tightly fitted. Soft types of garments give less distinct outlines and permit the sleeve lines to merge more readily into the body of the dress.

Cape or scarf may conceal arm in sleeveless dress. The sleeveless dress, particularly one of dark color, makes the arm more conspicuous. The woman with a large upper arm will find a dress made with a cape or scarf collar, with a drape hanging partially over the arm, much more becoming than the sleeveless dress with harsh, unrelieved armscye. The separate

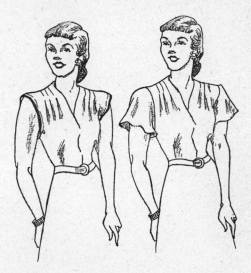

A cape, a scarf, an extended shoulder line, a loose short sleeve, is more flattering than a sleeveless dress on the figure with large upper arms.

jackets, which are so frequently part of the ensemble at all times of day, are especially becoming to the woman whose arms are too large. She will find it advantageous to wear them with all dinner and evening gowns. These jackets may also be added to the dress with transparent, too-revealing sleeves.

A contrasting fabric should never be used in the sleeve of a dress worn by a woman with large arms. It is as unbecoming as the sleeveless dress, having much the same effect as does a dark dress that exposes the arms. Likewise, if a woman whose arms tend to be big chooses a sleeveless dress, it will be more pleasing in a light color that does not contrast too decidedly with flesh tones, for contrast makes the arms more conspicuous.

Fabric should be employed in perpendicular feeling. Pattern in the fabric, even a slight rib in a weave, may greatly increase the apparent size of the arm unless it is employed to give a perpendicular instead of a horizontal line. Conspicuous

A sleeve cut in one with the blouse may make the upper arm look larger because the fabric over the arm is in a horizontal line direction; a set-in sleeve cut lengthwise of the fabric is more slenderizing.

or large-figured designs should be avoided, since only indefinite patterns of not too-vivid coloring are appropriate to the poorly proportioned figure, especially to one with large arms, since a sleeve must be unrelieved by the folds that may break the pattern in other parts of the dress.

Satin, because of its shiny surface, catches the high lights and unmercifully reveals bulging curves, and is especially unbecoming to the woman with large arms when it is employed with the sheen extending across rather than up and down the figure. Satin so employed causes the eye of the observer to travel across the figure from arm to arm, attracts notice to the arm, and centers attention on the width rather than the length of the arm.

Soft, lightweight, opaque fabrics are desirable. Bulky fabrics increase the apparent bulk of the figure, especially of the arms, causing them to stand out stiffly from the body. Stiff

A clinging, transparent fabric reveals the large upper arm; an opaque fabric is more becoming.

fabrics are equally disastrous to the woman with large upper arms.

A thin, transparent, clinging fabric reveals the arms in a most uncompromising manner. Large arms frequently appear more evident when a thin and clinging transparent covering attracts attention to them without concealing them than when no sleeves at all are worn. A soft, compact, lightweight, but not transparent or clinging fabric that conceals the actual out-lines of the arm is much more becoming than the too-revealing chiffons, georgettes, and laces. Double thickness of transparent fabrics, a double chiffon or georgette, a lace lining with chiffon or net, make these fabrics becoming instead of unbecoming to the woman with large arms.

CHAPTER XX

Footwear, Foundation for the Figure

THE GRACE OF THE ENTIRE FIGURE as well as that of the feet, ankles, and legs is affected by the suitability of footwear to the physique of the wearer and to the costume with which it is worn. Although the feet should be inconspicuously dressed, since not they, but the face, should be the center of interest, they should, nevertheless, appear graceful and well-groomed to the eye that does pause to examine them. The desirable foot is long and slender in itself, and aids in making the figure appear tall and slender.

Contrasts to Be Avoided

Contrasts in the color of the costume, the hosiery, and the footwear should be avoided whenever possible and always kept inconspicuous, so that a long line is preserved, which will give slenderness to legs, ankles, and feet and to the figure as a whole. Light hose contrasting with dark footwear, and both shoes and hosiery contrasting with the costume, make the legs appear much larger, not only because the light color itself increases their apparent size, but because horizontal lines are created by the contrast between the hose and dress and the hose and shoes. The ankles will appear much heavier because the line of the shoe is accented by the contrast with the hosiery. The line at the top, especially when oxfords or strapped shoes are worn, tends to lead the eye of the observer around the ankle, thereby increasing its apparent width.

When it is possible to have the dress, hose, and shoes of nearly the same color, as when beige is used in all three items, the feet and legs become relatively unimportant and inconspicuous, and even appear slender upon examination. When it is not possible to have these three items match, as when a dress of a color not used in hosiery and footwear is worn, an attempt should be made to have approximately the same color values (degrees of lightness or darkness) in the costume, hosiery, and footwear.

When a light or medium value is chosen for the dress or coat, beige or gray tones in hosiery and footwear may be chosen to give long, unbroken lines to the figure. When darker shades are worn, dark shoes may match the value of the dress, even though hosiery of lighter tones is worn. Darker tones of the modish hosiery shades tend to give additional height.

Although contrasting shoes are sometimes permissible, even advisable, those lighter than the costume are always poor costume design. A light color does not make a fitting foundation for a dark object, since it does not seem to give sufficient support. Light-colored footwear worn with a dark costume is therefore difficult for any type of woman, but especially so for the heavy woman, as the light-colored shoes make her feet seem an inadequate base for the massive dark bulk of the figure. Dark shoes with moderately dark hosiery in one of the darker tones of the mode will be much more pleasing. The ankles will appear less large than in light-colored shoes, and there will be less break in length of line, producing the effect of a firmer but less conspicuous foundation, which will give grace to the entire figure.

If footwear contrasting with the costume is worn, the color of the slippers should be repeated high on the figure, so that the eye of the observer is carried from the feet to the head in an uninterrupted sweep that gives an impression of height. Contrasting footwear, however, is most successful on the tall, slender figure.

The length of the foot and of the figure alike is shortened when shoes employing contrasting leathers are worn. A heel of contrasting color lessens the possible height of the figure by

A closed pump of solid color and one texture makes foot appear longer and more slender than does a shoe with contrasting colors.

the height of the contrasting heel. When the front and back portions of the shoe are of contrasting materials, the length of the foot is shortened while the width is increased by the horizontal line created by the contrast. If contrasting colors are employed, the break in line is even more evident than when contrasting leathers are combined. In either event, a shoe of one texture and one color is most likely to enhance the appearance of both the feet and the figure.

Long, Slender Shoe Gives Length to Foot and Figure

In shoes that are long and slender (they should, of course, fit the foot but should assume as long and slender lines as is possible with correct fitting), not only will the feet, ankles, and legs appear more slender, but the entire figure will appear to have gained added height and slenderness. The heavy woman who selects shoes too small for her makes her figure seem heavier, not only by the awkward gait produced by the small shoes, but by the inadequate foundation that noticeably small shoes give to the bulky figure. A longer, more slender shoe gives a foundation of better proportion and, at the same time, gives an impression of slenderness that may be transferred to the general impression one receives of the figure as a whole.

A shoe with a long vamp, peaked upward in front makes the foot seem long and slender; short vamp, low cut, lessens apparent length of foot, tends to slenderize ankles, but makes foot seem wider.

The tall, thin woman with an extremely long foot may find a moderately round toe, which may be worn shorter, in a length more closely related to the actual length of the foot, more becoming. It is the tall, thin woman, also, who may wear strapped pumps to advantage.

Straps shorten foot. The opera pump, the plain, strapless pump, displays the long lines of the feet and legs without making any break or division of their length. The wearer, therefore, appears taller, and her legs longer and slimmer, in footwear of this type. Strapped models tend to modify the length of the instep and make the ankles appear less slim. They, therefore, make the entire figure appear less tall.

Since opera pumps are not suited to all feet nor suitable for all purposes, it is important that the size and shape of the straps be considered carefully. Straps placed in a diagonal line, extending lengthwise of the foot and across it at the same time, are more slenderizing to foot and figure than are straps going straight across the foot.

A curving strap makes less horizontal break than one going straight across the foot. A wide strap gives a heavy feeling to the foot, creating horizontal lines, which add to the apparent width of the feet and ankles and frequently shorten the ap-

Intricate arrangement of straps centers attention on the foot, openness makes foot seem lighter. Large bow or buckle likewise makes feet conspicuous, makes ankles and legs seem smaller in contrast.

parent height of the figure as well. Two or three straps create much the effect of a wide strap, placing emphasis upon width. A single narrow strap is frequently the most becoming shoe the short, heavy woman can wear, for, correctly placed on a well-cut shoe, such a type of one-strap slipper supports the foot and prevents it from sagging at the sides.

Intricate elaborate arrangements of straps center attention upon the feet, making them so unduly conspicuous that the figure appears shorter because the eye of the observer is not allowed to travel to the top of the figure, appreciating the full height of the wearer. Numerous straps likewise break the length of the foot, making it appear shorter and wider than its actual size. A simple opera pump, allowing the eye to travel in an uninterrupted sweep down the length of the legs, ankles, and feet, makes the entire figure appear more slender and the feet and ankles appear especially slender and graceful. Many short, heavy women cannot wear the pump without straps because it gives insufficient support, causing the ankles and side of the foot to sag and the shoe to bulge at the sides. Those whose feet are strong enough to permit the wearing of the simple strapless pump usually find it very becoming.

The shoe with well-placed open spaces may, however, appear lighter weight, and therefore make the foot seem smaller and more delicate. If much of the foot is revealed it must be strong

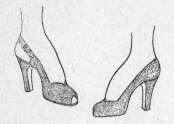

The open toe and sling or strap heel makes the foot seem shorter and lighter. The closed toe and heel make the foot seem longer and more slender.

and well shaped. The open shoe that reveals spreading feet and sagging arches is less becoming than sufficient leather to support the foot adequately.

The open-toed shoe may lighten its apparent weight. It likewise makes the shoe appear shorter. The open heel makes the shoe appear lighter weight. It is especially helpful in making low-heeled shoes seem lightweight and less utilitarian than they actually are. The flattering lines of the opera pump, combined with the lessened bulk of the open-heeled sling shoe, makes almost any foot appear small and well shaped.

Wing tip gives more slenderness than square. The shoe with a straight or square tip is usually more difficult to wear than the shoe with a wing tip, as the former lessens the apparent length of the foot, while the latter, even when of a contrasting color, tends to give accent to length, at least enough of a feeling of length to counteract the shortening influence produced by the contrast. If heavy stitching and perforations are used, either the straight or the wing tip is likely to make the shoe seem heavier.

The high heel makes the ankles appear more slender, the curve of the leg more graceful, and the foot smaller. It will therefore continue to be popular, even though many medical authorities believe that continuous wearing of extremely high heels thickens the ankles and weakens the feet and that the

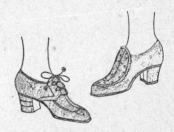

The oxford gives good support to the foot and may therefore improve posture, justifying the increased apparent size and heaviness of the foot.

woman who wears more moderate heels will have better looking feet in later life.

Although the extremely high heel adds actual height to the standing figure, it frequently so destroys good posture and carriage that the moving figure appears less tall. The moderately high heel inconspicuously adds an inch or an inch and a half of height to the figure, giving more apparent height than the extremely high heel, which obviously indicates that it is attempting to add height.

The heavy woman finds that the extremely high, slender heel gives insufficient support and, by seeming too fragile, emphasizes the bulk of her figure. A heel of moderate height, broad enough at the base to give a firm foundation, is more graceful on the average figure. As it is less likely to turn and become run-down, its wearer is more likely to appear always well groomed.

Even the smallest, daintiest foot appears large and rather mannish when an extremely low, flat heel and a heavy welt sole are worn. An oxford, with welt sole, heavy stitching, large perforations, saddles, tips, and other details breaking the length of the shoe and making it appear wider, is extremely difficult to wear. It not only makes the foot appear extremely large, but gives a heavy, masculine appearance to the foot and,

Platform shoes and wedges add actual bulk and apparent weight to the feet unless a contrast of texture, coloring or trimming makes it apparent that they are not part of the actual bulk of the foot. Solid texture and color may make the foot seem heavy and club-like.

if a woman is at all large, to her carriage and entire body. Except for golf or other active sports requiring this type of shoe, or orthopedic shoes requiring the bandaging effect of the firmly laced oxford, the modern, well-styled shoe of moderate and low heel height is a wiser choice than an oxford. Low heeled pumps, sandals, moccasins, and wedge-soled shoes supply the comfort and good carriage induced by low-heeled shoes without the heaviness and large, clumsy appearance most oxfords give the foot. The lightweight oxford with a turned sole, cut low at the throat, can be flattering and at the same time give the trim, tailored appearance required by some street costumes.

Other Considerations

Sport hose should not be conspicuous. Simple rib-knit sport hose of lightweight wool or lisle are much more easily worn than those of heavier texture or more elaborate construction. Solid colors are more likely to be becoming than those having a pattern emphasized by color contrast. The standard knitted silk hose are likewise more becoming to the woman with heavy legs and ankles than those of large or coarse mesh. The new dull textures are more slenderizing than shiny finishes.

Hemline affects grace of feet and figure. The narrow, close-fitting skirt with a straight hemline makes the feet, ankles, and legs seem larger than they actually are, for their size becomes more apparent in contrast with the close, narrow lines of the skirt. A skirt with fullness at the bottom makes the legs and feet seem smaller in contrast with the wide lines above them. An uneven hemline, which eliminates the horizontal straight hem, gives less width to the legs, ankles, and feet. A skirt with slender lines, but with fullness introduced in godets or other subtle handlings, which retain the slender lines of the skirt and give fullness above legs and feet, is usually most becoming to both feet and figure.

CHAPTER XXI

The Tall, Slender Woman

TALLNESS AND SLENDERNESS are universally prized in this age among women who aspire to dress well. Women of all types of figure strive to create the illusion of being tall and slim. Yet even the fortunate woman who is tall and slender may have need of illusions created by artful costume design. She may wish to take fullest advantage of her own distinctive lines, or she may feel that she is too thin and angular for her height, and wish to modify her not entirely pleasing figure.

Tall and Slim and Proud of It

The tall, slim woman with good carriage and pleasing proportions frequently appears most distinguished if she selects a costume that emphasizes her height and slimness. Particularly if she is young, the tall woman may make an asset of this striking characteristic.

The high-waisted dress, especially when combined with a full skirt, is extremely youthful, sometimes even childishly naïve in appearance. It frequently gives an extremely tall woman a little-girl aspect inconsistent with her figure. But even when the higher waistline is not actively unbecoming, it does not allow the tall, thin woman to capitalize her height and slenderness as does the long bodice giving a low waistline above which the upper part of the figure rises tall and slim. The long-waisted robe de style, with its full, long skirt, making the upper part of the figure seem smaller by comparison and adding to the apparent total length of the figure, emphasizes slim height while giving a much more sophisticated appearance than the short-waisted dress.

The short, pleated skirt, with its full, rippling movement, gives a youthful, jaunty appearance to the wearer, one that is attractive for many purposes, but which detracts from the distinctive height and slenderness of the tall woman. An intricately cut skirt with clinging lines and fullness ingeniously placed will give a knowing emphasis to length of line. Slender, tightly swathed hips, with fullness restrained to a low point in the skirt, increase the apparent height and slenderness of the figure and give an interesting silhouette. Bustles and panniers have much the opposite effect; they broaden the figure and reduce its apparent height.

The tall, thin woman who wishes to accentuate her unusual height and slenderness finds the dress made with a high, close-fitting collar; narrow, close-fitting sleeves; and close, sleek, straight lines throughout extremely smart and effective. The high collar that buttons at the side may sometimes be more becoming than the one that fastens at the front, as the side closing gives more width to the face and frequently permits softer, crushed lines or folds of fabric to be used to frame the face. A low, round neckline, wide sleeves creating round lines over the arm and hand, and a full blouse and skirt make the figure appear shorter.

The close-fitting suit with long, sleekly tailored lines, worn with a close-fitting turban and a tailored ascot tie, makes the wearer appear exceedingly tall and slim, well groomed, and smart. This costume is much more striking and, accordingly, much more difficult to wear than the suit cut on loose, easy-fitting lines, worn with a blouse of soft, feminine character and a hat with wider lines intended to give width and break height. The woman who is too tall and thin, whose contours are angular, should not attempt to adopt the severely plain, straight,

Deep, round necklines shorten the figure that is too tall and thin, deep V cut at back and long train give height to woman who is tall and slim and proud of it.

tailored lines. The tall woman who is essentially feminine in appearance wears these severe mannish styles to much better advantage than she who has a masculine appearance, which is accentuated by costumes of this character.

In no other costume does the tall, thin woman appear so strikingly, regally tall as in the evening dress with a deep, narrow *V* décolleté, ending in a long, narrow train, which carries the eye of the observer in an uninterrupted sweep down the length of the back. This type of costume, being extreme in type, makes the wearer conspicuous and, therefore, is suited only to the tall, thin woman of graceful and sophisticated bearing. A round neckline and a short, full skirt give more round,

Contrasting sash or girdle breaks the height of the tall, thin figure.

youthful lines and a more naïve appearance to the wearer, at the same time definitely shortening her figure.

Too Tall and Thin

The extremely tall, thin woman, the woman who is so tall and thin that it is desirable for her to make her figure appear less attenuated, must pay particular attention to space divisions and horizontal and perpendicular lines used in her costume.

Uninterrupted lines from shoulder to hem, particularly those without a break at the waistline, are unbecoming to the woman of unusual height and thinness. Because we are accustomed to a belt or horizontal seaming at the waistline, the figure without one seems unduly tall and the too-tall, thin figure extremely at-

A short or hip-length jacket makes the figure seem taller; a wrist or fingertip length jacket, particularly in a contrasting color, lessens the height of the figure.

tenuated. The princess line, with its long, slim, fitted, beltless silhouette, outlines the too-thin figure, emphasizing not only its length but its actual contours, and exaggerating the effect of the thin, angular figure. Horizontal seamings, belts, or swathed girdles break the height of the figure and give lines that induce width.

Coats that are full length, coming to or below the bottom of the dress, make the figure seem of much greater height than a shorter coat. A three-quarter or seven-eighth length coat breaks the length of the skirt, shortens the figure, and reduces the apparent length of the legs from thigh to knee—the proportion that frequently seems awkwardly long in the extremely tall, thin woman. ◦ A flaring, swagger cut, a short length with a wide, full hem, shortens the figure more than does a close-fitting, straight line. If there is a decided contrast between coat and dress, the figure seems shorter than when coat and dress are similar and the length of line is more decidedly broken.

A short jacket, one ending above the hip joint, gives awkward and unpleasing proportions to the woman who is extremely tall and thin. The legs are made to seem longer, and the torso too short for them. A jacket carefully selected so that its length breaks the length of the thigh creates the best proportion between the upper and lower parts of the body. The height of the entire figure is more effectively broken by the horizontal line of the jacket when the division comes near the center of the figure.

The extremely long jacket, that with long, close-fitting lines coming to the knee or near the bottom of the skirt, likewise increases the height of the figure and the length of the thighs and supplies much less pleasing proportions than does the suit with a jacket ending halfway between the hip and knee joints. A slight alteration that modifies the length of the jacket, perhaps changing it only an inch or two, may do much to improve the grace of the too-tall, thin figure.

Long skirts make the figure seem taller, greatly exaggerating the height of the already tall figure. The woman who wishes to minimize her height, therefore, should seek horizontal contrasts to lessen the apparent length of her long skirt. A contrasting border at the bottom, a long tunic with a skirt of contrasting color, are among the most becoming fashions for the extremely tall and slender woman. Skirt and blouse or coat of different colors make the height seem less. Contrasts

V necklines, seams from shoulder to hem, increase the height and emphasize thinness; high necklines, soft gathered, bloused fullness, wide gathered sleeves, full skirts, lessen thinness and angularity. A contrasting belt further decreases height.

supplied by gloves, by hosiery contrasting either in color or in value, by shoes with contrasts breaking their length, lessen the height of the entire figure. Hat with either contrasting crown and brim or contrasting band, or, more important still, a hat contrasting with the coat or dress, are extremely effective on the tall, slender figure. Since they are difficult for women of other figure types, the tall, slender woman does well to take advantage of her opportunity to wear styles that other women must forego.

The tall, slender woman can likewise wear wide and round capes, which would be disastrous on a less willowy figure. Drop shoulder lines are likewise becoming; but she should avoid raglan sleeves, which make her arms appear longer. Wide sleeves, horizontal lines in sleeves and bracelets, and many bracelets are effective in lessening the apparent length of the arm, thereby breaking the impression of length as applied to the entire figure.

CHAPTER XXII

The Tall, Heavy Woman

BY CLEVER COSTUMING, the tall woman who has become heavy, or who is naturally of large frame, may appear dignified and regal. If she fails to give this impression she is almost certain to look massive or unpleasantly imposing. Moreover, she must achieve her effects without emphasizing either her height or her breadth. She is barred from the use of methods minimizing height because they naturally accent width, and she cannot appear more slender by increasing her apparent height. Therefore, she must strive for a balance of horizontal and vertical line directions. Where one is employed the other must be used to counteract it. She cannot beg the question by avoiding the use of lines within the silhouette, for it is necessary for her to break up large surfaces by lines that cut their expanse.

Choice of Fabrics

Texture. A correct choice of fabrics is one of the greatest aids in giving the large woman a pleasing appearance. The texture of fabrics used may minimize or emphasize the bulk of the massive figure. All the types of fabrics listed in Chapter XIV as increasing apparent size or revealing silhouette are difficult for her.

Smooth, shiny surfaces high light both curves and angles.

They make the size of the tall woman of large frame unpleasantly apparent, whether she is thin or carries excess weight. She should choose dull fabrics, those with slightly rough, broken surfaces that absorb the light or that break it up into a soft, subdued reflection, with shadows in the depths of the folds.

Frilly, fine detail appears too dainty for the tall heavy woman and makes her seem masculine by contrast; soft lines giving simplicity without severity are most becoming.

Any bulky, cumbersome fabric tends to make the large woman appear massive. Rough tweeds and wool cloths are possible at all only because their weight is consistent with her size; she appears to have strength enough to carry them. Lightweight tweeds or firmly woven compact woolens, such as covert cloth, are becoming.

Thick, erect pile fabrics not only add appreciable bulk, much more apparent bulk than the actual dimensions added, but also create heavy, rounded lines, no matter how straight the lines of the design.   A soft pile on a lightweight pliable background or, better yet, a soft close nap giving a velvety appearance may be substituted.

Severely tailored suits make the tall woman appear mannish; softer, dressmaker suits are more becoming.

Long-haired fur, especially if used for an entire coat, greatly increases the apparent size of the tall, heavy woman. The very large woman usually finds a cloth coat more becoming than a fur coat; but if she selects a fur coat it should be one with flat, soft fur, with a soft pliable pelt; for a stiff fur, even though flat, will add bulk in the same way that a stiff fabric increases the size of the silhouette.

Transparent fabrics of fragile character are not appropriate to the costume of the tall, heavy woman, for they not only reveal the figure in its too-full proportions, but also make her appear more massive by contrast. When sheer fabrics are worn, it is important that they be used in a manner counteracting their sheerness. Double thickness of chiffon, or more closely woven fabrics that are not actually transparent, as crepe Roma or very heavy, closely woven georgettes or the sheer woolens, are becoming to the tall, heavy woman.

Clinging fabrics reveal contours and in this way call attention to unusual size. An elastic fabric, such as jersey, is particularly unbecoming. Two dresses made in the same style, one of jersey, the other of fine wool crepe, afford an excellent demonstration of the difference in becomingness to the large woman.

Designs correct for large women will assume incorrect lines when executed in stiff fabrics. The stiff material emphasizes angular bony structure or, if the wearer is overweight, high lights curves and creates additional ones. It adds apparent bulk by flaring away from the figure.

Color. Not only the texture but also the color and the pattern in the fabrics she chooses for her costumes influence the apparent bulk of the tall, heavy woman. Chapter XIV contains the principles of emphasizing or minimizing the figure by means of color.

The large woman must not forget that vivid, brilliant colors advance to meet the eye, making her appear larger and, at the same time, unduly conspicuous. Less intense or soft, grayed colors have the opposite effect.

Red, orange, and yellow—the warm colors—are more prominent than blues and greens, the essentially cool colors. The large woman should avoid large areas of warm color. If warm colors are suited to her own coloring, they should be chosen in softened or grayed intensities. Vivid color may be used as accents. Grayed, cool colors make her appear smaller and, at the same time, make her bulk as inconspicuous as possible.

The large woman dressed in white or in very light colors appears much larger than in dark colors. This effect is increased if the tints are warm, as yellows and pinks, and is still further increased if the coloring is bright and vivid. For occasions when other women may be wearing light colors, the tall, heavy woman will usually appear less conspicuous in grayed, light colors than in a dark costume.

Size and character of design in fabric. Small, dainty designs, those of fine, delicate character, emphasize the size of the large woman by their contrast with her large proportions. Designs that are less minute in scale, those of moderate size and more dignified character, are more consistent with the size of the tall, heavy woman.

Extremely large, sprawling designs, patterns so large that one or two seem to be sufficient to cover the entire figure, emphasize the unusual size of the area they cover. By its very magnitude, scaled though it is to the size of the wearer, the large design proclaims the expanse beneath it by leading the eye of the observer out over the massive bulk it covers. Allover designs of indefinite outlines are much more suitable.

Curved designs, especially those with large or unbroken curves, emphasize the curves in the wearer's figure, making her seem more rotund than she actually is. Designs that are neither entirely curved nor entirely geometric or angular, that neither repeat nor contradict sharply the curves in the tall, heavy figure, are more becoming than large dots or other pronouncedly curved designs.

Severely angular designs, those with bold, striking, modern feeling, are too pronounced for the woman of unusual size, since they make her conspicuous and thus emphasize her size. Broken or irregular geometric designs are much more becoming than regular plaids or checks or other severely geometric designs. Indefinite plaids, irregular placements of checks, or combined curved and straight lines are more appropriate to the costume of the tall, heavy woman.

The majority of designs have a feeling of movement that carries the eye of the observer in one direction or another and increases the apparent width or height of the wearer. The tall, heavy woman frequently appears to best advantage in designs having at least a slightly perpendicular feeling. These designs need not give pronounced emphasis to height, but they avoid increase in apparent width and add to the dignity of the wearer.

Stripes used entirely in one direction, either up and down or across the figure, are much more likely to emphasize bulk than are stripes ingeniously cut and combined so that they break the large surface they cover. Stripes must be carefully analyzed as to the direction in which they lead the eye. Those used to form oblique lines, especially V- or pointed lines, are likely to be becoming, if the oblique lines thus formed are not so long as to give too much emphasis to height. Wisely used, stripes may break up the surface in a manner that seems to lessen both the height and the width of the wearer.

The large surfaces of the tall, heavy woman's figure are sometimes effectively broken if patterned and solid-colored materials are used in combination. The design of the costume must, however, be carefully considered so that the figure is not shortened by abrupt divisions. If one type of fabric is used in the skirt and another in the blouse, an accent of that used in the skirt should be used near the face, so that the eye of the observer will be carried the entire length of the wearer's figure. An irregular line at the joining of skirt and blouse further adds to the becomingness of contrasting plain and figured fabrics. Unusual and ingenious cutting and combining of material, so essential to the smart costume today, add much to the becomingness and effectiveness of fabric combinations upon the tall, heavy woman.

The Large Woman's Hat

The hat should form a becoming frame for the face and preserve or create pleasing proportions between face and figure. Many types of hats fail to do these two things for the tall, heavy woman. Chapter IV gives specific principles for guidance in choosing hats.

Hats particularly unsuited to the tall, heavy woman are the close-fitting, brimless hat, which makes the features seem coarse and heavy, the head small, and the figure taller; the tailored, mannish hat, which gives a masculine appearance; the jaunty beret, which is too small and lacking in dignity; the tiny feminine hat worn with a veil over the upper part of the face, the sophisticated coyness of which is at variance with the dignity needed to make the tall, heavy woman appear to good advantage; the large hat with brim hiding the neck, or the hat with trimming hanging over the neck and shoulder, which shorten the figure and give it a stolid, massive quality; and any hat with elaborate bows, feathers, flowers, or other trimming that is dainty and frilly and very feminine.

The tall, heavy woman may wear a hat that is brimless in front if it has width at the sides. Her tailored hat should have a shaped brim, and perhaps several narrow bands with opportunity for color interest and less severe manipulation. A simple cloche may be worn when her more girlish companions wear berets. A well-selected small hat may be smart and sophisticated. A wide brim chosen with care may be particularly harmonious with her figure. All trimming should be simple and rather flat in character.

Footwear

The selection of footwear is especially important to the tall, heavy woman, since it must be not only becoming but comfortable to feet that must bear more than the average weight. Therein lies the key to her shoe selection. The footwear must appear comfortable as well as be comfortable, for if it seems inadequate to support the figure it is unpleasing to the observer. The tall, heavy woman usually has a large foot. Her feet and legs, therefore, should be inconspicuously neat and well groomed. Footwear of a lighter color than that of the costume is likewise an inappropriate support for the tall, heavy figure. If footwear does not match the costume it should be darker rather than lighter.

Shoes with fine, dainty straps; delicate detail; and extremely high, slender heels give the tall, heavy woman an awkward carriage because they not only appear to be but are inadequate to support her figure. On the other hand, the extremely stout, substantial shoe makes her foot appear large and clumsy, giving a heavy masculine appearance to her foot and to her carriage and entire body. Except for golf or other active sports, a walking shoe cut on simple lines with a heel of moderate height, one not too narrow at the bottom and with a lightweight turned sole, is much more becoming to the tall, heavy woman than is the shoe with a welt sole and flat heel. Close, narrow skirts and straight hemlines make feet and ankles seem larger, while soft fullness at the bottom of the skirt makes the feet and legs seem smaller in contrast with the wider lines above them. While the hemline should be kept inconspicuous, one that is somewhat irregular is more slenderizing than one with a rigid, straight line.

CHAPTER XXIII

The Short, Slender Woman

THE SHORT WOMAN of thin or slender figure has many advantages not shared by the woman of larger figure, but she likewise has limitations and restrictions incident to her small stature. Her problem is that of emphasizing her petite form in a manner that will be charming, and of avoiding the costume in which she appears small and insignificant.

Emphasizing Petite Charm

Striking accent may be needed. Although the costume should not usually be more striking than the physical personality, a dashing design prevents the small woman's appearing mouselike and inconspicuous. A very conservative costume, one without strong accent or distinctive styling, will make the small figure appear quiet and subdued. As there is comparatively little surface in the costume of the small woman, bright colors and striking detail are often more pleasing than upon the larger figure. The small woman of vigorous, alert bearing, with definite coloring and vivacious personality, may wear much more striking apparel than the small woman of uncertain, unassuming demeanor.

Demurely quaint style. The small woman wears picturesquely demure styles extremely well. The period dress made with close, slim-fitting bodice and full skirt is often extremely

In a very conservative dress the small woman seems subdued and insignificant; fine, dainty, soft detail with interest centered high near the face is becoming.

A short skirt is girlish and becoming; added length of skirt, instead of adding height, makes the dress look too large for the wearer.

224

becoming. The demure dress, simply and artistically conceived, is much more becoming than the period dress of more massive proportions, especially that with wide skirt and wide, dropped shoulder line, which build out the figure so that it appears either too wide or so small as to be submerged under the bulk of clothes.

Modified princess. The short, thin woman who desires to increase her apparent height and to avoid emphasis on width finds both perpendicular and oblique lines helpful. They must, however, be correctly placed so that they give pleasing space divisions without overemphasizing the thinness of the figure.

When the little woman selects costumes with perpendicular lines to make her appear taller, unfortunately she increases her apparent thinness. If she chooses dresses with horizontal lines, they reduce her apparent height, making her abnormally short and ill-proportioned. An unbroken surface, like that of the modified princess dress, without pronounced lines in either direction and without prominent space divisions, therefore, is suitable for the short, thin woman, because it decreases none of her proportions.

Combined lines counteract each other. The use of both horizontal and perpendicular lines may be another solution of the short, thin woman's problems. When lines going in both directions are employed, one giving height, the other tending to increase apparent width, the wearer may appear slightly larger and more impressive than when an unbroken surface covers her small figure. Other space divisions that break the surface in both directions may make the entire figure appear smaller. Too many space divisions and too-intricate or heavy designs should be avoided lest they become massive, overpower the slight figure, and hide its petite beauty.

Long, flowing lines. The perpendicular effect created by long, unbroken folds, or by drapes hanging in long, unbroken lengths, markedly increases the apparent height of the short, thin woman and conceals undue thinness, as well as softening contours in a flattering manner. Drapes with short, broken lines, or with folds forming lines that produce a horizontal effect, are much less suitable for the short, thin woman.

Not too long a skirt. The short, slender woman should avoid skirts that are slightly longer than the mode, which give her dress the appearance of being too large for its wearer. Some short women like to wear longer dresses in the belief that they give an impression of greater height, but by so doing they lose their appearance of dainty petiteness. Short skirts, as short as is consistent with the mode, make the small woman appear girlish and youthful, giving pleasing emphasis to her petite stature.

Space Divisions

Normal waistline. As the short woman is frequently inclined to have a high natural waistline, great care must be used in the placement of the belt. Dresses designed with a high waistline may be quaintly pleasing on a few short, slender women (particularly those with narrow shoulders), but, as a rule, they appear awkward and ill-proportioned. A normal or slightly lower than normal waistline usually gives much better proportions.

Equal lengths of skirt and blouse should be avoided. Great care should be taken that the skirt and blouse do not divide the figure exactly in the middle. This is particularly likely to occur when the skirt is short and the waistline is between the hips and natural waistline. Adjustment of skirt length must

Low necklines, yokes and gilet effects make the small figure seem shorter than it does in higher, softly draped necklines which are especially becoming to the small figure.

Horizontal lines lessening height can make the short, slim figure appear heavy and stocky, diagonal or slanting lines give interesting surface interest without perceptibly lessening height.

frequently be accompanied by a change in the waistline if the proportions of the costume design are to be retained and the grace of the wearer's figure preserved. The hemline should be placed to avoid showing equal lengths of leg, skirt, and blouse. As the short woman is likely to be especially short in certain measurements—from hip to knee, for instance, or hip to ankles, or sometimes from hip to shoulders—spacings become especially important.

Short jacket ending above hips difficult. Like the high waistline or belt placed high, the jacket that is short, ending above the hips, is extremely difficult to wear. It greatly lessens the wearer's apparent height, in some instances making her appear like an awkward, growing child whose legs have become too long for the upper body. Fingertip jackets designed for taller figures, with skirt and sleeves shortened for the short, thin woman, should likewise have the jacket length reduced from its original measure. If a belt is worn with the jacket or overblouse, the proportions become changed and the ill-advised effect of two equal space divisions is less likely to result. As the belt creates another horizontal spacing, double care must be used in determining these space divisions.

Contrasting skirt and blouse should be avoided. The short woman will greatly lessen her apparent height and make her figure appear unduly short and insignificant if she wears either a jacket or a blouse that contrasts with her skirt. The short woman who wishes to employ contrast in a jacket ensemble may do so by choosing a jacket and skirt of matching color for wear with a blouse of a contrasting color. The jacket will reveal a long, narrow panel, with either V- or narrow, perpendicular lines of contrasting color. If the jacket hangs too-widely open, the horizontal line at the end of the contrasting blouse may be too apparent and shorten the figure or even give it a semblance of heaviness. Obviously, the costume planned with a contrasting blouse should never be worn without the jacket by the short, thin woman; she should always be aware that her costume has this limitation.

Wide belt of contrasting color difficult. The wide belt is much less becoming to the short, thin woman than one of very narrow proportions. If the belt is of contrasting color, it is especially difficult to wear in wider widths. A narrow belt of self-fabric gives least horizontal break, while it serves to define a waistline that emphasizes the slenderness of the short, thin woman.

Long coat. Three-quarter or seven-eighth coats, which tend to break the long line of the figure, are to be discarded by the small woman in favor of the full-length coat.

Keeping in Scale

Soft, delicate textures. Delicate, dainty fabrics of supple, soft quality enable the small woman to emphasize her petiteness in an attractive feminine manner. Heavy, bulky fabrics, out of scale with her size, hide her dainty proportions and make her appear either awkward or submerged by the bulk of her costume.

Small, dainty design. The scale of the design or figure on the material should likewise be in scale with that of the wearer. Small designs of delicate feeling, which would be totally out of place on the woman of extremely large proportions, are consistent with the size of the small woman and aid in emphasizing the daintiness of her figure. A rich brocade of elaborate, elegant character is too formal, too impressive, for the short, thin woman.

Coiffure. If the head is made to seem larger than its actual proportions, the body will seem shorter and less graceful. While a slightly larger than normal head may give a youthful appearance to a young woman, since children's heads are larger in proportion than adults', the head that is perceptibly larger appears awkward, shortens the figure, and makes it top heavy. It is possible to have a close, yet not sleek, coiffure that will soften the features without increasing the apparent size of the head.

Hats. A heavy hat is more actively unbecoming than a large hairdress, for it is not so easily recognized as the cause of the large proportions of the head. A turban following the natural proportions of the head and giving a close, trim appearance, which increases the apparent height of the figure, is frequently becoming to the short, thin woman. The turban draped in soft folds that carry the observer's eye up to the top of the head is usually becoming to both the face and the figure.

The wide brim, particularly one that is wider than the shoulders, appears too heavy for the short, thin figure to carry. It hides the neck and shoulders, especially if its lines are drooping, thereby making the figure seem short and top heavy. A moderately wide brim is more becoming and a brim smaller in the front and back than at the sides is more easily worn. The brim that turns up at one side or at the front carries the eye of the observer beyond the actual height of the figure and thus makes the small woman seem taller.

Accessories. Accessories out of scale with the petite figure likewise destroy its apparent grace. Large, heavy beads, many strands of beads, numerous bracelets, especially those of heavy character, appear too heavy for the small woman to carry. They, therefore, make her appear awkwardly small. A single strand of smaller beads, a chain of lighter weight, a lightweight bracelet—in general, the use of fewer accessories and those few in scale with the figure of the wearer—contribute more to the costume of the short, thin woman.

The large handbag of a color contrasting with the costume of the wearer is unsuitable for the small woman. It not only makes her seem small and insignificant in comparison with its conspicuous bulk, but it creates a contrasting line or spot in the center of the figure that breaks its apparent height as much as would a contrasting belt. A handbag of the same color as the costume, of moderate size and inconspicuous design, is most easily correlated with the smaller woman's costume.

Large, heavy bows and many details unsuitable. The woman of petite figure should avoid costumes with large bows and other heavy details. Simplicity, absence of many details, keeping those details that are used in scale with the small figure on which they are to be worn—these are essentials of the costume that becomes the smaller woman.

Large fur scarf dwarfs figure. The fur scarf made from a large pelt makes the upper part of the figure appear too heavy and, at the same time, hides the neck and shoulders. The scarf made of several smaller skins is more in scale with the small figure, gives longer lines that tend to increase apparent height, and softens the neck-and-shoulder line without hiding the natural proportions.

Considerable experiment may be necessary to determine the number of skins and the arrangement that creates the most becoming line. Many conventional arrangements are entirely too heavy and create broadening lines very unbecoming to the short woman. Fur scarfs of any description have a tendency to make the small woman appear matronly; she frequently appears better without a fur scarf. If she owns one that is becoming with some costumes, she cannot wear it indiscriminatingly with as many different types of apparel as can her taller sisters.

Footwear. Since the woman of small stature usually has small feet and slim legs, she has less difficulty in selecting becoming footwear than do most other types. Extremely low, flat heels and simple, broad-toed shoes may give her some of the awkward characteristics of the growing girl. An extremely high heel will make her taller, but sometimes the extreme height of the heel is too obvious and makes the figure appear stilted. Shoes of the same color or of the same value as the costume add height and slenderness. Large buckles and intricate details are ill-placed on the shoes of the small woman. They not only appear too heavy for her to carry gracefully, but they attract undue attention to the feet. Conspicuous heavy sport hose likewise are unsuitable.

CHAPTER XXIV

The Short, Heavy Woman

THE SHORT WOMAN who is overweight, or who has large bust or hips, unquestionably has difficulty in obtaining a fashionable silhouette. She, therefore, presents an interesting problem in the study of line direction and optical illusion. Women of every type may learn about dress from her, for she presents striking examples of the effect of slenderizing and broadening lines. She may likewise learn about dress from other women. She must avoid those means by which the tall, angular woman strives to appear less attenuated and those by which the short, thin woman strives to appear taller. She must make more effort than the short, thin woman to appear tall, for she seems much shorter than a thin woman of the same height. Some of the devices employed by the tall, heavy woman she cannot employ, either because they do not give sufficient emphasis to height or because they require height to carry them well.

She will do well to remember that her figure is not an asset, and that the face and not the figure should always be the center of interest. Since nature has so frequently compensated overweight with an enviable complexion, the short, heavy woman more often than not possesses a definite asset in her face. Therefore, she should make every effort to enhance her face and to keep her figure inconspicuous. She should wear becoming, actively flattering colors, always remembering, however, that the body of the costume itself should not be of a bright conspicuous color, which calls attention to short stature and too-generous girth.

To Keep Figure Inconspicuous

When the short, heavy woman has acquired lists of fabrics she may and may not wear, she is far on the road toward being well dressed. Her choice of textures, as well as of colors and designs, is more limited than for any other type of figure. She must avoid all fabrics that are striking in any way. Yet she need not think of these restrictions as negative. They are her means of centering interest away from unpleasing proportions.

Fabrics that add actual bulk and those that reveal contours are equally unbecoming. Tweeds; any rough-surfaced fabric; any erect-pile fabric; any material that is shiny, stiff, or cling-ing; long-haired fur, even in trimming; transparent material—these are taboo. A definite design, particularly if it is large or in contrasting colors, will spoil the effect of the most carefully chosen texture.

Once she has her peculiar requirements in mind, the short, heavy woman will find an adequate choice of pleasing fabrics. Lightweight woolens, or, better yet, fine worsteds, for suits and dresses; a close-napped wool fabric with a soft, suede finish for her coat; soft, supple silks or transparent velvet of rich deep luster, but of a texture that absorbs light—these are her stand-bys. Jersey may be used over a slip that prevents clinging. Semi-sheer materials will look and be cool, without actually re-vealing contours or breaks in line. Indistinct designs are often more pleasing than a perfectly plain surface.

A soft, close fur, fairly flat, with little luster, one that can be manipulated much like a fabric, may be used. Furs should be

Details of costume should never add to actual width of silhouette.

Interest centered low or scattered shortens figure; interest centered high gives height and emphasizes face.

worked so that their markings create long, slenderizing lines. Horizontal placement of fur is poor, whether in collar, cuff, or band at bottom of coat.

Dainty detail in trimmings and accessories is too fine in scale for the short, heavy woman. Bulky, heavy details weigh her down and seem to shorten her figure. She needs simplicity of design and few accessories, those few being of moderate size in scale with the wearer.

The short, heavy woman must be careful to avoid adding actual bulk at the sides of her figure. Wide sleeves, large bows placed out over the shoulders or hips, heavy drapes, full, loose lines, and bulky fabrics all materially increase the size of the silhouette and make the figure seem shorter and heavier. Drapes and folds should be placed within the silhouette, not added to it.

Many lines and intricate details in the skirt of a costume give the wearer a squat, heavy figure. Even when arranged in perpendicular lines for slenderness, skirt detail should not be profuse. A few simple lines extending the length of the figure are invariably better.

One of the surest ways of keeping the short, heavy figure inconspicuous is never to permit color contrasts or other breaks to form horizontal lines. Coats should always be worn full length. Hip-length jackets should be worn with matching skirts. Hat and shoes should continue rather than contrast with the color of dress or coat.

To Improve the Figure

The short, heavy woman finds that most becoming garments fit somewhat loosely. The one-piece, beltless dress with seam-

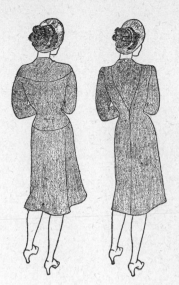

Curving lines in seams or trimming add to rotundity of figure; V-shaped and pointed lines lessen apparent roundness.

Too high shoulder pads, necklines high about throat, make the short, heavy figure seem square and awkward.

ings that suggest the princess silhouette, but actually do not possess the closely fitted lines of that silhouette, is frequently very flattering.

One-piece dresses fitted with inconspicuous darts and perpendicular seaming, perhaps with a center seam front and back that permits the introduction of subtle fullness, are frequently more becoming than those cut with skirt and blouse joined at the waistline.

Carefully fitted shoulderlines are especially important. The shoulder pad and the width of the shoulder should be just wide enough to assure that the hips appear in good proportion and that the upper arm does not protrude. Too heavy a pad, especially one that is too high, makes the neck seem shorter and the entire figure more stocky.

Center of interest should be high. Interest centered high on the figure adds to its apparent height. When the interest is lower or scattered, attention is directed to broad proportions instead of being led to follow and accent height. The neckline or the hat should be designed to draw the eye of the observer upward. The face thus gains its opportunity to hold the interest.

The optical illusions by which the short, heavy woman improves her appearance are based on her desire to look taller and more slender. Curved lines and round details are to be avoided by the woman who possesses too full natural curves. The use of straight or diagonal lines removes emphasis from the curves in the figure, and, if they are wisely placed, increases apparent height. Wide and square lines across the neck and shoulders increase the width of the face, neck, and figure as a whole. They are especially unbecoming if the lower part of the face is broad and full, as they emphasize sagging double chins, short, fat necks, and round shoulders, all of which too frequently accompany the short, heavy figure.

V-shapes used near the face are a most effective means of making the face, neck, and figure appear longer and more slender. A deep, narrow *V* creates a greater illusion of length than a wider one. It is frequently advisable to emphasize the *V*-neckline by means of color contrast or other striking but not fussy or elaborate detail. A necklace of decided character, perhaps held in *V*-line by a pendant, may give a *V*-feeling to necklines of other shape.

Yokes used at the shoulders usually make the figure seem shorter and wider. A *V*-yoke may be actively becoming if the shoulders are not wide and heavy. Groups of tucks or perpendicular seamings that break the surface and give a well-fitting line to the shoulders may be used instead of a yoke.

If a *V*-rather than straight seaming is used at the waistline, the usual horizontal break may be avoided. A self-color belt is preferable to one of contrasting color, and a narrow one is more easily worn than a wide one.

Horizontal lines in the skirt are especially bad, but *V*-shaped tiers, or a series of *V*-lines, are sometimes extremely effective on the short, heavy figure.

One of the most important guiding principles for the short, heavy woman is that her costume should never hide or shorten the length of her neck. It may be covered, but never merged into the head or the width of the shoulders. Shortening her neck makes the short, heavy woman square and awkward as nothing else will. The shoulder-length bob, the veil hanging down over the neck, the hat brim or trimming covering the neck, the large coat collar or heavy furs, all should be avoided by the short, heavy woman.

Hats

Although her conflicting problems make many hats unsuitable for her, the short, heavy woman need not find the choice of a hat too discouraging. It is an important part of her costume. It should attract interest, should enhance her face, and, at the same time should be carefully analyzed for its effect on her figure as a whole. Hats should always be studied on the standing and walking figure, from side and back views as well as when seen from the front.

As a rule a small, brimless hat seems to add height to the figure, but the short, heavy woman usually has a broad face, which requires width at the sides of the hat as a background. Her problem is to find one that does not add width to her figure, nor prevent the eye of the observer from traveling the entire length of the figure.

The small, draped turban may be actively becoming if the folds are kept flat and width is introduced where needed for background. A diagonal line may be very successful. Two diagonal folds producing a pointed formation may do much to increase apparent length of both face and figure.

A small, close-fitting hat with flaps or "ears" at the sides, covering the neck, sometimes gives a slender line over the cheeks and may seem to be becoming to the face of the short, heavy woman. It is, however, destructive to the grace of the figure as a whole.

A large brim may be particularly becoming to the large face, but it should never be chosen by the short, heavy woman. Instead, she may wear a brim of moderate size, larger on one side than on the other, and slanting up on one side and down on the other. The brim that turns up all around may be the most height giving of all, but it should not be too large or heavy, or too round in outline. The round breton hat adds to the rotundity of the figure, but the breton with lesser curves, larger on one side than the other, may be extremely flattering to the short, heavy figure.

The drooping. brim is bad for both broad face and short, heavy figure; the upturned brim is good on both.

The crown of the short, heavy woman's hat should never be large or bulky. It should follow the contours of the head. If it fits closely at the sides, it may be slightly high or pointed at the top, for height.

Any break in the height of her hat must be avoided by the short, heavy woman. Contrasting color, contrasting bands, or, more especially, contrasting crown and brim produce a horizontal line that breaks the height of hat and figure.

A hat that contrasts in color with that of the costume, especially one much lighter or darker in value, will shorten the apparent height of the figure almost as many inches as the actual measurement of the poorly chosen hat. If contrasting colors are introduced they should create perpendicular lines.

A hat of self-color for each costume is not only advisable but almost imperative for the short, heavy woman who would appear at her best. An occasional exception, after due consideration, may be made in the hat intended chiefly for restaurant dining. If the hat is of good design with height-giving lines, and if it is truly flattering to the face, it may successfully contrast with the inconspicuous background dress.

Footwear

The short, heavy woman must take great pains to keep her footwear inconspicuous. Since she usually has a short, broad foot, she should select models that are as long and slender as is possible in a well-fitting shoe. This will make her feet, legs, and entire figure seem more slender. The short, heavy woman who selects too-small shoes makes her figure seem heavy, not only by the awkward gait produced, but by the inadequate foundation that the too-small shoes give to her figure. Like the tall, heavy woman, she must avoid delicate, dainty shoes that seem inadequate to support her figure. She must even more carefully avoid shoes that add weight and heaviness to her feet and figure—wide straps, heavy stitching and perforations, heavy leathers and soles, and contrast either in the shoe or between the shoe and the costume as a whole.

Contrasting footwear, difficult for any short figure, is particularly disastrous to the short, heavy figure. This is especially true if the footwear is lighter than the costume. Pronounced contrasts in hose, footwear, and dress or coat perceptibly shorten and broaden the figure.

Dark footwear should be worn with a dark costume, and relatively dark hose, as dark as permitted by the mode. Sheer hose of dark value make the legs seem less heavy and smaller than do heavier hose of either light or dark value. At the same time they permit the wearing of darker hose that would appear dowdy and unfashionable in heavier weights. With a costume of medium value, hose and shoes of a neutral "natural" shade may be worn, or neutral hose of medium value and inconspicuous shoes of a darker color. If brown shoes do not conflict with the costume color or with other accessories, they blend best with the natural shades of hosiery and therefore give a longer line. Matching hosiery and shoes are in theory most slenderizing, but, when colored hosiery is not in fashion, they defeat their purpose by making the legs unduly noticeable. As white and other light colors increase apparent size, light hosiery of a neutral color is much more slenderizing than white hosiery worn with white shoes. For this reason, white hosiery has been out of fashion for many years.

CHAPTER XXV

Line in Relation to Mood and Character

*T*HE WHOLE FUNCTION OF LINE in relation to the figure has not been fulfilled when the desired effects of height and slenderness have been achieved. Every costume has a character of its own. Every occasion has a tone to which certain types of costume are suited. Some women have physiques and temperaments so marked that they choose always costumes preeminently suited to themselves, but others make of themselves what they will by suiting the costume to the mood. It is understandable that a woman might wish to appear dignified while shopping or traveling, merely youthful in her own home of an afternoon, and to transform herself into a sophisticated creature for an evening at the theater or for some important social function.

While the personality may be greatly modified by the lines of the costume, it cannot be completely changed. Designs that are entirely contradictory to the personality of the wearer make, by their very opposition, the conflicting personality more apparent, but do so in a way that makes both the individual and the costume seem awkward and lacking in harmony.

Curved Lines Lend Youth and Roundness

Rounded contours and curved lines are distinctly youthful. They give animation and gaiety to the young girl wearing them. The lines of her face and figure are softened, made to seem more girlish, or even childish, if extremely rounded effects predominate in the costume.

Circular fullness and soft, rounded folds of soft fabric contribute a subtle feeling of roundness, sometimes more effective than the more obvious round necklines; straight, round skirts; round capes; and curved seamings or trimmings. Round beads, particularly large round beads used in short round chokers and round ball earrings, contribute decided roundness of effect to the costume. Curves in hat crowns and brims, the round loops found in bows, are likewise important.

Gay, youthful, round shapes, which make the girl of round youthful contours seem younger, may, by their very youthfulness, emphasize the age of the person who is no longer young. Modified rather than pronounced curves, combined with other lines, will be more becoming to many girls and women.

Straight Lines Give Dignity, Simplicity, and Maturity

Straight lines predominating in a costume lend an appearance of poise and dignity. They give an air of decisiveness, yet of severity and maturity, in contrast to the appearance of youthfulness lent by curved lines.

Unbroken straight lines, straight, stiff edges of fabric, and straight horizontal or perpendicular lines may unduly emphasize severity and dignity, making the wearer seem staid and mature. Straight lines around the face and neck are for this

245

reason difficult to wear, suitable only for the very young girl who wishes to add to her apparent age. Too many pronounced straight lines emphasize unyouthful angularity in the thin figure. They make the plump figure seem heavy and extremely mature. Pleats and soft folds give a straight line in softened effect and are much more easily worn than more severe, stiff, straight lines. The use of scarfs or necklines creating transitional lines frequently relieves this trying effect.

Diagonal, Pointed Lines Are Subtle, Sophisticated

Slanting, diagonal, or oblique lines are decidedly sophisticated, lending interest to the costume and to the wearer. The diagonal line, well placed, shows more subtlety, more imagination, than either the straight or the curved line. Less youthful than curved lines, less mature than straight lines, yet possessing much of the animation of the former and the dignity of the latter, the diagonal line gives distinction and sophistication.

Bias cuts and draping of fabric give oblique lines and diagonal feeling to the costume. Pointed and *V*-formations composed of converging diagonal lines give much the same feeling to the design, though their effect is more obvious than that of the diagonal. The restrained use of *V*-shapes may give interesting space divisions within the costume. Too many pointed formations, particularly if poorly placed, may be angular and unpleasing.

Curved, straight, or diagonal lines, used singly or, more frequently, combined in the costume design, may greatly influence the apparent youthfulness, sophistication, or dignity of the wearer. The unwisely chosen costume will subdue the most charming personality and hide or distort perfection of face and figure. One wisely chosen will enhance a personality that other-

246

wise would lack distinction. It will give an illusion of perfection to face and figure.

The individual who wishes to be becomingly and suitably dressed should never forget that both her physical appearance and her innate character are continually being modified. Garments from past seasons may be unbecoming because the contours of the face and figure have changed, because the complexion has altered, because the expression of the face and the nature of one's entire carriage and motion are that of a much different person.

The happy, vivacious woman can wear colors and styles that might seem too animated on the sad, worried woman. On the other hand, conservative styles gain character from the spirited personality, but may seem drab when worn by the colorless individual. Most women find that their self-confidence and poise is increased when they are wearing actively becoming apparel. Therefore the woman who has learned to dress becomingly may find that her costumes become increasingly more interesting without overpowering her personality.

Part III

Ages of Women

CHAPTER XXVI

Children's Clothes

Individualized Infants' Clothing

FOR COUNTLESS YEARS infants' apparel has been lacking in style consciousness, in individuality, in color interest. It has been chosen on the basis either of utility or of daintiness—daintiness conventionally pretty but seldom truly beautiful. Even prettiness is lost in excess of fine, delicate details, of too-intricate, finely scaled trimmings believed to be in character with the small wearer.

Color interest. Many women go through life clinging to the mistaken notion that pale, delicate, baby blues are becoming, that "blue is my color" simply because they were dressed in pale blue from babyhood up. *Baby blue,* almost invariably found on all baby clothes that are not trimmed with an equally uninteresting pink, is usually less becoming than a less conventional color would be. A soft blue-green will be found much more interesting, more distinctive, and, in most cases, more flattering to the baby with so-called blue eyes. A true blue, in a softened, not too-pale tint or a blue-violet, even a pale violet or orchid tone, might be used.

A delicate, pale red-orange rather than pink, one of the colors variously known as *peach* or *apricot,* is more interesting than pale pink, and, in soft, pastel tints, equally delicate and suitable. Soft, pale yellow may be charming for babies' clothing. Soft, creamy tones, for some purposes, are more pleasing than pure whites, although pure whites in materials that will retain their clearness after many washings are especially suitable for the foundation of babies' wardrobes. The colors may be used as an accent or an occasional garment.

While the very young infant may be dressed usually in white and very pale pastel colorings, the colors may become slightly stronger, more vital, in larger sizes for the more active baby, whose individuality as well as size is increased.

The baby who is energetic and vivacious may wear definite colors, color schemes of several colors in interesting harmony, although small-patterned prints in scale with the size of their diminutive wearer should always be chosen.

Small designs composed of two or more colors, but with the area so broken that the effect is that of a monotone or indistinct spotting of color on a light ground, will usually be more pleasing than bold and definite patterns. The extremely delicate, naturalistic, sprigged floral design, youthful and dainty in effect, is suitable for the first figured materials worn by the infant; but more interesting designs, especially those having amusing nursery designs, are to be recommended for the child who is old enough to enjoy them. It is becoming customary to remove the frilly, feminine emphasis from the clothing of the baby boy to give young masculinity the distinction of more simple, forceful lines and colors, and to replace each outgrown garment with something of more masculine character.

Little Girl Wants Clothes Like Mother's

Nothing delights the little girl more than clothes that are enough like big sister's or mother's to make her feel important and grown-up. Mother, however, is likely to object to models that are too decidedly grown-up in aspect. Mother and daughter fashions, the two dressed alike except for the necessary modifications in cut and scale, may be charming when the mother has a youthful face and figure. If her appearance is mature, nearly identical mother and daughter fashions increase her apparent age rather than making her look like an older sister. Sister fashions are attractive but most likely to please the younger sister. Big sister is likely to object if she feels that her clothes are too juvenile, too much like her little sister's. Since children's costumes, even those more or less staple in style, are inspired or modified by those worn by the more mature feminine world, there are always points "just like mother's."

Similarity in design. The high waistline, so girlish on a child's dress, which, with its full skirt and other youthful detail, may be very different from mother's, gives a point of similarity that may be stressed to the delight of the child and the satisfaction of the mother who wishes small daughter to like her clothes.

A buckled belt has a simple, schoolgirl air, which makes it suitable for both the girl of school age and the smaller girl of preschool age. Because belts are incorporated in so many models for the adult, the belt may be pointed out to the child as an important grown-up detail.

An essentially youthful and simple dress may have a suggestion of the fitted silhouette if it is made with a straight, close-fitting, but not tight, bodice and a full skirt, making the bodice seem slimmer by contrast.

Although the child's skirts are necessarily shorter than those of the adult, they may assume the silhouette of long skirts with the low-placed flare, if they are cut and seamed to release fullness near the hem. This gives a graceful ripple over the knees that is becoming and permits active movement. Collars and cuffs with round lines essentially youthful in character are frequently incorporated in children's styles. The child herself will become more interested in her dress if she is told that big sister and mother also are wearing collars and cuffs. Although the lingerie touches on adults' costumes are very different in character, the little girl feels that it gives her dress an air of importance.

Color. There are enough bright, clear colors that are simple in character so that it is possible for little sister, big sister, and mother all to wear the same hue, and all to be correctly and modishly dressed. There are some colors, especially the violet hues and black, that are sophisticated in appearance and less fresh and youthful than the blues, greens, and reds. Some tans and browns are adaptable to children's clothing, the lighter tans being most easily worn and combined with other colors. Some children may wear yellow and softer orange tones. The little girl with clear, wholesome coloring may wear fairly bright colors. Light, delicate tints, even those so dainty that they may appear weak and characterless on the adult, are frequently becoming to the child, although the little girl who appears only dainty in pale, light blue may seem much more interesting, much more definitely an individual, in a more emphatic color. The turquoise or blue-green shades will frequently be pleasing. Deeper blues of middle values will be more becoming, as well as more practical, in most instances.

Ensemble idea. The ensemble interests the child in her clothes, not only because her mother's and big sister's clothes are usually planned in this manner, but because she may grasp the idea of matching colors and planning costumes. If one especially becoming color is chosen as the basis of the wardrobe, for the coat, hat, and for one or two dresses, other dresses may be of lighter or darker shades of the same hue or of contrasting hues that will combine harmoniously with it.

Simple adjustments. Children learn self-reliance by dressing themselves. Clothing should be so constructed as to permit this. Adjustments should be so simple that the child will not make mistakes and become discouraged.

Hygiene Requirements of Growing Girl

Although clothing for the growing girl should be becoming to her, it is even more necessary that it be designed and selected with due consideration for its hygienic features. It is extremely important that the clothing of the growing girl be not so heavy that it is a burden to carry around, and that its weight be distributed so that it does not pull the vital organs down out of place or induce habits of poor posture.

Constriction and interference with posture. Almost all mothers appreciate the importance of clothing that is loose enough to avoid constriction, and of the absence of tight bands that might interfere with the circulation or cramp the abdominal region and interfere with digestion or other bodily functions. They like garments that have loose neckbands and cuffs or wristbands, especially if they provide room for growth. Not all mothers realize that constriction may occur because of a badly fitting sleeve, which twists and pulls upon the child's body. The body bones of the small child are easily pulled or pressed out of shape and may become set in malformations that will be carried through life. Shoulder and sleeve adjustments that induce correct posture and those designed to coax the body into good posture if a poor condition exists are, therefore, as necessary as is mere lack of tight, constricting bands.

Socks and short hose eliminate the constriction that hose supporters may produce. For this reason, and because removable long outer pants supply greater protection outdoors without overheating the child indoors, socks are almost universally worn by modern American children.

Underclothing should not bind, nor should it twist and pull upon any part of the body. No garment of this type should be worn after it has been outgrown. Clothing that becomes twisted and worked out of place upon the body is either poorly shaped or incorrectly adjusted.

Shoulder support best. Garments supported from the shoulders are considered most hygienic. Separate skirts are best when hung on underbodies that bring their weight to the shoulders. If they are on yokes or belts so that they may be worn with tuck-in blouses, the weight should be placed over the bony structure of the pelvic girdle, never over the soft and easily constricted portion of the body that comes at the natural waistline.

The growing girl should be taught the correct method of wearing and adjusting her garments so that their weight will always come at the proper structural points of the figure. Skirts that are too long to be worn low at the waistline should be shortened, not pulled up so that they pull and press downward at the natural waistline.

Distribution of weight. Even when the weight is borne by the shoulders, it must be carefully distributed with special care that garments are not heavier in the front than in the back, making the girl stoop and develop a posture that is awkward as well as unhygienic. A well-fitted shoulder and sleeve will aid in distributing weight evenly, in keeping the dress or coat in place, and in preventing it from pulling forward and interfering with comfort and posture.

Garter belts, provided they fit over the bony structure at the hips rather than drag down at the waistline, are preferable to round garters worn about the legs. Such belts should not be fastened too tightly, especially those that are worn in front, for if they are too tight they will pull downward on the abdominal organs even when worn low. Garters placed at the sides and back are less likely to be injurious.

Although garter belts are popular among young girls wearing long hosiery, many health experts believe that a smooth but not tight-fitting one-piece garment is more hygienic. It not only provides garters whose weight is borne by the shoulders or is evenly distributed over the torso, but it also gives a foundation that prevents other garments from cutting in at the waist or pulling down over the abdominal region. Separate skirts are more easily and more hygienically worn over a lightweight, well-fitting foundation of this character. A smoother line is provided for fitted dresses.

Garments that remain adjusted. Clothing for the growing girl should be of the type that remains adjusted and stays in position during the entire day. The active, growing girl, who, though interested in attractive clothes, does not remain conscious of them during the day, is likely to appear untidy and will appreciate the type of clothing that is structurally well fitted and does not pull out of place. Flying ends, sashes, and panels are not for the growing girl's everyday costumes. Belts should possess sufficient body so that they do not easily turn and twist, and they should either have straps to hold them trimly in place or be securely fastened in position.

Room for growth. During the age when most girls grow very rapidly, it is desirable that their clothing be constructed in such a manner that there is room for growth. Even when the expense of replacement is not an important consideration, as it is in the majority of families, it is essential that the clothing allow for some growth and development; otherwise it is likely to restrict growth or cause bad posture before the wearer and her mother realize how tight it is. For comfort in well-fitting garments choose models having fullness over the developing bust, and raglan sleeves or saddle shoulders cut so that they conform easily to the figure. Inverted pleats at the back of a waist or coat of the type that is so frequently used in adults' active sport apparel give the growing girl room for development and freedom of movement. Wide seams and deep hems, which permit of alteration, increase the length of service that may be obtained from the growing girl's clothing.

Warmth and weight. Lightweight woolens, which do not cause the body to become overheated and which prevent it from feeling sudden changes of temperature, are preferred by many mothers for winter dresses. Others feel that these are too warm for heated buildings, that cotton or simple silk dresses are more suitable, that extra warmth and protection should be supplied by outer garments, while indoor clothing should be sufficiently lightweight and porous in construction to permit ventilation and evaporation of moisture from the skin.

Although the growing girl herself and many mothers do not believe woolen underwear is desirable for the girl who is indoors much of the day, lightweight woolen hosiery is usually considered desirable. In attractive colors, which harmonize with the colors and the character of the dress and coat, it will not be objectionable to the girl, although she will probably prefer silk hose. Lisle hose is smart for active sport wear.

Color Diminishes Awkwardness

The colors employed in the costumes of the growing girl may do much to lessen the awkwardness so characteristic of the growing period. It is important that colors be considered first from the standpoint of their becomingness to the individual and then from the standpoint of creating a harmonious wardrobe with little liability of error in combinations of apparel. The growing girl herself, unless she is under constant and careful supervision, is too likely to combine colors that should not be used together simply because she likes each color individually.

The young girl with a radiant, healthful complexion has much greater freedom in her choice of colors than does the girl whose coloring is sallow or who is bothered with adolescent skin difficulties. Bright colors, which are so essentially youthful, may, therefore, be worn by the young girl who has no serious defects in her complexion.

The girl whose skin is less perfect must avoid extremely bright colors, and she must likewise avoid those natural beiges that are similar in color to her sallow skin. Whatever her general coloring, if her skin is sallow and imperfect, she should avoid vivid blues and all violet shades and bright oranges and yellows. Yellow-browns must likewise be avoided.

She will find among the most flattering colors dark, but not too vivid, blues, dark greens, especially dark blue-greens, dark reds, and particularly dark wine-reds that verge on the violet-red and dark red-oranges that include the red-brown range. Off-whites with a light, warm tint, pastel red-orange, and light blue-greens, if not too vivid, are likewise generally becoming.

The growing girl will appear clumsy and awkward if she clings to the characterless "baby blues," "candy pinks," and similar colors in which babies and small children are usually dressed. Combinations of two well-chosen colors, or occasionally of three harmonious ones, will do much to make each costume more interesting and to emphasize the individuality of the youthful wearer.

CHAPTER XXVII

The Miss in Her Teens

Almost all young girls are strongly influenced by a desire to have others comment favorably about them and their appearance. Young girls of high-school age usually fear being thought different. They dress as nearly as possible like their classmates and friends. Only the very courageous and daring, those few who set the fashion in their group rather than follow it, will be happy in wearing styles that are not already universally accepted in their small world.

The slightly older girl, who has passed through the imitative stage, desires to be individual and distinctive as strongly as the younger girl fears being queer. She may wear unbecoming styles simply because they are new or different. For this reason she needs more guidance than does the girl who wears more standardized types of apparel.

The younger girl is frequently difficult to fit because she does not wear foundation garments. Even though her figure be straight and slim, it is seldom firm enough, or its lines smooth and flowing enough, for many of the styles of the present day. Pleated skirts, or full gathered or flared skirts in which the fullness does not begin too far down, may frequently be combined with a slim, fitted bodice, thus emphasizing the slimness of the figure without making the unrestrained hips too apparent.

Casual jackets and skirts seem especially suited to the youthful and immature figure.

Little care. The young girl has seldom learned to take good care of her clothing, to make the constant small repairs, and to do the cleaning and pressing necessary to keep a wardrobe in good condition. As she is usually hard on her clothes, because she is both active and careless, her wardrobe should be of materials and styles that require little attention.

Colors and fabrics that do not show spots easily and that will not pull apart at the strain of seams are almost as necessary to the girl who is nearly twenty as to children.

Comfort and freedom. Youth, almost without exception, demands apparel that permits freedom of movement, clothes that will not pull apart and appear untidy at vigorous, unthinking activity. For this reason, many girls, even those who wish the extremely long skirt for formal evening wear, cling to the extremely short skirt, shorter than that approved by fashionists today. For active sports this is still considered correct and may appropriately be worn for all activities with which the longer skirt would definitely interfere. For street wear the slightly longer skirt, long enough at least to cover the bend of the knee, is usually more becoming.

The one-piece dress, which has returned to high favor, is suited to the young girl because it cannot pull apart and become untidy at the waist or hipline as the two-piece dress frequently does. The tuck-in blouse or sweater, if long enough to extend well down under the skirt, and to blouse enough to permit raising the arms without disarranging the costume, is especially appropriate and appealing to the junior. Jumpers provide the contrast and variety of the separate blouse, but are more easily worn. They are more slenderizing than the separate skirt and they remain neat and tidy without constant effort on the part of the wearer. Jackets and sweaters giving the requisite comfort and freedom of movement are also to be recommended. They have the added advantage of covering the figure that is imperfectly proportioned or that has not the smooth hipline that is needed with the tuck-in blouse.

Revealed forehead. The hats with the exposed forehead are youth's own style. They are thought to have been created because the so-called American flapper insisted on wearing her hats perched on the back of her head. It usually interests the young girl to realize that this smart mode was created expressly for her and that only the youthful face appears to advantage in the severe line of the almost completely exposed forehead.

Fabrics. The tweeds, the knitted fabrics, the soft plain crêpe in the mode today are especially appropriate to the needs of the young girl. Tweeds require little care; knitted fabrics possess the same advantage and the added comfort incident to their elastic character, which permits freedom of movement. Soft crêpes hang in graceful, youthful lines, being both comfortable and becoming. The young girl appears best in these fabrics and should choose them and avoid the regal, intricate brocades, the metallic fabrics with hard gleam, which are too sophisticated to be in character with costumes becoming youth.

Adaptability. The type and color of the accessories, and frequently of larger items, must be carefully considered, as the girl usually possesses a smaller number than the woman. She must often wear the same top coat, the same hat, shoes, gloves, and other items with many different types of dresses and for numerous occasions; for this reason it is important that they harmonize.

A frequent mistake of the young girl is that of wearing hats, coats, and dresses, each of different colors or of colors that neither match nor harmonize, thus giving an untidy, poorly groomed appearance.

Apt and Inapt Age Emphasis

The junior girl, who has reached the age when her individuality should be recognized and accented by means of her apparel, may make many mistakes in attempting to find garments suitable to her type. She may wear costumes too important and mature or she may err by choosing too-youthful costumes. An understanding of her most frequent mistakes aids in the selection of appropriate and becoming costumes.

Sometimes, in the attempt to appear older and more dignified, sometimes because of lack of knowledge, the junior buys apparel with lines so straight, stiff, and mature that they seem very obviously created for a much older woman.

Straight lines need not be avoided entirely; in fact, their use is essential in many types of simple, practical costumes. When employed in the costume for the junior, they should, however, be combined with rounded or curved lines. Soft folds that, in themselves, produce rounded contours may take the place of actual roundness of outline.

Just as the young girl who has never had long hair likes to experiment with its highly feminine effect, so does the girl who has never worn long skirts like to wear them whenever they are fashionable. She wants her formal evening dresses extremely long—longer than are graceful or practical for the young active figure. Her long evening dresses will be most becoming and more comfortable if they clear the floor by an inch or two, so that she may dance without fear of tripping on them. Trains, even though they be slight and graceful in themselves, are only awkward on the girl who has not learned to handle them gracefully.

In the daytime the miss in her 'teens likes to wear her skirts the accepted adult street length, which, in the days when short skirts are fashionable, usually gives her a decided advantage over older women who usually do not find them so becoming as she does. When longer skirts are fashionable, the adolescent girl still does well to wear her skirts fairly short, remembering that one of the chief reasons for longer skirts is that of flattering the more difficult figure.

The long skirt made of soft material draped or hung in a simple manner may be very charming on the junior. Full, gathered skirts are more likely to be becoming than those wrapped in close, swathed lines or those with intricate trains or flying, dangling parts, for the young and active person seldom has either the carriage or the patience to wear trains successfully. Her walk is seldom leisurely enough to give graceful flutter to loose panels, which fly out awkwardly with her brisk, vigorous movements.

While many mothers welcome the longer skirt, they usually like to see their daughters attired in a simple, youthful manner, in a style more youthful than the daughter herself may desire. The daughter may sometimes be discouraged from wearing trains and intricate types of skirts if she is reminded that they are difficult to dance in and are usually heartily disliked by young men.

The higher waistline and the fitted, slender waistline are pre-eminently youthful fashions, which appear to best advantage on the youthful, slender figure. Not all junior girls, however, have the requisite slender figure to wear the definitely fitted waistline or the high normal waistline. Many adolescent girls, either because they are not well proportioned or because they are not wearing foundation garments that give a smooth, unbroken line to the figure, look best in waistlines slightly below normal and in belts that are not drawn tightly so as to cause a definite indentation at the waistline.

Periodically the fashion of drawing the belt very tight, of tying a tight belt around a heavy coat, of a straight, one-piece dress or even a sweater so that it is gathered into a tiny waist becomes the mode of the moment among adolescent girls even though it is not even remotely related to recognized adult fashions. Sometimes it is a fad in only one school, or one section of the country, sometimes it is widespread. To all but the taller and more slender girl with a well-proportioned figure it is extremely unbecoming.

The junior girl, just beginning to wear interesting and individual apparel and to attend important social functions, is often tempted to wear too-intricate and regal types. Our customs and conventions permit the young girl to wear styles that would be considered unsuitable for the European girl. No junior, however, should make the mistake of wearing really elaborate apparel in costly, highly decorative fabrics, with intricate detail. She should especially avoid costumes that require a studied carriage or constant manipulation, which may destroy the simple naturalness of her manner. Many and ornate accessories and elaborate slippers detract from rather than add to the interest of a junior girl.

The costume of the girl in her 'teens should not be devoid of interest; simplicity should not be carried to the extreme. Softened lines are better than severity; unusual, interesting, and, sometimes, striking detail may be employed; but the accents should not be so strong and conspicuous that attention is detracted from the youthful wearer and concentrated, instead, upon her costume.

Heavy folds of fabric, too-straight lines, unfitted garments giving a straight rather than a naturally curved silhouette make the figure seem heavier and more mature than it actually is. By choosing the type of dress planned to hide the bad lines of the more mature figure, the junior associates herself with the heaviness and maturity these lines were contrived to conceal.

The dress that reveals the natural lines of the figure accentuates the youthfulness of the wearer, yet reveals the "young lady" silhouette, which differentiates the junior from her younger sister and from the straight, casually fitting apparel that she has been wearing most of her life.

The junior who clings to extremely short garments and very rounded outlines, as round collars and short, full skirts, has much the appearance of being overgrown and awkward. Her apparel, because it is too childish, appears too small, the outgrown old clothes of past seasons.

She may choose slightly longer skirts than children wear, and have them pleated or youthfully flared, and she should choose less obviously rounded lines and a youthful jacket of straight but casual character. She may wear the sport coat with jaunty, wide, notched lapels, but not the narrow, straight lapels of the older woman or the round collar of her younger sister. Her costume as a whole should show greater individuality in the selection of details than the apparel of the little girl.

Many juniors and the elders who advise or supervise them in their selection of apparel make the mistake of combining essentially youthful, even childish details with those that are sophisticated and mature. One sees the young girl wearing longer, uneven hemlines with low-heeled, round-toed slippers, even with oxfords. She wears the softly feminine draped or flared costume with the boyish beret, at once too youthful, too informal, and too round in line for the longer lines of the new silhouette.

It is possible to have a combination of youthful details and more sophisticated interest, to employ soft, youthful lines, rounded contours, and the longer outlines of the new silhouette together with all parts of the costume chosen to harmonize with each other.

Junior Types

Girls of the so-called junior age neither look alike, act alike, nor think and feel alike. That they should not be dressed alike, except in those camps and schools that make clothes unimportant by means of uniforms, is a conclusion with which there will be little dispute. The junior girl's own interests and tastes influence the apparel selected. Sometimes, however, her own diagnosis of her type, of her difficulties and problems, as well as of her assets, may be inaccurate and misleading.

A junior of small, rounded figure, of youthful but rather fragile, childish appearance, announced that she could not wear anything but sport clothes, because she was of the athletic type. Her problem is that of selecting soft, flattering lines that will permit free, active movements. Of course, for active sports she should still wear apparel designed for that purpose, but more casually tailored, with more feminine detail than the mannish tailoring that she has hitherto worn.

Conflicts between the problems of physical characteristics and activities or of preconceived notions of apparel are frequent. While these several factors influence apparel selection, the physical characteristics of face and figure should usually be the first consideration.

Youthful, childish type. Many junior girls still appear much like younger children. Sometimes this is because they are less mature than the average girl of their age, sometimes because they have the small frames and rounded contours that will always make them appear younger than their actual years. While this will be an asset in later years, the junior girl is sometimes sensitive and frequently feels at a disadvantage.

The very youthful junior must avoid both very young round lines, which emphasize her youthfulness, and those mature, straight lines and heavy, important fabrics that obviously are not suited to her, and which, by their very contrast with her youthful face and figure, make her appear even younger. Discreet use of more sophisticated, interesting detail and avoidance of that which is entirely youthful, coupled with apparel that focuses attention on the wearer by emphasizing some pleasing feature, will prevent this type of junior from passing unnoticed as a child.

Petite, sophisticated type. Very similar in size to the youthful, childish type, but with less round, childish contours, the petite, sophisticated type appears more definitely individual. She tends to appear older than she actually is. Sometimes she has deliberately chosen to appear older, but very frequently she wishes to appear more youthful without wearing childish types that obviously are unsuited to her.

Her mother and other adults in her family are usually even more desirous of having her appear young, fresh, wholesome, rather than sophisticated. They may choose styles that are simple and smart without being extreme, which introduce enough rounded lines and soft folds of fabric to give a fresh, youthful appearance.

Tall, slender, youthful type. The tall, slender, youthful girl, considered typical of American youth, has little difficulty in selecting her apparel. Her problem becomes that of choosing from many becoming styles rather than that of finding any that are suitable. She should not, of course, choose styles too dignified or important, but if she does select these older ones, she has less difficulty in carrying them without appearing stolid or mature or ridiculously overdressed than do the other junior girls. When occasion or mood demands, she may wear very youthful styles.

Tall, overgrown girl. The girl who is actually too tall and overgrown rather than tall and well proportioned, whose arms and legs seem too long for her to handle gracefully, who seems awkward because her figure is not fully developed and is angular rather than rounded, who has not learned to carry her new height easily has a difficult time selecting becoming apparel. Sometimes she appears best in lines designed to lessen height, and to give increased width, for usually she is very thin as a result of her rapid growth. Garments that fit loosely, casually, yet carefully enough so that they do not appear untidy and do not become disarranged easily, are most suitable. The girl of this type has seldom learned to wear her clothes well and should not have garments that require constant adjustment or measured and graceful carriage.

Well-developed, mature type. The large girl with a well-developed, mature figure tends to appear much older than she is, usually so much older that it makes her embarrassed and unhappy and robs her of pleasant contacts with others of her own age. Much of this mature appearance may be removed by well-chosen apparel, by lines that are sufficiently rounded or curved to give a youthful feeling, but not so rounded that the figure becomes rotund by reason of the curves emphasized in the cos-

tume. Soft materials hanging in graceful but not too volumi-
nous folds, garments that fit neither too loosely nor too tightly,
and, above all, simplicity without severity are especially apt for
the junior girl of mature figure. She should avoid wearing
skirts longer than the mode, as they will give her a heavy appearance; yet she cannot wear them shorter, for this, too, would
make her conspicuous and, in many cases, would reveal heavy,
solid-looking legs. All extreme styles attracting undue attention should be avoided, and interest should be centered as near
the face as possible so that the maturity of the figure will be less
apparent.

Solid, overweight type. The heavy, overweight girl, especially the girl of large proportions, appears solid and mature,
much older than her years. Her movements are likely to be
awkward because of the large bulk she possesses, although occasionally girls who have always been large are surprisingly
graceful.

Fussy, frilled clothing and dainty, fragile fabrics give her
an extremely awkward appearance; they seem so inconsistent
with their wearer's lack of personal daintiness that they may
appear ridiculous. Fine, minute detail should likewise be
avoided, as its scale is not in keeping with that of the wearer.
Simple outlines with space divisions that break the surface,
making size inconspicuous, are most becoming. Too many
straight lines will emphasize maturity. Striking colors or designs and bulky fabrics are always to be avoided.

One piece dresses and jumpers should be chosen rather than
skirts and blouses or sweaters. Jackets must match the skirt
rather than contrast with it. Full length rather than short coats
should be worn.

Short, rotund type. The short girl who is overweight is

likely to seem much shorter and heavier, much more poorly proportioned in comparison to her actual overweight than is the tall, large-framed girl who is too heavy. The short girl does not appear so mature as does the girl of larger frame. Because her round lines give a youthful, even a babyish, appearance, she may wear straight, perpendicular lines, which will increase her apparent height and lessen width without making her appear too mature. The heavy girl of large frame frequently finds that these slenderizing lines must be softened to relieve the maturity that they emphasize in her figure. Horizontal lines created by contrasts between skirt and blouse or sweater or by contrasting jackets should be avoided by the short, round girl. She too will find long coats more becoming than short ones, one-piece dresses or jumpers most becoming.

The short, rotund girl must avoid all round and curved lines; even soft, rounded folds of fabric will increase the roundness of her face and figure. Bulky fabrics, adding even a fraction of an inch to her actual width, will make her appear appreciably heavier and more round, or, sometimes, if the lines are heavy, square rather than round.

Campus Costumes

Where does the junior live? Where does she go to school? Is she still in high school, preparatory school, or college? Where is the school located? What are her social contacts in and out of school? Wardrobe requirements are influenced by the location of the school—in country region, small town, or large city—and by whether or not it is coeducational.

The college located in the country, with many acres of wooded campus, grass, gravel walks perhaps, and paths, demands apparel of a casual character. High-heeled, thin-soled, low-cut shoes would be neither practical nor comfortable for daily wear. Berets, casual felt hats, or a total absence of head covering is much more usual than the smart, carefully fitted hat that would be worn in town. Comfortable, casual sport clothes of the type suited for activity, if not for specific sports, are more suitable than tailored street costumes or even sport apparel of the spectator type.

Wool dresses, preferably of lightweight wools that are not too warm for heated buildings, but which offer some protection against the sudden changes of temperature, are needed in the wardrobe of the girl on the large campus where buildings and classes are some distance apart. While simple silk dresses are worn, especially in warmer weather, they are less important than in the city college. Skirts and blouses or sweaters and jackets in the more casual manner compose practical and youthfully becoming suits. Leather jackets and coats of tweed and camel's hair are more necessary for daily wear than those of less sturdy fabrics and more formal character. Waterproofs are always needed.

The types of clothes needed for off-the-campus occasions and for activities other than those that are part of the daily routine will vary according to the individual and the college. All girls will need at least one smart street and traveling costume. Some girls will find a suit of a less casual character more becoming and practical; others will choose separate daytime dresses and coats.

At least one simple afternoon dress of becoming color and well-cut, youthfully draped lines is needed for teas, informal dinners, and evening occasions for which formal wear is not required, but for which the sportswear usually worn throughout the day is unsuitable. In some colleges the majority of girls have little need for dinner gowns or semiformal evening dress, and require formal dress only for one or two proms or other important dances. In others, formal evening wear is less needed than semiformal wear.

The number of week ends permitted away from the campus as well as the social contacts of the individual will largely determine the formal clothes required by each junior. Suitable accessories for each type of costume must be included. The junior, however, wears fewer and simpler accessories than the woman.

The girl who attends a city school, perhaps while living at home and going back and forth in subways or surface cars, needs much more tailored and formal apparel. Her daytime costumes, while they should be simple, practical, and youthful, must be appropriate for the street and systems of public transportation. Her suits must be less casual, her accessories more formal; she must wear gloves and a hat. While she may have tweeds, camel's hair, and other practical wool coats, she has less need of garments intended for more active outdoor pursuits. Her waterproofs are best in somber tones, in finishes that give them the appearance of a street coat rather than of a raincoat. The city schoolgirl may use more simple silk and fewer wool dresses than the girl on a campus in the country. Shoes with low or medium heels are most suitable to the school girl. In the city, shoes of the moccasin type, the not-too-open sandal, wedge-soled shoes, and tailored oxfords are more suitable than the flat-heeled saddle oxford. Stockings or bare legs well tanned or with liquid make-up are more appropriate than bobby socks for the adolescent girl who must use public transportation.

CHAPTER XXVIII

The Young Woman

OUNG WOMEN are and can afford to be more highly individual in their selection of apparel than women of any other age. Young girls necessarily have certain problems in common dictated by school and social custom and by the similarity of the childish figures. Middle years and the later years of life likewise produce many characteristics that are similar in women of like age; but we do not think first of the young woman as a young woman, but as an individual. The young woman will find her costume requirements dictated by her figure and face type and by her daily activities. Since she is usually more active both in business and social life than women of other ages, she frequently has need for more types of clothing. She may learn to establish with consistency various identities suitable for her business and social life. She must not forget that her apparel should minimize defects of face and figure as much as possible, and at the same time emphasize her most attractive characteristics.

Accenting Individuality

The young woman who has reached early maturity, who has the self-confidence and poise usually lacking in the young girl, and who has yet suffered none of the destructive effects of time that lessen physical charms has much less difficult dress problems than does the woman of more advanced years. Individual characteristics become important; there are fewer problems common to all women of this age.

The first requirement that the younger woman should make of her costumes, and the one that she frequently either consciously or unconsciously does make, is that of consistency with her type. A garment that, in itself, is perfect in design and execution is pleasing and correct only if it is consistent in feeling with the face and figure of the wearer, which is the structural basis of the design.

Not only the actual proportions of the figure or the actual shape of the face should be considered when selecting designs, but also the more subtle distinctions based upon feeling and personality. Some persons seem so reserved, so quiet in physical and mental personality, that costumes of striking design, of vibrant character, would be inconsistent and inappropriate. Other persons are so energetic and forceful that apparel of delicate, fragile character seems totally out of place when worn by them. Still other persons are so dainty in appearance that apparel of harsh texture or severe mannish lines seems obviously not to belong to them. It is possible for each woman to determine the type of apparel that is most appropriate to herself and to recognize designs that seem to have been created for her.

Most women can increase their own interest and pleasure in their clothes and make their personalities more varied and interesting to others by varying the type of their costumes. While most individuals are limited as to the types of apparel that they may wear, few women are so limited that they may successfully wear only one type. Many women limit themselves to a single definite type of apparel, so that all their costumes appear alike. If this one type is well selected and is truly suited to the wearer, the mistake, although it does create monotony and makes the wearer less interesting than she need appear, is not so serious an error as wearing unbecoming clothes.

The young woman who is fairly well proportioned, who has no serious defect of face or figure to overcome, can readily change her appearance and her apparent personality by varying her costume. In dressing suitably for each occasion, but in accordance with her type, the woman who has many activities will obtain sufficient variety in her costumes. She will find active sport types, tailored types, and softer and more formal types of apparel that will express her personality. The woman who has fewer activities, who does not dress for so great a variety of occasions, must strive more consciously to vary her type. The woman with pronounced defects of face or figure must be even more careful, for she must avoid extreme types that might tend to focus attention upon defects.

Not only the activities of the individual, but her temperament, carriage, and movements limit or extend the types of apparel that are becoming and suitable to her. The woman who moves slowly, with rhythmic, graceful movements, may wear floating drapes and intricate details that would appear awkward on a woman with quick, jerky movements. On the other hand, the woman who moves slowly but heavily cannot wear the flowing draperies that add grace to her more languid sister; and the woman who is forceful and energetic, with even, quick motions, needs apparel that will express her force and vigor without interfering with her freedom of movement.

Color, always a vital consideration in costume design, is extremely useful in establishing distinctive individual dress becoming to the wearer and making her a distinct personality. Some persons characteristically wear certain colors and establish their individualities by this means. If the color is at all unusual in tone, this may be an extremely effective means of appearing more imaginative than the majority of women, who wear given colors merely because other women are wearing them and make themselves parts of the masses rather than distinctive individuals. It is especially important that the color be becoming, for an unusual color that is not flattering to the wearer serves only to attract attention to undesirable characteristics.

The woman striving to emphasize individuality need not fear monotony in confining herself to a few becoming colors. There are usually three or four hues and two or three tones of each hue that the individual will find becoming and that will add vitality and charm to her appearance. Thus, the woman who looks best in greens may be able to wear both greens and blue-greens and find them becoming in several values and intensities. She may, therefore, adapt these colors as the keynote colors of her wardrobe, habitually wearing them either in duller intensities for the foundation of her wardrobe or in smaller notes as an accent. For variety, she may wear the opposite or complementary colors, the red and orange tones, which may be used as accents to dull grayed greens or by themselves in dull intensities with accents of the greens and blue-greens.

The Very Feminine Woman

The woman of soft, feminine personality, the passive type with a suggestion of fragility and gentleness, should be costumed to emphasize her delicate, dainty charm. If she wears clothes that are too forceful, too strong, and too striking, her personality is submerged and weakened. It is her problem, therefore, to emphasize her soft, feminine quality, neither submerging it nor lessening its beauty by apparel totally lacking in distinction and character.

Color is especially important to the woman of soft, gentle personality. If she wears dull, drab, uninteresting colors, she herself, with her none too-definite or striking personality, may become insignificant in appearance and lacking in distinction. If she wears colors of subtle, softened intensity, with interesting arrangements of unusual but not too-bold or striking color harmonies, she gains in distinction and charm. Lacking vivid, forceful coloring herself, she must not choose colors so neutral that they give a monotonous appearance to the combined colorings of the costume and herself.

While the dull, neutral colors will prevent her being seen at all, extremely vivid colors will cause the costume to become very evident, but the wearer will sink into the background. Colors should be chosen that will enhance the personal coloring of the wearer, overcome defects of complexion, give added life and vitality to the hair, and deepen the coloring of the eyes.

Dainty, filmy fabrics, cobwebby laces, and even crisp, transparent finishes emphasize the dainty, fragile character of the soft, feminine type. Heavy clothes, stiff fabrics of elaborate, elegant character require much more dignity than the dainty woman possesses to carry them successfully; their wearer appears less important than the imposing costume.

The demure, restrained costume emphasizes the repose and gentleness of the wearer and makes her appear a more distinctive and interesting individual; her costume becomes a background consistent with the character of the wearer. Simplicity of design, raised to distinction by means of dainty, feminine detail, wise color accent, and perhaps the contrast of lingerie touches at neck and wrist, emphasizes the quiet charm of the less aggressive personality. Details centered near the face aid in drawing attention to this feature, which should be the center of interest in a costume that expresses the gentle personality of the wearer.

The Forceful, Energetic Woman

The young woman who belongs to the more vigorous type should wear costumes that express her own forceful personality. A basic rule of costume design is that colors should never be more forceful than the physical personality of the wearer. This permits the woman of forceful, energetic character to wear definite, decided colors that are denied many women. Weak, pale colors may make her own coloring appear coarse, while forceful colors further vitalize her appearance. Distinctive and characterful, even bold, color contrasts are frequently advisable.

The quick, active, energetic movements of the forceful woman are at variance with costumes designed with many soft floating ends, fluttering details that appear untidy and bedraggled on the woman of quick, brisk movements. They give her an appearance of being agitated, of poor poise. Simple tailored lines should characterize her costume, with details manipulated so that the entire costume moves with the wearer rather than fluttering out away from the figure. Freedom of movement, so essential to the grace of the woman of brisk, energetic action, should always be permitted by the costume.

Round lines, giving softer, more feminine contours, are hardly consistent with the personality of the woman of strength and vigor. Short, broken lines, destroying the harmony of her vigorous, clear-cut outlines, should never be recommended for the active, aggressive type of woman. Straight, unbroken lines, both in perpendicular and diagonal arrangement, are usually becoming to the vigorous personality, emphasizing dignity and poise.

The person of vigorous, aggressive character may sometimes wish to appear more daintily feminine than her natural personality. She may, if she so wishes, wear costumes with softer details, slightly more feminine in aspect than her own personality. She should not, however, make the mistake of wearing extremely dainty garments, which, by their contrast with her more vigorous personality, will give her a suggestion of masculinity.

The severely tailored costume should not have masculine details or accessories, but rather those with a youthful, boyish note. Only the young, fresh-looking woman can afford to strive for a masculine effect, either boyish or mannish. Usually the severely tailored costume is most pleasing when relieved by simple accessories that show feminine thought and imagination.

Designs of striking character, those employing definite, clear-cut outlines, decided contrasts in vivid colors, can be worn by the woman of forceful personality. Opaque materials that assume simple, clear-cut lines or sturdy fabrics that have a strong vigorous character readily lend themselves to costumes that enhance the personality of the vigorous, active woman.

CHAPTER XXIX

The Middle Years

*N*o woman desires to appear middle aged. As a matter of fact, women of middle age usually appear either years older than their actual age or, if they have attempted to remedy this defect, years younger. There is a long period between youth and age during which time a woman's appearance should express her individuality without giving an impression of any age.

Women of middle age frequently have more distinct personalities than they had when younger, although some of them have become submerged by their home duties, by lack of attention to their clothing, and by nondescript costumes. The clothes of the middle-aged woman should express the experience and the importance which years may bring, and thus give her a distinction that youth lacks.

The middle-aged woman frequently fails to see the changes that the years have made in her face and figure. She sees in the mirror the image that was there ten or even twenty years ago. She clings to youthful styles, not in a determined effort to retain youth, but because she has not seen their unsuitability for herself. It is better to err on the side of apparel more staid than the actual years justify than to lack dignity entirely. The conservative costume may make the face seem young by contrast.

The young girl with the beauty that nearly always accompanies youth and health may wear inexpensive materials, "junk jewelry," and other devices that give an "effect"; the woman of middle age finds that genuineness and quality are needed to give her grace and dignity. A high grade of simulated pearls or other well made costume jewelry of good design may, of course, be worn, but it is best to restrict the middle-aged woman's jewelry to one or two good pieces that have definite relation to the costume with which they are worn.

Another frequent error is that of choosing lace for wear with costumes with which it is inconsistent. Many middle-aged women, as well as older women, place great value on "real" lace, that is, lace that is hand made, which does, of course, possess quality and genuineness, but which is not always suitable for the costume. On the other hand, fine qualities of machine-made laces may be most appropriate and pleasing for an entire gown for the middle-aged woman, yet she may reject them because to her they are not "real" lace. Other middle-aged women err on the opposite side, wearing coarse, inexpensive machine-made laces, in large amounts and with fabrics and lines with which lace is utterly inappropriate.

Simplicity Gives Distinction

Simplicity and quality should be the keynotes of the middle-aged woman's costume. Simplicity gives an essentially youthful appearance. A garment giving a youthful effect removes many years from the apparent age of the woman who habitually wears elaborate effects. Intricacy of cut and fine detail are found in many smart garments that retain an effect characteristically simple. Although many persons are inclined to believe the contrary, a great many smart fashions are designed for the mature woman.

The well-designed costume should never be more forceful in appearance than the personality, both mental and physical, of the wearer. As the middle-aged woman usually has a less alert carriage, less definite and forceful coloring, less clear-cut features, and, usually, slower speech and manner of thought than the younger woman, there is greater likelihood of her personality being submerged by a conspicuous costume. Striking lines, vivid colors, the extreme and bizarre, detract both from her dignity and her personality. Occasionally, a woman of middle age may still have a vivacious manner and definite physical beauty, which will permit the wearing of forceful apparel.

As the middle-aged woman tends to be heavier, with less free movement than the younger woman, heavy, clumsy effects in clothing must be studiously avoided. Dark, heavy, thick materials and lines that suggest bulk and weight—particularly those that appear poorly balanced, and, therefore, awkward and difficult to carry—should be eliminated from the middle-aged woman's costume.

Textures become especially important at middle age, for they may materially add or detract from the grace of the figure. Soft, supple fabrics, those that hang in graceful folds without clinging unduly, are most flattering. Bulky fabrics create angularities and accentuate any defects of figure or movement. Stiff fabrics, as taffeta, are likewise difficult; only the woman with an exceptionally youthful face and figure finds them becoming at middle age. Fabrics with an indefinite pattern possess richness and a sophisticated interest that the woman of middle years may effectively carry. She may find fabrics with designs of subtle character more becoming than those of solid color, though the latter are almost always more pleasing than designs of striking character. Beads, flowers, or other decorative detail added to a patterned fabric create too much design in the costume and give it a confusing, elaborate character that robs it of all distinction, while conferring upon the wearer a heavy, middle-aged appearance.

Defects of figure, accumulations of flesh, unequal distribution of flesh are common at middle age. Some women must consider methods of reducing the apparent size of the hips; others, of the bust or abdomen and diaphragm; while still others have a large upper arm or round shoulders and a lump of flesh below the back of the neck. The chapters in this book discussing methods of minimizing these defects, therefore, are of especial interest if studied in their relation to the problems of the woman of middle age.

The Hairdress

The hairdress frequently discloses the age of the woman of middle years. The woman who does her hair in careless, ill-groomed, or obsolete styles, or in incongruously youthful modes, emphasizes her years. If, on the other hand, the hairdress is simple, modish, and becoming, the observer is less likely to think consciously of either age or coiffure, but rather of the personality of the individual.

Although modern knowledge of diet, of protective foods that give vital minerals and vitamins, may postpone gray hair beyond the middle years, to many women it is the most distressing sign of advancing years, the change that first makes her feel that she looks middle aged. Well kept, smartly styled gray hair may be extremely flattering, providing a soft frame for the face. It may be more becoming than dyed hair, even though it is dyed to approximate the natural color that it was originally.

Every woman who gives thought to becoming dress should seriously consider the problem of gray hair in relation to her appearance and her personal habits. The woman who cannot afford the time or the expense of regular and rather lengthy visits to the hairdresser should usually relinquish all thoughts of dyeing her hair, as the slightest showing of gray hair at the part or the hairline is much more ageing than an entire head of gray. The woman who thinks that she can dye or retouch her own hair usually fails to do a thorough job unless she has help.

Even though careful dyeing and retouching can be maintained, careful consideration should be given to the becomingness of gray or colored hair. When the first gray hairs are beginning to be evident, hair pieces or transformations of gray and of white hair should be tried on and studied in relation to the skin, eyes, and shape of the features. A visit to a hairdresser specializing in styling who will allow sufficient time for the study of the true becomingness of hair color may be a better investment than the purchase of a new costume. It should not be forgotten that hair dyeing is a lucrative part of the hairdressing business, and that the actual decision, to dye or not to dye, should be the individuals, aided by family and trusted friends, and by experienced clothing advisers.

If the decision is to dye the hair rather than to let it become gray, perhaps the first step is the use of colored rinses that tint the few gray hairs after each shampoo. As the gray hairs increase, dyeing is usually more successful. The good hairdresser, experienced in dyeing, tries to avoid the lifeless look of hair dyed too solidly one color. Nature's color shows variations in shading which, if subtly simulated when the hair is dyed, make dyed hair more flattering and more natural looking.

In an attempt at careful grooming, some middle-aged women make the mistake of having their hair dressed with a set pattern of tight, small waves. A loose, natural-appearing wave, soft curling ends, following the natural contours of the head, is almost always most becoming.

The hair tends to recede from the forehead and to thin out at the temples as the years advance. This gives a high, square

Soft ringlets on the top of the head may be very becoming to the woman of middle years.

A simply waved hairdress, parted at one side and combed up off the forehead in a slanting line, but soft about the face and over the ears, is becoming to most women.

When the forehead is good, the hair may be combed up to give additional length to the face, if there are waves or soft curls at the temples and over the ears.

line and the dreaded middle-aged appearance unless the hair is arranged over the forehead. Concealment of wrinkles and the thick, lifeless skin, which often occurs on this part of the face, is made possible. It also makes the eyes appear darker and deeper and tends to erase the tired lines around them. The ears, which tend to enlarge and coarsen with age, are also best concealed or partially concealed by the hair. The coiffure arranged in simple soft lines over these features, therefore, is much more becoming than one in which the hair is combed away from the ears and forehead. The woman with long hair that has never been cut, frequently has so much that it cannot be arranged otherwise than in stiff, hard, heavy masses, which make her appear aggressive and top heavy. The woman who has pride in long hair, yet who longs for a modish headdress and the

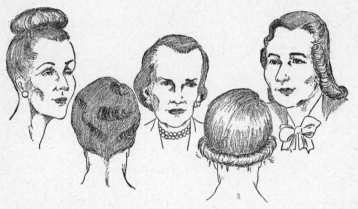

Top-knots or masses of hair at the top of the head alter its actual contours and make the head seem heavy.

The shingled neckline is not only unpleasant to the eye, but it dates the wearer as being sufficiently old to cling to the hairdress of a generation ago.

When the hair is thin at the temples, the forehead has square lines that should be concealed rather than revealed.

A stiff smooth roll is less becoming than short, loose curls, especially if there are short straight wisps of hair at the back of the neck.

The simple smooth lines of the pageboy or shoulder length bob are too youthful for the middle years.

smart, close-fitting hats it permits, can enjoy both by having her hair expertly thinned or shortened so that smaller bulk remains. She must learn to do her hair in soft lines without knots or bunches, which give the effect of having been added to the head.

Untidy back-hair is ageing as well as unpleasing. If the hair is combed up at the back, short ends must be avoided with the aid of a wave that helps to hold them in place, and by the use of waxes or lacquers. Untidy curls and frizzled ends are especially bad when the hair is gray and give it the appearance of steel wool unless it has a smooth, glossy, brushed appearance.

Hair combed up away from the back of the neck gives an untidy, poorly groomed appearance, for there are always short ends that cannot be successfully kept up. As hair combed up from the back usually necessitates a group of curls, a knot, or a bunch of hair, the natural contours of the head are destroyed and the head size becomes unduly large.

A knot placed low on the neck, centering attention upon a feature that is no longer young and graceful, is unbecoming to the woman of middle age. It accentuates the thickened line of her neck and the lump of flesh that is frequently found at its base. A knot placed higher, just at the hairline, makes the neck appear much more slender and the shape of the head much more pleasing.

The Hat

The hat worn by the middle-aged woman may add many years to her apparent age, or subtract appreciably from it. Amusing and ridiculous hats call attention to defects of face and figure. Round, unbroken lines call attention to irregular contours of the face as well as to rotundity of face and figure. Soft, irregular lines, brims that partly shadow the face, are more easily worn than stiff, rigid shapes and off-the-face hats. The latter may be becoming if the hairdress it reveals is truly flattering. All hats should be considered in relation to the hair style. Most millinery designers have a definite hair style in mind when they design each model, and the best design is not complete unless complemented by the lines of the hair. The middle-aged woman is likely to overlook this if she is unaccustomed to changing her hair style frequently.

Hats that are too small for the face and the figure and those that are too large and too heavy are equally unbecoming to the middle-aged woman, yet both are frequent errors.

The youthful, poke-shaped hat with unbroken, round lines is far less becoming to the woman of middle age than is the hat with less regularly rotund contours. The brim that is longer

The rigid round hat emphasizes rotundity and irregular contours of the face. Softer, irregular lines, are flattering to the middle years.

at one side, or that employs pleats or other manipulation of cut or draping to break the round lines, is less likely to emphasize facial defects. An unbecoming hat may frequently be made becoming by cutting the brim (if of felt), or by folding it into less regular lines.

The typical matron's hat is heavy, awkward, and unbecoming largely because its crown has little or no relation to the shape of the head. In many hats of this type the crown is up above the head so far that it destroys the balance of the entire figure. The crowns are frequently square rather than rounded. A hat made with a crown that follows the contours of the head, fitting closely so that it becomes an integral part of the figure, is much more becoming and makes both face and figure appear to better advantage.

When the head size is large enough to make the crown appear large, as is often the case when a woman has long hair, the apparent proportions may be improved if the surface of the crown is broken by tucks or seamings. Even a fold or a crease put in with expert fingers may serve to increase the becomingness of a hat with a plain crown. The middle-aged woman frequently makes the mistake of buying a hat in a too-small

The elaborately trimmed, heavy hat is dated and matronly. A beret may be softly flattering, supply slenderizing diagonal and upward moving lines, a smart part of the costume.

head size and wearing it high on her head rather than pulled down over the forehead, the ears, and the back of the head. Many women who realize that their hats are not smart or becoming do not know that the fault lies with the manner in which the hat is worn.

Another error sometimes made by the woman of middle age is that of selecting an elaborate, heavily trimmed hat, one that is a decorative addition to the costume rather than a part of it. Hats that are intricately cut and manipulated in an unusual and interesting manner, yet simple in effect, are more satisfactory.

The hat with a brim shading the eyes, concealing tired lines around them and giving a background to the face, which makes the features seem smaller and any irregularities less evident, is more becoming than either the brimless hat or the hat with a brim that turns abruptly away from the face.

A brim with a slanting, irregular line, higher at one side than at the other, is preferable to one that droops at both sides. Drooping brims emphasize the drooping, sagging lines in the middle-aged face.

The well designed beret can be especially smart and becoming to the middle-aged woman. It can supply sufficient width to form a background for the face without being so wide or heavy that it is unbecoming to the figure. It should have a diagonal line, higher at one side than the other, and should not be too round.

CHAPTER XXX

The Elderly Woman

*M*OST OF US KNOW at least one woman who has grown old so gracefully that she is affectionately termed a "dear old lady." Such women, who have had the grace and wisdom to acknowledge and thus minimize the ravages of time and to accent their remaining points of beauty, serve to indicate solutions for the costuming problems of women of declining years.

Hairdress and Make-Up

The older woman can remove years from her apparent age and add vitality and interest to her personality by doing her hair in a becoming manner and by wearing carefully selected and meticulously applied make-up.

Obvious make-up on an old woman is at once ridiculous and pathetic, but faint touches of rouge of soft, not vivid, red (usually red that is faintly red-violet) give an appearance of vigor and vitality. If color is used on the lips, it should be a soft, delicate salve or cream rouge that may be rubbed in to give a faint, shaded coloring. A definite outline on lips that have lost the firm contours of youth emphasizes the age of the wearer. A rather dark, natural, or flesh powder is usually best, as the skin of the older woman, in most instances, has darkened with age. Eye make-up is almost always a mistake for the older woman. An oil or petroleum jelly may be used to darken gray eyelashes and brows slightly.

The forehead, which usually grows higher as well as more wrinkled with advancing years, should be at least partially concealed by the hair. The ears also appear very large in proportion to the face. Few, if any, older women have lovely ears, yet the majority of older women, following the hairdress of their youth, comb the hair off the ears as well as off the forehead, revealing these unpleasing features.

Hair combed up exposing the ears, with or without the old-fashioned top-knot, betrays age; softly waved hair partially concealing ears, is ageless and becoming.

The hairdress, according to all rules of good structural design as well as the edicts of the present mode, should follow the contours of the head. The older woman too frequently advertises her advanced age by disregarding this principle.

One still sees older women who wear their hair drawn back from the forehead and ears in a coil that can be called only a knob placed directly on top of their heads. This hairdress appears on many older women of evident wealth who buy modish apparel in Fifth Avenue shops. Other older women wear aggressive bunches of hair at the back of their heads, usually too high up to permit hats to fit smoothly, and greatly altering the contours of the head. Flat, loose coils would be much more youthful and would give softer, more flattering lines.

A few older women, with alert, piquant faces, may success-fully wear skillfully cut hair, but straight, harsh lines and severe, boyish cuts should always be avoided. Short hair should be combed to give the appearance of a soft coiffure following the outlines of the head. Occasionally, an older woman looks well

Kinky or fussy hair seems to repeat the wrinkles and crepey skin, soft, loose waves are flattering.

The center parting reveals every irregularity of facial contour; a parting at one side is more easily worn.

with her hair in soft ringlets covering the entire head. Most older women, however, do well to avoid short hair, for unless the hair is naturally wavy or very scrupulously cared for, it is likely to become straight and stringy and to hang in wisps that make the older woman seem aged and forlorn.

The present generation has learned the flattering effect of soft waves so large and simple that they give a natural effect. The older woman should adopt these large, soft waves and avoid the crinkled, fuzzy hair which usually accompanied artificial curls in the days of her youth. Softly waved hair is usually much more becoming than straight hair, especially as it aids in making thin hair appear thicker.

The older woman will usually find that her hair may be most becomingly arranged if it is parted at the side, rather far to one side if the face is long and narrow, rather high on the side if it tends to be broad. A parting directly in the middle may be quaint and distinctive on the older woman who possesses very fine and regular features.

Hats

A few older women still cling to the old-fashioned "old lady's" bonnet, which, in former days, was considered the only correct head covering for the older woman. To some fragile,

Small, narrow brims and rigid crowns are too severe; wider brims cast flattering shadows.

delicate "old ladies," it is decidedly becoming; it gives them a charming, quaint air, for the lines of the bonnet with the strings and bow under the chin are softening and becoming. Larger or more vigorous older women may, however, be made to appear ridiculous.

The traditional old lady's hat, which has largely supplanted the bonnet, is less becoming than the bonnet. It is neither quaint nor modish. It assumes stiff lines, is usually placed too high on the head, and appears an addition to the silhouette rather than a part of it. Yet the average older woman replaces one such unbecoming and unmodish hat with one equally uninteresting.

The older woman frequently makes the mistake of wearing her hat too high on her head, a style reminiscent of the days

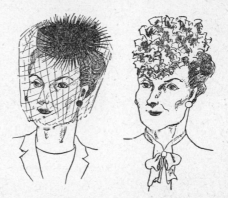

Small hats may appear like old ladies' bonnets when they are perched high on the head; a small turban of soft lines, partially covering the forehead, may be flattering.

when hats were perched on bandeaux. When fitted with a correct head size, the older woman often wears her hat far back from the forehead, revealing lines in the forehead and about the eyes. A hat worn low on the head, covering the forehead and the ears and shading the eyes, is becoming to the older woman. For this reason she may always wear her hats slightly lower than the mode dictates, thus attaining a maximum of concealment without appearing queer.

The small, close-fitting turban, failing to shadow the face or to give it background, reveals sunken cheeks and lined, wrinkled skins. Difficult as it is for even the younger woman, unless she has perfect features, many older women persist in wearing this style, which, particularly in stiff, severe textures and lines, gives little chance for charm in the older woman's appearance.

A small hat, but not too small to extend slightly beyond the widest part of the face, may be becoming to the older woman. A slight brim that shades the eyes and soft folds rather than severe, stiff lines and textures aid in obtaining the appearance of graceful, attractive old age.

The older woman who wears an exaggeratedly large hat with wide, drooping brim is too obviously trying to cling to youthful

Jaunty, youthful shapes contrast with the aged face; dignified and irregular lines are suitable and becoming.

styles—the reverse of growing old gracefully. She attracts undue attention to her aged skin and the drooping contours of her face.

If the too-large hat is bulky and overtrimmed, it further submerges the wearer. As large hats were more elaborately trimmed in her youth, the older woman who chooses a large hat frequently makes the mistake of selecting one that is virtually a flower garden or bedecked with many bows, rather than the smart simplicity considered good style today.

Round, youthful shapes appear at variance with aged faces. Jaunty, sport types of hats for women who are obviously long past the age that engages in sports, or of a generation that never indulged in them, are so unsuitable as to be almost ludicrous.

A moderately large brim may gracefully shadow the face and conceal the lines and aged texture of the skin. Lines that are neither too rounded and too curved nor too severely rigid and straight are most pleasing on the older woman. They give an appearance of simple dignity that makes the older woman appear at her best. It is possible every season to select smart hats that are becoming to the older woman, hats of simplicity and dignity.

The woman who has grown old gracefully, who neither denies nor emphasizes her years, usually selects with consideration of its color, texture, and lines, a smart, modish hat, one that makes her figure and her features appear to the best advantage. She allows neither the years nor the fashions to dictate to her.

Necklines

How frequently the older woman appears at her best when wearing a coat! How frequently many years seem to be added to her age when she removes it! The reason is usually the soft, flattering fur collar that covers the wrinkled and discolored skin of the neck and provides a softening frame for the face. An important consideration in selecting becoming costumes for the older woman is that of obtaining necklines with softening outlines similar to those produced by the fur collar.

Long-haired furs of soft, fluffy character are most becoming to the older woman, as they seem to fill in hollows of the neck and face and veil wrinkled, crepy skin. The coat collar that is swathed high about the neck covers the tip of the chin and hides its sagging lines as well as the wrinkled neck. A model that comes high at the back of the neck, fitting close at the sides, is more becoming than styles that are more open.

The scarf coat collar may be arranged so that it covers the throat. When it is made of a supple, pliable fabric that readily assumes soft folds, it may be as pleasing as the long-haired fur collar. The scarf or stole collar of stiff, bulky fabric or flat, sleek fur creates stiffer, less gracious lines.

The scarf collar or a draped scarf neckline is particularly de-

Straight, rigid lines in coat collars open to reveal the neck are less flattering than those of soft, long-haired furs covering neck and tip of chin.

sirable on dresses as, more than any other style, it hides the neck, at the same time giving soft, casual lines that do not call attention to the features they are intended to conceal.

Most elderly women should have a scarf to complement each costume. Many dresses that at first seem unbecoming to the older woman will prove actively becoming when a suitable scarf is used. With the evening dress a scarf of net tulle, of chiffon, or other diaphanous tissue will usually prove successful. Chiffon, georgette, crepe de Chine, and other soft silks are pleasing with afternoon dresses, while flat crepe, radium, and other soft but firm silks combine well with more tailored day-time dresses. The older woman should avoid bold and striking designs, particularly those of pronounced sport character. The scarf offers a splendid opportunity to place softening, becoming colors near the face.

The little formal jackets made in soft casual styles, of rich materials, are a most useful feature of the present mode, one that is particularly becoming to the older woman who finds the

The collarless neckline is extremely unbecoming; a soft scarf or collar partially concealing the neck is flattering. A dog collar only serves to center attention on the old neck.

low décollétage and sleeveless character of evening gowns un-becoming. Velvets, double chiffon, and other soft fabrics are more becoming than crisp or stiff silks, glittering sequins or paillettes, or hard metallic cloths. Those that fit high at the back and the sides of the neck are more pleasing than those that are cut low and wide at the neckline.

Dress necklines, if they are to be worn without a scarf, are most pleasing when they fit close at the sides and back. A small collar, fitting high at the back and sides, may end in a narrow, slender *V* at the front. The lines should be in accordance with the accepted mode, but modified so that they conceal the neck as much as possible.

The high, tight collar, either attached to the dress or worn as an accessory to a dress with another neckline, is in most instances extremely unbecoming to the older woman, as, instead of supplying a softening frame for the face, it reveals it relentlessly. The tight collar pushes up the loose folds of skin of the neck and chin and makes the chin line much poorer than it actually is. Tight ribbon bands or "dog collars" do not add to

Beads or other ornaments worn directly over the wrinkled throat call attention to it. Jewelry contrasting with the dress rather than the skin is more easily worn.

the attractiveness of most older women, proclaiming, as they do, that they are devices used to hide wrinkled necks, yet at the same time attracting attention to the neck that is only partially concealed.

Strings of beads, chains, and other necklaces worn on wrinkled, discolored necks attract attention to the aging skin. As it is impossible to wear a sufficient number of ornaments to cover the wrinkled skin (though some women literally attempt to do this), it is best to avoid them entirely after the neck becomes badly aged.

Fabric and Color

Soft, supple fabrics and dull textures are most becoming near the face and hence should be chosen by the woman whose skin is aged. Velvet, which is both soft and lustrous, is much more becoming than satin, which has a hard, shiny finish. Shiny-surfaced fabrics reflect light on the face, in this way emphasizing hollows, wrinkles, and discolorations of the skin.

When one remarks an older woman who appears years younger than her actual age, the colors she wears are usually instrumental in creating this youthful effect. She appears younger in contrast to other women of her age who wear black. A charming woman of seventy, who is usually believed to be about fifty years old, wears soft rose color almost exclusive of any other color. Even her coats and hats are of soft dull rose, of the shades known as bois de rose or ashes of roses. Occasionally she chooses an extremely rosy beige, not a yellow or a gray beige.

Color, too much or too vivid color, or its absence in drab, neutral tones, has even more influence on the appearance of older women than upon other persons. The subdued coloring, the faded and usually yellowed skin, hair that has turned gray or white, and eyes that have become less bright and frequently lighter with the years, are easily submerged by too-forceful, vivid colors. These vivid colors will likewise accentuate discolorations and blemishes in the skin. On the other hand, dull blacks tend to absorb color from surrounding surfaces, making the wearer paler and more colorless. Dull, neutral beiges and grays may be so similar to both the skin and the hair of the wearer that they make her appear monotonous and uninteresting. As too-vivid colors overpower the coloring of the older woman and too-neutral colors lessen her own coloring, the logical solution is that of not wearing definite colors, but those that have been partially softened or grayed; in fact, those colors about halfway between neutral and vivid intensities. When black or neutrals are worn, color or white should be used with them, counteracting the unbecoming effect.

Light colors are most becoming near the face. Grayed, somewhat neutralized colors (but not dead or totally neutral gray) are more becoming than intense colors, which may reflect unpleasing color on the face or make it appear more faded by contrast. Off-whites and light, softened, warm colors are usually preferable to dead white. They are frequently the most pleasing colors to use in scarfs or collars, serving as a transition between the color of the dress and that of the face. Light, grayed violets, blues, and greens are pleasing on many older women, but frequently more becoming when an off-white is used next to the face.

The older woman frequently finds that she may wear colors with her gray hair that were definitely unbecoming in her youth. Chapter XI gives more specific information relative to the problems of women with white and gray hair.

The Lines of the Mode

Women of advanced years too frequently make the mistake of dressing in utter disregard of the mode. This wearing of styles of days gone by serves to emphasize and exaggerate age. The "old-fashioned" costumes, so different from the styles our eyes are accustomed to see, seem awkward and graceless.

While definitely old-fashioned apparel should be avoided, a quaint note is frequently pleasing on an older woman, giving an appearance of having grown old gracefully, of having kept pace with the years, yet of retaining some of the demure charm of other days. For this reason the slender old lady of alert carriage frequently finds modern adaptations of period styles extremely becoming. Softer materials than the stiff taffeta the younger girl affects when she chooses these quaint designs are more becoming to age. Lace and chiffon or other soft silks may be given some of the feeling of *bouffant* frocks without being harsh in texture or outline. The bodices of these gowns should not be so tight fitting as they were in the older woman's youth. The tight-fitting bodice makes the garment appear old-fashioned rather than quaint and reveals the defects of figure and posture that the older woman is almost certain to possess.

Many older women still cling to old-fashioned, rigid corsets, which give them a too-definite waistline and a stiff, graceless figure. In more natural corsetry they may be much more becomingly costumed. Whether or not the corsetry is rigid, the dress should not fit closely, with a tight, natural waistline belt—a style that usually gives the figure awkward proportions.

The loose, shapeless dress, which apparently does not touch the figure at any structural point and hangs in loose, baggy lines from neck to hem, makes the old woman look characterless and uninteresting. If, as is frequently the case, the too-loose dress is combined with the too-long skirt, the wearer is almost entirely submerged under the unshapely bulk of her costume.

Garments that definitely fit the wearer, not too closely or too loosely, but which hang in soft, flowing lines related to the structure of the figure, give the older woman at once grace and dignity. While a tight bodice and belt should be avoided, garments that fit the shoulders and hips rather closely, not in a strained, but in a close line, are becoming. A girdle that is swathed in soft lines at the hips may give shape to a formless, too-loose dress and make the wearer appear more youthfully alert.

The older woman who selects daring lines that greatly change her silhouette, modes such as bustle drapes or flaring peplums, accents her age, since she no longer has the vivacity necessary to carry them successfully. Too elaborate models also submerge the wearer and betray that she has belonged to a generation that considered elaboration and profuse decoration desirable.

Much of the older woman's tendency to overdress, to wear too-elaborate detail, is due to a misunderstanding of the fact that the older woman of leisure may wear richer materials than were suitable to her youth. The very elegance of these materials, however, calls for simplicity of design, for restrained, but not severe lines. Soft, rich silks, supple, clinging velvets, brocades, and patterned materials of indefinite design and inconspicuous pattern may give true dignity to the older woman, may give her an appearance of sophistication, of having lived fully and grown old gracefully. Soft, flowing lines, soft drapes, and self-trimming are more pleasing on the older woman than either stiff severity, dashing lines, or profusion of detail.

Shoes

The woman of advanced years too frequently betrays her age by wearing footwear reminiscent of the days of her youth, by assuming modes neither becoming nor smart.

The unduly small foot in a too-small shoe is attempted only by the older woman. In her youth, a tiny shoe peeping from beneath long skirts was considered an ideal of feminine beauty. Too-small shoes increase the stiff, uncertain gait that so often results from added years. Wrinkles and other signs of age may also directly result from painful footwear. If the ankles have thickened with the years, the too-small shoe will make this defect more apparent. If the body has become heavy, the seemingly inadequate foundation makes it appear even larger and more ungainly by contrast.

Exaggeratedly high, slender heels tend to make walking difficult for a woman of any age. When the older woman, whose joints are stiffer and whose gait is somewhat uncertain, wears extremely high heels with a narrow, inadequate base, she is likely to appear weak and tottering. Her entire figure is thrown out of balance and her posture is made stooped and awkward.

The heel of moderate height, neither extremely low, as in sports and children's shoes, nor extremely high, is most graceful on the older woman. The heel should be somewhat curved —not straight, flat, and shapeless, nor curved so much that it has almost no base—for the older woman needs a foundation that is both firm and graceful.

CHAPTER XXXI

"She Wears Her Clothes Well"

A SMARTLY DRESSED, attractive businesswoman nearing forty was recently heard to remark, "It took me twenty years to learn to dress so that I am reasonably good looking. If I had only known when I was eighteen or twenty what I know now about clothes, my life would have been very different. No one ever thought I was a pretty girl, but when I look at my snapshots of school days, I learn that I was very badly dressed.

"Flappers were in fashion then, and I wore my hair in wild disorder—wind-blown bobs, I remember, they were called. My clothes were designed to be cute—on other girls, but they made me look only awkward. Yet, as I remember it, I was never bad looking. I had large eyes, a clear skin, and dark-brown hair with a slight, natural wave. My weight was normal, and my height average or very slightly less.

"My figure has not improved with the years—quite the contrary—yet I seem to have a much better figure now than I had twenty years ago, because I have learned what clothes are becoming to me. I make the most of my natural wave now, though, of course, if I didn't have a natural wave I would get a good permanent or wear my hair straight and simple.

"Since my complexion is still good I use little make-up other than lipstick, carefully applied, and a slight touch of mascara to emphasize my eyes, which are still my best feature. As a result I am considered a good-looking woman, and I look young enough so that my age is never considered a detriment by my employers; yet I have known other women who, before they reached forty, found that they looked too old to compete with the younger women in their line of work.

"But," she concluded, "if I'd only known twenty years ago what I know now about clothes, I'd have had much more fun as a young girl and probably much more attractive chances at matrimony; and maybe I would not be an efficient business-woman thinking about competing with the younger generation of businesswomen."

It is true that a great many women have, by the time they have passed their first youth, learned by the trial-and-error method what to wear and what not to wear. There are also a great many women whose choice of apparel seems to become worse year after year. Very often those of the latter group were pretty, slender girls who looked well in anything.

Sometimes these women who dress less attractively each year make the mistake of continuing to wear clothes that look well in the shop window or on the woman with good coloring and slender figure. Other women realize that their apparel does not enhance their appearance, but they are uncertain of just how to obtain clothes that really flatter them. Some of them feel rather helplessly that their only beauty is about gone and that nothing can make them look as they wish to look. Others feel that it takes unlimited time and money to achieve the attractive appearance for which they long.

Granted it takes thought and some time to plan becoming

costumes, and granted also that money is always helpful, many women could look far better than they do and spend much less money if every item of apparel was purchased in accordance with a carefully conceived plan.

The first thing a woman should do in making her costume plan is analyze her face and figure, basing the analysis on the information in this book. She will then know, in a general way, which lines and colors are most likely to be becoming.

Her own clothes' closet will give her definite and concrete help in avoiding future mistakes and in making only wise selections in the future. Her clothes may be divided into three groups—those that she really enjoys wearing; those that are "all right," or almost "all right"; and those that she thoroughly detests.

Starting with the last and hated group, each costume should be studied before a mirror. They should be examined carefully from the front view, profile view, and the rear reflection. What makes them unbecoming? Is it because the fullness comes at just the wrong place in the blouse and so makes the figure look too "busty?" Is it because there is too much material or trimming on the sleeves that the shoulders seem too broad? Do these sleeves add bulk at the waist or hipline? Perhaps the lines of the dress are basically good, but the dress is too tight, in which case the owner may learn not only that she must cease buying dresses that are too small for her, but also that a few weeks of careful dieting might make even her detested dresses becoming.

Next, the unexciting, but not definitely unbecoming clothes should be tried on. What do they lack? Very frequently they need only an accent which will give them distinction and which will call attention to the wearer's best features. Well-chosen accessories that add accents of becoming colors may redeem these borderline clothes. Almost always, their general cut and design is such that the wearer's worst features are hidden or minimized, otherwise these garments would not have been placed in the middle or "all right" class.

When the clothes that are hated and those to which the owner is indifferent have been critically studied, it should be a joy to analyze the clothes that have proved becoming and which she likes to wear. But even this group must be analyzed ruthlessly. Perhaps she enjoys wearing a certain coat because it has pockets into which she can put her hands. Possibly after she sees herself walking toward a mirror with her hands in her pockets she will sew up the pockets and thereby avoid the slouched, hunched-over appearance which walking with the hands in the pockets gives to most women. Then, too, she may enjoy wearing a dress because she thinks the color is flattering or because the color is a favorite; yet the actual dress itself may be unbecoming either because of its lines, or because the coloring is not actually flattering.

As a general rule, however, the clothes one enjoys wearing, especially if one enjoys wearing them after they cease to be new, are becoming. Comments of friends and family also give a clue to true becomingness. The majority of the clothes one enjoys wearing are garments that have won renewed admiration even after repeated wearings. From these clothes one can learn a great deal.

Each individual's becoming clothes probably have certain traits in common. If her face is broad, the individual will probably find that all of her becoming clothes have *V*-necklines. If her face is too thin she is likely to find that her becoming clothes all have softly rounded necklines. If the hips are large, one will doubtless find that none of the becoming clothes are tightly belted or swathed at the hips. Probably many features will confirm the information in this book; some may seem contradictory. But if, after careful study, one finds lines and devices becoming or unbecoming, they should be adopted whether or not the book recommends them.

As seasons change and new fashions come into being, one should look for similar lines or textures or colors in the new styles. Always consider possible changes in face and figure. If one is gaining weight or losing weight, or if the face is tired and haggard today and fresh and rested tomorrow, one may be able to wear many styles in the future which are not becoming today, or vice versa. If among your favored garments you have some clothes that you have been wearing for several years, not because of necessity, but because you loved them, be sure that they are still becoming and not simply profiting by their past becomingness.

If you have a dress or a hat or a coat that you have found becoming in the past, try to determine whether it is the line, the texture, or the color which makes it flattering. If you think it is the line, try to create a similar line in other colors, watching carefully to see if it really is becoming in other colors. A hat that is extremely flattering in blue or green or black might be very unbecoming in bright red or in brown. Likewise, a coat that is successful in black might be a mistake in beige or in brown.

If you have a good dressmaker or are one yourself, it may be very wise to have your most becoming dresses copied exactly or copied with slight modifications which bring them up to date in fashion. It may also be wise to use the same pattern for several dresses if the cut and lines of the first one have been un-usually successful.

In doing this do not fail to consider the effect of texture on the lines of the dress. You are almost sure to be disappointed if you have copied, in heavy or stiff fabric, lines that were perfect in a soft, non-bulky fabric.

The purpose of this book is to train the critical eye in the intelligent choosing of wearing apparel. Having chosen becoming and suitable garments, one must, in order to wear them successfully, adjust them so carefully that one does not remain conscious of them. It is the unself-consciousness born of self-confidence that gives true poise and beauty.

The more consideration one gives to clothes before wearing them and while putting them on, the less thought need be given them while they are being worn. Clothes should be fitted so that they will not restrict movements of the wearer, yet will fit the body closely enough to remain in place and to reveal its most graceful contours. While ideally one should stand erect and thus make figure and clothes appear to the best advantage, one should not stand erect while being fitted unless very sure to do so while the clothes are being worn. If an erect body, with head up and shoulders back in a natural position, trunk elongated and spine straight, has not become habitual through exercise, the conscious effort to hold the body in this position in order to make the clothing fit will lead only to awkwardness and self-consciousness.

Clothing should be worn pulled up at the shoulders so that it fits well about the neck and so that the sleeve is of the proper length. A well-fitting coat may lose its lines unless it is care-fully put on, but it is not a well-fitting coat unless it retains these

313

lines without effort to the wearer after it has once been carefully adjusted. The hands should be put into the sleeves in such a manner that the seams are straight and untwisted and the cuff in the position most becoming to the hand. Underarm seams should fall straight, not twist either forward or backward. In a well-fitted, carefully adjusted dress, they should remain in this position during normal movements.

Readjustments of clothing should be avoided, unless necessitated by wind or body movement. Many a woman destroys the effectiveness of her clothes as well as her appearance of poise by constant "fussing" with her apparel. She needlessly changes the angle at which her hat is worn, the amount of hair that is showing, the color in her cheeks, or various lines in her costume. If this is accomplished without the aid of a mirror or with a small mirror that shows only a portion of the face and figure, the result is likely to be less pleasing than the original effect.

One can best forget one's clothes while wearing them if each costume has been studied carefully before it is worn. A brief but careful analysis before a mirror will reveal disarrangements that are likely to occur when the figure is in motion and will indicate the correct position. It is particularly necessary to learn to put on hats and coats guided by a sense of "feel," since one must often adjust them in theaters or elsewhere where mirrors are not available or cannot be inconspicuously employed.

The figure should be studied in motion. As we all appear at our best before a mirror, since we instinctively stand straighter and move more gracefully, the figure should be studied in natural motion. Snapshots taken when the individual is unaware will do much to reveal faults of carriage and proportion. Home movies, where available, might also be used for the same analysis. A triple mirror, or mirrors arranged on opposite walls so that they show front and back views, are especially helpful. A critical eye is needed only for analysis of other persons. Few persons in this age are willing to undergo the discipline required to achieve good carriage. Yet many of us could profitably practice walking along a straight line without bending the knees, perhaps even carrying a book balanced on the head, until our muscles acquire the feeling of graceful rhythmic movement.

The person with a critical eye has become conscious of defects. This book is largely concerned with such defects as can be hidden in the course of emphasizing good points. The trained critic will inevitably become sensitive to defects owing to carelessness and to lines and blemishes that can be corrected when once their existence is recognized.

A person who has been using the same rouge daily does not observe that it is not the actual hue of the natural color. Likewise she may tend to put on more rouge day by day, the gradual increase in color blinding her to the fact that too much coloring carelessly applied does not appear either attractive or natural to others. Hair and complexion can often be markedly improved by care. Overweight, likewise, can be overcome by one who recognizes it to a degree that reconciles her to consistent abstinence. Garments themselves may be meticulously cared for. All such measures add to the self-confidence at the basis of wearing one's clothes well.

The purpose of this book is to train the critical eye. But, after all, it is the eye, not the book, that is the final judge of becomingness and suitability. It is well to scrutinize carefully any color or design that experience indicates is not pleasing for your figure, coloring, and personality. But please do not discard anything that your eye tells you is good in favor of something that the book says ought to be good. And please do not judge others as unskillful dressers merely because they affect costumes the book *seems* to condemn for them.

Have confidence in your own eye!

Index

A

Abdomen, minimizing enlarged, 163-175
  beltline, 170
  boleros, 166-167
  cut of bodice, 167-170
  decorative details over, 170-171
  foundation garments, 163-164
  hemline, 170
  jackets, 166-167
  maternity wear, 171-175 (see also Maternity wear)
  V-line at waist, 171
  weight of dress, 164-165
Accent, striking, 223
Accessories:
  color of, 116
  for short, slender woman, 230-231
  for teen-age miss, 263, 266
Acid rinse, hair, 69-70
Age:
  adaptation to, 104-110, 251-316
  advanced, apparel for, 293-307
  emphasis, apt and inapt, 264-268
Analogous colors, 114
Analysis:
  color and line, 77
  individual coloring, 75-81 (see also Individual coloring: analysis)
  of face, 310
  of figure, 127-131, 310
Angularity, 20, 46, 49, 206-213
Ankles, beautifying, 197-198, 200, 201, 202

A

Arms:
  bare, 138, 139, 193
  capes or scarfs concealing, 193
  large upper, 191-196 (see also Large upper arm)
  loose bodice, 192-193
  shape of, 130
Armscye:
  carefully placed, 167, 183-184
  for large upper arm, 191-192
  small, 181
Ascot tie, 31-32
Asymmetric trimming, hats, 39-40
Athletic figure, heavy fabrics for, 148
Awkwardness, eliminating child's, 259-260

B

Baby clothes, 251-252
Back, masses at, 186
Bangs on forehead, 8
Bare arms, 138, 139, 193
Beads, 230-231, 302
  on dress fronts, 167
  size of, 18-20
  short strands of, 19
Beauty parlor, 6
Beige, in wardrobe, 94, 120
Belt, 158, 160
  contrasting, 212
  for maternity wear, 173, 175
  for teen-age miss, 266
  garter, 257
  inner, 166
  low, 177, 178

Belt (*Cont.*)
  self-color, 239
  shoulder-support, 256
  wide contrasting, 229
Beltline, 170
  curved, 175
Beret, 291, 292
Black, 92, 93, 99, 102-103, 112
  in wardrobe, 64, 117-118
Blonde (*see also* Cool coloring):
  colorful, 86-87
  color for, 71
  drab, 82-86
  eye make-up for, 72-73
  neutral, 82-86
  pale, 82-86
  vivid, 86-87
Blouse (*see also* Bodice):
  contrasted with skirt, 228-229
  equal length of skirt and, 226, 228
  large, loose, 181
  length of, 226-228
  light-colored, 181-182
  peasant-style, 174-175, 183
Bloused line, 158-159, 169-170
Blue-black hair, 73, 87
Blue eyes, 99-103
Blues:
  analysis of, 75-76
  navy, 117, 118-119
Bluing, 70
Bluish-gray apparel, 110, 120
Bobbed hair:
  for elderly women, 295
  long, 6
  pageboy, 9
Bodice (*see also* Blouse):
  bloused, 158-159, 192-193
  cut of, 167-170
  full, 158, 174-175, 183
  joining of skirt and, 159-160
  loose, large upper arm, 192-193
  tight-fitting, 181

Body, proportion of head to, 127-128
Bolero jacket, 140, 141, 165, 166-167
Bows, 185
  at neckline, 31
  concealing round shoulders, 185
  large, heavy, 231
  on shoes, 201
  over abdomen, 169
Boyish note, 281
Bracelets, 230-231
Brassière, 129-130, 130-131, 163-164
  uplift, 176
Brimless hats, 39
Brimmed hats, 40-44, 47, 48, 54-55
Broad face (*see* Wide face)
Broken lines, 161
Brooches, 16-17
Brown, in wardrobe, 117, 119-120
Brown eyes, colors for, 97-99
Brown hair, 70-72, 79, 98-103
Brunette, 82 (*see also* Warm coloring):
  colors for, 87-95
  Latin type, 94-95
  vivid, colors for, 93
Brush, lipstick, 60
Brushing hair, 6, 69
Buckles, 170
  on shoes, 201
Bulky fabrics, 215-217
Businesswoman, smartly dressed, 308-316
Bust, modifying large, 176-182
Bustles, 207
Bustline, 129

C

Calves, 131
Campus costumes, 272-274
Capes, 139, 141
  circular, 188
  collars, 139, 141, 193
  for tall, slender woman, 212-213

Capes (*Cont.*)
  large upper arm, 193-194
  long, pointed, 188-189
Care of clothing, 262
Carriage (*see* Posture)
Center line, narrow, 132, 133
Center panel, 133, 134
Center part, hair, 7-8
Character, line related to, 244-247
Cheeks:
  color in, 61
  hair curved over, 11, 12
  hue of, determining, 77
Childish type, junior, 269
Children's clothes, 251-260
  growing girl's, 255-259
  individualized infants', 251
    colors, 251-252
    designs, 252
  little girls', 252-255
    color, 254
    ensemble idea, 254-255
    like mother's, 253-254
Chin:
  double, 25
  protruding, 52-53
  receding, 51-52
Choker necklace, 18-19, 28
Circular cape, 188
Clinging fabrics, 149, 195
Clips, 16-17
Close hairdress, 9-10
Clothing:
  care of, 262
  readjustment of, 314
  collars, 30-36 (*see also* Collars: coat)
  colors, 118, 119, 120, 121
  flaring, 141
  for tall, thin woman, 210
  full-length, 140, 141
  fur, 119-120
  lapels, 32-34

Clothing (*Cont.*)
  long, 229
  short, 141
  three-quarter length, 140-141
Coiffure:
  short, slender woman, 230
  unnatural, 6
Collars:
  and face, 25
  and figure, 139-141
  at back, 186
  cape, 139, 141, 193
  coat:
    band or contrasting lapels, 32
    fur, large, 34-36
    lapels, 33-34
    open at throat, 30-31
    pointed, 33
    scarfs or tab ends, 31-32
  contrasting, 139
  "dog," 302
  fur, 30, 32
    large, 34-36
  high, close, 25, 26
  loose, soft, 177, 179
  points on, 33-34
  round, 26-27, 28, 35
  scarf, 193, 300
  shawl, 35-36
  tie, 31-32
  to conceal defect, 187
  tuxedo, 35
Collarless neckline, 187
  for elderly women, 301
College costumes, 272-274
Color:
  analogous, 114
  analytical selection of, 75-81
  and texture of hair, 79-80
  basis for wardrobe selection, 117-121
  becoming, 81
  becomingness, devices that change, 63-66

Color (*Cont.*)
black, 64, 92, 93, 99, 102-103, 117-118
bright, 153
changed by hats, 66
classification of, 81
combinations (*see* Combinations of color)
contrast, 64-65, 111-112, 115-116
cool (*see* Cool coloring, woman with; Cool colors)
dark, 152-153
determined by hue of skin, 82
diverse, 115-116
dull, 153-154
eyes and, 69, 72-74
flattering, 66-68
for blonde, 71 (*see also* Blonde)
colorful, 86-87
brown eyes, 97-99
brown hair, 70-72, 79, 98-103
for brunette, 87-95
for daytime, 76
for elderly woman, 303-304
for fair skin, 97-103
for feminine type, 279
for gray or white hair, 104-110
for growing girl, 259-260
for infants' clothing, 251-252
for intermediate type, 96-103 (*see also* Intermediate type)
for red-haired type, 70, 71, 88, 89-93
for small girls' clothing, 254
for tall, heavy woman, 217-218
for young woman, 277-278
hair and, 69-72
harmonious combinations, 111-121 (*see* Combinations of color)
high value, 61-62
in cheeks, emphasizing, 61
in children's clothes, 251-252, 254
in prints, 152

Color (*Cont.*)
intensity, 113
light value, 63-64
low value, 61-62
neutral, 87, 92-93
for pale blonde, 85
neutralized, 94
of cheeks, 61
of eyes, altered by make-up, 72-73
of gloves, 139
of handbags, 231
of hats, 66
of hosiery, 197-199
opposite, accents of, 115-116
readings, rating scale for, 76-77, 78-79
related, 114
relating, to skin, 56-68
silhouette, size, affected by, 144-154
skin:
powder should match, 57-58
rouge should match, 58-59
textures change effect of, 65-66
treatment of, 3
unbecoming, 81
décolletage softens, 64
vivid, for white hair, 107-110
vivid hues, 62
warm, 88-95 (*see also* Warm coloring, woman with; Warm colors)
wearable, 81
Coloring:
cool, colors becoming to, 82-87 (*see* Cool coloring)
individual, analysis of, 75-81 (*see also* Individual coloring: analysis)
warm, 82, 87-95 (*see* Warm coloring, woman with)
Combinations of color, 111-121
analogous colors, 114

Combinations of color (*Cont.*)
  basis for wardrobe selection, 117-121
  color interest, 111-113
  hues:
    contrast of, 111-112
    matching, 113-114
  intensity, contrast of, 113
  related colors, 114
  value, contrast of, 112-113
Comfort, dress, 262-263
Complexion, 56-57
  poor, color for, 66-67
Confidence in self, 316
Contours, loose folds and, 180-182
Contrasts:
  costume, hosiery, footwear, 197-199
  cuffs, 139
  for tall, slender woman, 212
  hues, 111-112
    decided, 115-116
  intensity, 113
  maternity wear, 173
  skirt and blouse, 228-229
  value, 112-113
Cool coloring, woman with:
  color accent needed, 82-86
  colors becoming to, 82-87
Cool colors:
  combined with warm, 115
  flatter all figures, 154
Corset, 164, 176, 305
Costume:
  campus, 272-274
  character of, 244
  confusing, 126
  hosiery and footwear contrasts, 197-199
  well-designed, 126
Costume jewelry, 16-24
  color in, 65, 116
  for maternity wear, 171-172
Crowns of hats, 43, 44

Cuffs:
  contrasting, 139
  heavy, 138
Curls, 11
  elderly women, 295
  stiff, sculptured, 14, 15
Curved lines, 160, 245

D

Dark colors, 152-153
Dark eyes, 97-99
Dark skin, color for, 63
Décolleté gown, 64
Decorative details:
  dark, 64
  over abdomen, 170-171
Defects of face, correcting, 46-55, 315
  angular lines, 49
  double chin, 53-54
  drooping mouth, 47
  glasses, 54-55
  haggard lines, 47
  irregular features, 47, 49
  large nose, 50-51
  protruding chin, 52-53
  receding chin, 51-52
  round face, 48
  turned-up nose, 49-50
  unpleasing lines, 48
Demure styles, 223, 225
Design:
  fabric:
    small, 229
    tall, heavy woman, 218-220
  infants' clothing, 252
  small girls' clothing, 252-253
Details:
  at back of neck, 185
  feminine, 279-280
  fine, dainty, soft, 224
  for short, heavy woman, 235-236
  for short, slender woman, 231
Diagonal lines, 134, 135-137, 246-247

Diaphragm, minimizing enlarged, 163-175 (*see also* Abdomen, minimizing enlarged)
Diet, gray hair and, 285
Dignity, 245-246
Dirndl skirt, 174-175
Distinction, simplicity and, 283-285
"Dog" collars, 302
Doll's hat, 44
Double chin, 25, 53-54
Drab blonde, 82-86
Draped hip, 158, 159
Draped neckline, 227
Draperies, 159
  loose, floating, 149
Dress:
  conservative, 224
  high-waisted, 206
  long-waisted, 206-207
  loose, shapeless, 305
  one-piece, 165, 166
  sleeveless, 138, 139
  two-piece, 165-166
  weight of, 164-166
Dressmaker, 312
  suits, 216
Drooping brims, hats, 41-43
Dull textures, 144-146
Dyed hair, 70, 285-286

E

Earrings, 21-24
Ears:
  hairdress revealing, 8, 9, 11, 14, 15
  hair revealing tips of, 12
  hats revealing, 43
Elderly woman, 293-307
  fabric, 303-304
  footwear, 306-307
  furs, 299-300
  hairdress, 293-296
  hats, 296-299
  lines of the mode, 304-306

Elderly woman (*Cont.*)
  make-up, 293-296
  necklines, 299-302
Energetic woman, 280-281
Ensemble idea, child's clothing, 254-255
Evening dress, teen-age miss, 264-265, 266
Eyebrow line, hats, 40
Eyeglasses, 54-55, 72
Eyelashes, darkening, 72-73
Eye pencil, 73
Eyes:
  accented by matching hue, 73
  blue, 99-103
  brown, 97-99
  circles under, 63
  color and, 69, 72-74
  colored eye shadow, 73
  gray, 73-74, 99-103
  green, 99-103
  hazel, 74
  hues of, 80
  intensifying color of, 74
  make-up and, 72-73
Eye shadow, 73

F

Fabrics:
  and color, 65-66
  bulky, 215-217
  clinging, 149, 195
  contrasting, 193-194
  design in, 218-220, 229 (*see also* Design)
  for elderly woman, 303-304
  for feminine type, 279
  for middle-aged woman, 284-285
  for short, heavy woman, 234
  for tall, heavy woman, 214-220
    color, 217-218
    design, 218-219
    texture, 214-217

Fabrics (*Cont.*)
  heavy, bulky, 147-148
  in perpendicular feeling, 194-195
  knitted, 149
  large upper arm, 194-196
  lightweight, 147-148, 195-196
  opaque, 147, 148
  printed, 150-152
  shiny surfaced, 214-215
  soft, 147, 148
  stiff, 145, 146, 195
  thin, 147, 148
  transparent, 147-150, 195-196, 217
Face:
  analysis of, 310
  broad, 4 (*see also* Wide face)
  brooches, clips, pins and, 16-17
  center of interest, 3
  ·changed by rouge placement, 59-60
  color contrast near, 64-65
  color of, devices that affect, 61-63
  dark color value near, 64
  defects, hats and, 40 (*see also* Defects of face, correcting)
  hairdress and, 5-15
  light color values near, 63-64
  minimizing yellow in, 62-63
  narrow (*see* Narrow face)
  necklaces and contour of, 18-20
  necklines and, 25-36
  ornaments and contour of, 16-24
  outlines of, and hats, 38-44
  oval, 3-4
  shadows in, 63
  small, hats, 43
  square, 4
  veils over, 45-46
  wide (*see* Wide face)
Fads, 126
Fair skin, color for, 97-103
Fall apparel, 119
Fashions:
  for elderly women, 304-306

Fashions (*Cont.*)
  in hairdress, 6-7
  new, 312
  quaint, demure, 223, 225
Fat, excess, 163-164
Features:
  irregular (*see* Irregular features)
  size of, and hairdress, 12-14
Feet, 131
  hemline and grace of, 205
  slenderizing, 199-200
Feminine personality, 278-280
Figure:
  critical analysis of, 127-131
  details, 138-143
  diagonal lines, 135-137
  height of, 127-128
  hemline and, 205
  horizontal line, 137-138
  optical illusions affecting, 127-143
  perpendicular lines, 131-135
  posture, 128-129
  proportion of:
    head to body, 127-128
    shoulders, bustline, hips, 129-130
  studied in motion, 314-316
  teen-age miss, 265-266, 267
  weight, 128
Fingernails, 67-68
Flappers, 308
Flower, 25, 185
  at neckline, 29
  hats, 39
Footwear, 197-205 (*see also* Shoes):
  contrasts to avoid, 197-199
  elderly woman, 306-307
  short, heavy woman, 241-243
  short, slender woman, 232
  tall, heavy woman, 221-222
Forceful woman, 280-281
Forehead:
  bangs on, 8
  hair low on, 8

Forehead (*Cont.*)
  hair off, 8
  showing, hats, 42, 49, 51, 52, 54
Foundation garments, 163-164, 257, 261
  maternity wear, 174
  one-piece, 164
Freedom in dress, 262-263
Frills, 29
Full skirts, 156, 157, 174-175
Fur, 66
  as sleeve trimming, 139
  coats, 119-120
  color of, 72
  facings, 181-182
  for elderly woman, 299-300
  for short, heavy woman, 234-235
  for tall, heavy woman, 216-217
  scarfs, 30, 231-232

G

Garter belts, 257
Gilet effects, 227
Girdle, 159, 171, 209
Girls' clothing:
  growing girl, 255-260 (*see also* Growing girl)
  small girl, 252-255
  teen-age miss, 261-274 (*see also* Teen-age miss)
Glasses:
  eye make-up and, 72
  hats and, 54-55
Gloves, of contrasting color, 139
Golden hair, 86
Gray:
  colors, 105-107, 110
  in wardrobe, 120
Grayed colors, 94, 105, 106
Gray eyes, 73-74, 99-103
Gray hair, 70, 71
  and diet, 285
  colors for, 104-110

Green, dark, in wardrobe, 120-121
Green eyes, 99-103
Growing girl:
  color for, 259-260
  constriction, 255-256
  distribution of weight, 256-257
  garments that remain adjusted, 257
  hosiery, 256
  hygiene requirements, 255-258
  posture, 255-256
  roomy garments, 258
  tight clothing, 255-256
  underclothing, 256
  warmth and weight, 258-259

H

Hair:
  and round shoulders, 190
  blue-black, 73, 87
  blonde, 82-87
  bobbed, 7, 295
  brown, 70
  care of, 69-70
  center part, 7-8
  changing color, 70
  color and, 69-72
  covering neck, 9
  curved over cheeks, 11, 12
  cut, 7, 295
  enhancing color of, 70-71
  golden, 86
  gray, 71
    colors for, 104-110
  knot of, 13
  long, 288
  low on forehead, 8
  luster of, 69-70
  mixed dark and gray, 105
  red, 70, 71, 88, 89-93
  off forehead, 8, 10-12, 14
  revealing tips of ears, 12
  shampooing, 69-70
  shingled, 7, 295

Hair (*Cont.*)
  texture of, color and, 79-80
  value contrasts emphasize, 71
  waves, and size of features, 13-15
  white, colors for, 104-110
  yellow, 70-71, 97-98
Hairdress:
  and size of features, 12-13
  back of head, 14
  close, 9-10, 12, 13
  curls, 11, 14, 15, 295
  coronet braids, 11
  ears exposed, 8-9, 11, 12, 14, 15
  exaggerated, 12
  for elderly woman, 293-296
  for middle-aged woman, 6-7, 285-289
  for narrow face, 7-10
  for short, slender woman, 230
  for teen-age miss, 263
  for wide face, 10-12
  for young women, 6
  loose, 11, 12, 13, 15
  pompadour, 7, 11
  profile, 13, 14
  shapes face, 5-15
  simple, 5, 13, 15
  to avoid, 4-6
  to widen face, 7-10
Hairdressers, 6
Hairline, concealing, 8
Handbag, 231
Hands, grooming of, 67
Harmonies, color, 111-121 (*see also* Combinations of color)
Hats:
  amusing, 37-38, 44
  and shoulder defects, 189-190
  brimless, 39
  brims, 40-44
    and glasses, 54-55
    drooping, 41-43
    turned up, 42

Hats (*Cont.*)
  coloring changed by, 66
  contrast, to emphasize features, 48
  correct facial defects, 46
  crowns, 43, 44
  dark, 64
  double chin, 53-54
  drooping brimmed, 142-143
  eyebrow line, 40
  facial contour and, 37-55
  flower, 39
  forehead showing, 42, 49, 51, 52, 54
  for elderly women, 296-299
  for middle-aged woman, 289-292
  for short, heavy woman, 240-241
  for short, slender woman, 230
  for tall, heavy woman, 220-221
  for tall, slender woman, 212-213
  for teen-age miss, 263
  for wearers of glasses, 54-55
  importance of, 37
  irregular lines, 40-41
  large nose, 50-51
  lines following natural contours, 43-44
  lines of, and figure, 141-143
  ludicrous, 37-38, 44
  off-the-face, 39, 42, 49, 51, 52, 54, 142-143
  protruding chin, 52-53
  receding chin, 51-52
  repetition, to emphasize lines, 47
  sailor, 40, 41
  slanting-brimmed, 142-143
  small, close-fitting, 38-39, 44, 45
  stiff, 45-46
  tiny, 37-38
  transitional lines, 48-49
  tricorne, 50
  trimming, asymmetric, 39-40
  turbans (*see* Turban)
  turned-up nose, 49-50
  veils on, 45-46

Hats (*Cont.*)
  wide-brimmed, 142-143
  with brims, 40
Hazel eyes, 74
Head, proportion of, to body, 127-128
Health, clothing and, 255-259
Heavy fabrics, 147-148
Heavy woman:
  and high heels, 203-204
  perpendicular lines for, 131-135
  prints for, 150-152
  short (*see* Short, heavy woman)
  tall (*see* Tall, heavy woman)
Heels:
  high, 203-204
  low, flat, 204
Hemline, 170
  effect of, on grace, 205
Henna, 70
High-heeled shoe, 203-204
High-waisted dress, 206
Hipline:
  closely fitted, flare below, 157
  V-seaming at, 136, 137
Hips, 129-130
  concealing large, 155-162
  proportion of shoulders and bust-
    line to, 129-130
  skirt fullness to conceal, 156
  swathed, 158, 159
Horizontal lines, 137-138, 227
  and large bust, 178
  and large hips, 156-158, 159-161
  combined with perpendicular lines,
    225
  tall, thin woman, 210
Hose supporters, 257
Hosiery:
  costume and footwear contrasts,
    197-199
  for growing girl, 256
  shades of, 197-199
  sport, 205

Hues:
  background and foreground, 75
  colors and skin, 82
  contrast of, 111-112
    decided, 115-116
  eyes, 80
  few, preferable to many, 81
  in rating scale, 76, 78-79
  lips, cheeks, 77
  matching, 113-114
  of skin, color and, 82

I

Individual coloring, analysis:
  cautions, 80
  eyes, 80
  rating scale, 76-77, 78-79
  skin tones, 77, 79
  texture of hair and, 79-80
Individuality, accenting, 275-278
Individualized infants' clothing, 251-
    252
Infants' clothing, 251-252
Instep, 200
Intensity, contrast of, 113
Intermediate type:
  brown hair; gray, green, blue eyes;
    fair skin, 99-103
  brown hair, eyes; skin medium or
    fair, 98-99
  colors for, 96-103
  yellow hair, cool skin, brown eyes,
    97-98
Irregular features:
  hairdress and, 15
  hats and, 49
  necklines and, 29-30
Irregular lines, hats, 40-41

J

Jabot, 167-169
  for maternity wear, 174
  long, draped, 177-179, 180

Jacket:
  bolero, 140, 141, 165, 166-167
  ending above hips, 228
  fingertip, 210, 228
  flaring, for maternity wear, 172
  formal, 301
  for tall, thin woman, 210, 211
  hip-length, 140, 141, 210
  minimizing enlarged diaphragm,
    166-167
  separate, 193
  teen-age miss, 262, 263
  types of, 166-167
  worn open or close, 168
  wrist-length, 210
Jewelry:
  color in, 65, 116
  costume, 16-24
  for elderly women, 302
  for middle-aged woman, 283
Jumpers, 262-263
Junior types, 268-272
  childish, 269
  mature, 270-271
  overgrown, 270
  overweight, 271-272
  petite, 269
  rotund, 271-272
  short, rotund, 271-272
  solid, overweight, 271
  sophisticated, 269
  tall, overgrown, 270
  tall, slender, youthful, 269-270
  well-developed, 270-271
  youthful, 269-270

K

Kimono sleeves, 183, 184
Knitted fabrics, 149, 263

L

Lace, 283
Lapels, on coats, 32-34

Large upper arm, 191-196
  cape or scarf, 193-194
  fabrics for, 194-196
  loose bodice, 192-193
  loose sleeve, 191-192
Latin type brunette, 94-95
Legs, 131, 201
Lemon rinse, 70
Lightweight fabrics, 147-148, 195-196
Lines:
  curved, 160, 245
  daring, 306
  diagonal, 134, 135-137, 246-247
  irregular, hats, 40-41
  long, flowing, 226
  of the mode, elderly women, 304-
    306
  pointed, 246-247 (see also V-lines)
  radiating, 171
  related to mood and character, 244-
    247
  straight, 245-246
Lips, hue of determining, 77
Lipstick, mouth changed by, 60-61
Loose folds, 180-182
Low neckline, 26, 27, 28, 30

M

Make-up:
  eye, 72-73
  for elderly woman, 293-296
  lipstick, 60-61
  nail polish, 67
  powder, 57-58
  relation to skin, 57-61
  rouge, 58-60
Mannish effect, 281
Mascara, 72
Mass at back of neck, 185-186
Matching hues, 113-114
Maternity wear, 171-175
  belt, 173, 175
  contrasts of color and texture, 173

Maternity wear (*Cont.*)
flaring jacket, slim skirt, 172
foundation garments, 174
jabots and revers, 174
larger sizes for, 175
loose garments, 173
low fullness, 174
plain surfaces, 173
wrapover models, 172-173
Mature girl, 270-271
Maturity, 245-246
Middle-aged woman, 282-292
conservative costume, 282
dyed hair, 285-286
hairdress, 6-7, 285-289
hats, 43, 289-292
jewelry, 283
personalities of, 282, 284
Miniature hat, 44
Moccasins, 204
Mode, 126
lines of, for elderly women, 304-306
Mood, line related to, 244-247
Motion study, figure, 314-316
Mouth, changed by lipstick, 60-61
Muscles, sagging, 163

N

Nail polish, colored, 67
Narrow center line, 132, 133
Narrow face:
collars and, 30-36
earrings and, 21-24
hairdress for, 7-10
necklaces that broaden, 18-19
necklines that widen, 25-27
Navy blue, in wardrobe, 117, 118-119
Neck:
close lines at, 177, 180
hair covering, 9
short, heavy woman, 239
Necklaces, 28
and contour of face, 18-20

Necklaces (*Cont.*)
choker, 18-19
Neckline:
and face, 25-36
closely fitted, 180
collarless, 187
coat collars, 30-36 (*see also* Collars: coat)
draped, 227
for elderly women, 299-302
for irregular features, 29-30
high, close, 25-26, 28
bulky, 35
low, 26, 27, 28, 30, 64, 227
round, 186-187
ornaments at, 28-29
pointed, 186-187 (*see also* V-neck-lines)
round, 26-27, 28
scarves and, 25-26, 29-31
square, 26, 27, 186-187
tall, slender woman, 208, 212
that lengthen face, 27-29
that widen face, 25-27
too many details, 29
V-shaped, 136-137 (*see also* V-neck-lines)
Neutral colors, 87, 92-93
Neutralized colors, 94
Nose:
hairdress and, 14
hats correct defects, 46-51
large, 50-51
turned-up, 49-50

O

Oblique lines, 160
Off-the-face hats, 39, 42, 49, 51, 52, 54, 142-143
Olive skin, 94-95
One-piece dress, 236-238
teen-age miss, 262-263
Opaque fabrics, 147, 148

Open-heeled sling shoe, 202
Open-toed shoe, 202
Opera pump, 200-202
Optical illusions affecting figure, 127-143 (*see also* Figure)
Ornaments, 170-171
  and contour of face, 16-24
Oval face, 3-4, 46
Overgrown girl, 270
Oxfords, 203, 204

P

Pageboy bob, 9
Pale blonde, 82-86
Panels, 132, 159
  center, 133, 134
  long, loose, back, 189
  side, 133-135
Panniers, 207
Pearls, 19-20
Peasant blouse, 174-175, 183
Perpendicular lines, 131-135, 178, 179
  and large hips, 158, 159
  combined with horizontal lines, 225
  increasing slenderness by, 131-135
  tall, thin woman, 210
Individuality:
  accenting, 275-278
  feminine, 278-280
  middle-aged woman, 282, 284
Peters, Dr. Lulu Hunt, 128
Petite charm, emphasizing, 223-226
Petite type, junior, 269
Pigmentation:
  of eyes, 72-74
  of hair, 69-72
  of skin, 56-68
Pill box hat, 39
Pinkish-gray apparel, 120
Pins:
  and contour of face, 16-17
  at neckline, 29
  in hat, 44

Platform shoes, 204
Pleats, 159
Pockets, 158
Pointed lines, 246-247 (*see also* V-line):
  cape, long, 188-189
  collars, 33-34
  drape, 135
  hemline, 135-136
  neckline, 136, 137
  panels, 135
Poise, 275
Pompadour, 7, 11
Posture, 128-129
  and high heels, 203
  of growing girl, 255-256
Powder, matching skin, 57-58
Princess dress, 210
  modified, 225
Printed fabrics, 150-152
  selecting, principles, 150
  striped effects, 150, 151
Profile:
  hairdresses, 13, 14
  view, 310
Proportion:
  head to body, 127-128
  importance of, 125-126
  shoulders, bustline, hips, 129-130

Q

Quaint style, 223, 225
Quality, and distinction, 283

R

Radiating lines, 171
Raglan sleeves, 183, 184
Rating scale, color readings, 76-77, 78-79
Readjustment of clothing, 314
Red hair, 70, 71, 88, 89-93
Redingote, 134
Related colors, 114

Retroussé nose, 49-50
Revers, maternity wear, 174
Ringlets, 11, 14, 15
  elderly women, 295
Rouge:
  matching skin, 58-59, 315
  placement, face changed by, 59-60
Round earrings, 21
Round face (see also Wide face):
  earrings and, 21-24
  necklines and, 25-27
Round necklines, 26-27, 28, 208
Round shoulders:
  capes and, 188-189
  collars and, 187
  earrings touching, 22
  hair and, 190
  hats and, 189-190
  lines that improve, 183-190
  mass at back of neck, 185-186
  neckline, 186-187
  shoulder seams and, 184, 185
  sleeves and, 183-184
  waistline and, 189
Ruffles, 29

S

Saddle shoes, 204
Sailor hat, 40, 41
Sallowness, 63
Sandals, 204
Sash, 159, 209
Scarfs, 25-26, 29-31, 167, 169, 185
  color in, 64, 65
  concealing large upper arm, 193-194
  for elderly women, 300-301
  for maternity wear, 174
  fur, 231-232
School costumes, 272-274
Seaming, pointed, 136-137
Seams:
  curving lines in, 237
  shoulder, 184, 185

Self-confidence, 275
Semiprecious stones, 116
Set-in sleeves, 183-184
Shampooing hair, 69-70
Shawl collar, 35-36
Shingled haircut, 7
Shiny fabrics, 65-66, 144, 145, 181
Shoes:
  for elderly woman, 306-307
  for tall, heavy woman, 221-222
  high-heeled, 203-204
  hosiery and costume contrasts, 197-199
  long, slender, 199-200
  moccasins, 204
  open-heeled, 202
  open-toed, 202
  opera pump, 200-202
  oxford, 203, 204
  platform, 204
  round-toed, 200
  saddle, 204
  sandals, 204
  square tip, 202-203
  straight tip, 202-203
  wedge-soled, 204
  with contrasting leathers, 199
  with long vamp, 200
  with open spaces, 202
  with straps, 200-202
  with wing tip, 202-204
  with welt soles, 204
Short, heavy woman, 233-243
  center of interest, 238-239
  footwear, 241-243
  hats, 240-241
  improving figure, 236-239
  keeping figure inconspicuous, 234-236
Short, slender woman, 223-232
  accessories, 230-231
  design, 229
  details, 231

Short, slender woman (*Cont.*)
  footwear, 232
  fur scarfs, 231-232
  hairdress, 230
  hats, 230
  keeping in scale, 229-232
  petite charm, emphasizing, 223-226
  space divisions, 226-229
  textures, 229
Shoulder-length bob, 239
Shoulder-line, broad, 157
Shoulder pads, 129, 130, 184
  too high, 237, 238
Shoulders, 129
  closely fitted, 180
  proportion of hips and bustline to,
    129-130
  round (*see* Round shoulders)
  seams, 184, 185
  severe lines at, 177, 180
Shoulder-support belt, 256
Side panels, 133-135
Side part, hair, 8
  high, 10
Silhouette:
  broad base triangle, 155-156, 157
  dark colors reveal, 152-153
  heavy fabrics conceal, 147-148
  maternity wear, 174-175
  shiny textures reveal, 144, 145
  stiff fabrics conceal, 146
  transparent fabrics reveal, 147, 148-
    150
Simplicity:
  and distinction, 283-285
  in hairdress, 5-6, 13-15
  in straight lines, 245-246
  teen-age miss, 266
Size:
  dark colors decrease, 152-153
  heavy fabrics increase, 147-148
  shiny textures increase, 144, 145
  stiff fabrics increase, 146

Skin:
  cool, 97-98
  fair, 98-103
  hue of, determines colors, 82
  medium, 98-99
  olive, 94-95
  relating colors to, 56-68
  rough, 58
  tones, analyzing, 77, 79
Skirt:
  bouffant, 146
  contrasted with blouse, 228-229
  dirndl, 174-175
  equal length of blouse and, 226, 228
  for tall, slender woman, 211-212
  full, 156, 157, 174-175
  joining of bodice and, 159-160
  medium length, 226
  narrow, 177, 178
  pleated, 207, 261
  short, 224
    pleated, 207
Sleeveless dress, 193
Sleeves:
  close-fitting, 138
  contrasting, 193-194
  kimono, 183, 184
  long, narrow, 138
  loose, large upper arm, 191-192
  raglan, 183, 184
  set-in, 183-184
  short, 138, 139
  types of, 138-139
  wide, 138
Slenderness, gaining, 127
Slender woman:
  short (*see* Short, slender woman)
  tall (*see* Tall, slender woman)
  veils for, 46
Slips, 148-149
  tight-fitting, 181
Socks, 256
Sophisticated type, junior, 269

Sophistication, 246-247
Space divisions, short, slender woman, 226-229
Sport hosiery, 205
Sport shoes, 204
Square face, 4
Square necklines, 26, 27, 186-187
Stiff fabrics, 145, 146
Stiff hats, 45-46
Stout women (see also Short, heavy woman; Tall, heavy woman):
　colors for, 154
Straight lines, 245-246
Straps:
　intricate arrangement of, 201-202
　on shoes, 200-202
　types of, 201-202
Striking accent, 223
Stripes, for tall, heavy woman, 219
Styles, 126 (see also Fashion)
Subtlety, 246-247
Surplice closing, 134, 135, 169
Swagger coat, 141
Swathed hip, 158, 159
Sweater, 262-263

T

Taffeta, 146
Tailored costume, 281
Tall, heavy woman, 214-222
　fabrics, 214-220
　footwear, 221-222
　hats, 220-221
Tall, slender, youthful girl, 269-270
Tall, slender woman, 206-213
　too tall and thin, 209-213
　with pleasing proportions, 206-209
Teen-age miss, 261-274
　accessories, 263, 266
　adolescent, 265
　awkward, 267
　belts, 266
　campus costumes, 272-274

Teen-age miss (Cont.)
　care of clothing, 262
　comfort and freedom, 262-263
　elaborate apparel, 266
　evening dresses, 264
　fabrics, 263
　figure, 265-266, 267
　hairdress, 263
　hats, 263
　skirt lengths, 264-265
　types, 268-272 (see Junior types)
Texture:
　changes effect of colors, 65-66
　dull, 144-146
　for middle-aged woman, 284-285
　for tall, heavy woman, 214-217
　of hair, color and, 79-80
　silhouette, size, affected by, 144-154
　shiny, 144, 145
　soft, delicate, 229
Thin figure, stiff fabrics for, 146
Throat, collars open at, 30-31
Tight clothing, growing girl, 255-256
Top-knot, 7
Train, 209
Transitional lines, hats, 48-49
Transparent fabrics, 147-150, 181
Tricorne hat, 50
Trimming, hats, asymmetric, 39-40
Tunic, short, 134
Turban, 41, 141-143
　narrower than face, 38, 39
Turned-up nose, 49-50
Tuxedo collar, 35
Tweeds, 263
Type, consistency with, 276-277

U

U-lines, 160, 162, 179
Underclothing, growing girl, 256
Upper arm, large, 191-196 (see also Large upper arm)
Upswept hairdress, 10-12, 14

V

Value, contrast of, 112-113
Veils, 37, 45-46, 239
Velvets, 66
Vivid brunette, 93
V-lines, 160-162, 179-180, 246-247
  at waist, 171
  for elderly women, 301
  for short, heavy woman, 237
  in jackets, 228
V-necklines, 27, 28, 29, 30, 32, 34, 35,
    36, 136-137, 186-187, 208, 209,
    212, 311
  ornaments and, 17
V-shaped cape collars, 139, 141

W

Waist:
  bloused, 181
  full, bloused, 158-159, 169-170
  straight, hanging, 189
  V-line at, 136, 137, 171
Waistline, 130-131
  and round shoulders, 188, 189
  closely fitted, 158
  normal, 226
Wardrobe selection, color, basis of,
    117-121
Warm coloring, woman with, 82
  colors for, 87-95
  Latin type, 94-95
  red-haired types, 89-93
  types of individuals, 88-89
  vivid brunette, 93

Warm colors:
  combined with cool, 115
  hard to wear, 154
Warmth of clothes, 258-259
Wedge-soled shoes, 204
Weight, 128
  of clothing, 258-259
  of dress, 164-166
Waved hair, 14
  elderly woman, 294
  middle-aged woman, 287
White hair, colors for, 104-110
Wide face:
  collars and, 30-36
  hairdress for, 10-12
  necklaces that slenderize, 19-20
Wine color, in wardrobe, 121
Wing-tip shoe, 202-204
Wrapover models, 172-173

Y

Yellow, minimizing, in face, 62-63
Yellow hair, 70-71, 97-98
Yokes, 227, 239
  and hipline, 158
Young woman, 275-281
  individuality, accenting, 275-278
  forceful, energetic, 280-281
  very feminine, 278-280
Youthful type, junior, 269-270

Z

Zippers, 132